I dedicate this book to my wife, Rebecca, and my wonderful children, Claudia and Christopher—you are always an inspiration to me and are the greatest blessing in the world. Thank you for everything!

Contents at a Glance

Foundations of WPF

An Introduction to Windows Presentation Foundation

Laurence Moroney

Apress®

Foundations of WPF: An Introduction to Windows Presentation Foundation

Copyright © 2006 by Laurence Moroney

ISBN-13 (pbk): 978-1-59059-760-6

ISBN-10 (pbk): 1-59059-760-5

Printed and bound in the United States of America 9 8 7 6 5 4 3 2 1

Lead Editor: Ewan Buckingham
Technical Reviewer: John Grieb
Editorial Board: Steve Anglin, Ewan Buckingham, Gary Cornell, Jason Gilmore, Jonathan Gennick,
    Jonathan Hassell, James Huddleston, Chris Mills, Matthew Moodie, Dominic Shakeshaft, Jim Sumser,
    Keir Thomas, Matt Wade
Project Manager: Denise Santoro Lincoln
Copy Edit Manager: Nicole Flores
Copy Editor: Kim Wimpsett
Assistant Production Director: Kari Brooks-Copony
Production Editor: Ellie Fountain
Compositor: Gina Rexrode
Proofreader: Linda Marousek
Indexer: Michael Brinkman
Artist: Kinetic Publishing Services, LLC
Cover Designer: Kurt Krames
Manufacturing Director: Tom Debolski

Distributed to the book trade worldwide by Springer-Verlag New York, Inc., 233 Spring Street, 6th Floor, New York, NY 10013. Phone 1-800-SPRINGER, fax 201-348-4505, e-mail orders-ny@springer-sbm.com, or visit http://www.springeronline.com.

For information on translations, please contact Apress directly at 2560 Ninth Street, Suite 219, Berkeley, CA 94710. Phone 510-549-5930, fax 510-549-5939, e-mail info@apress.com, or visit http://www.apress.com.

The source code for this book is available to readers at http://www.apress.com in the Source Code/ Download section.

Contents

About the Author

 **LAURENCE MORONEY** is a technologist based in Sammamish, Washington. When he started writing this book, he worked for Mainsoft, the cross-platform company, as a technology evangelist helping customers make the most of their investments in Microsoft code. By the time the book reaches the shelves, he will have taken a job at Microsoft as a technology evangelist for Windows Presentation Foundation and Windows Vista, a task to which he is really looking forward! As someone who has worked with Microsoft technology in a number of industries—in such diverse environments as jails and casinos, financial services, and professional sports—he is excited by the direction .NET technology is taking in version 3.0 and beyond and by how it is going to change the overall experience of developers and users alike.

About the Technical Reviewer

 **JOHN GRIEB** lives on Long Island, New York, and works for Reuters as a technical specialist. He is currently the lead developer of a project to migrate Reuters Messaging to Microsoft Live Communications Server 2005. Prior to that, he spent several years in Reuters' Microsoft R&D Group and Innovation Lab gaining experience in a broad range of Microsoft products and technologies by participating in many of Microsoft's beta programs and by developing prototypes demonstrating how they could be leveraged within Reuters' products and services.

John has been married for 25 years to his wife, Eileen, and has an 18-year-old daughter named Stephanie and a 16-year-old son named Robert.

Preface

The Windows Presentation Foundation is one of the new "foundations" being introduced by Microsoft in .NET 3.0, along with the Windows Communication Foundation and the Windows Workflow Foundation.

The Windows Presentation Foundation is a vital component to the future of application development, allowing developers to take control of the sheer power that is available at the desktop to develop rich, interactive, media-enhanced user interfaces.

My first professional programming experience was to model the unproductive text-based interface used for programming and configuring surveillance systems as a Windows-based graphical user interface using Visual Basic 3.0. The productivity enhancement that this brought allowed large-scale systems to be configured in minutes instead of in hours or days. Going from Windows user interfaces to rich-media user interfaces using Windows Presentation Foundation will start yielding the same productivity and user experience leaps.

This book is based on the July Community Technical Preview of Windows Presentation Foundation, and by the time the book is in your hands, the technology may be slightly different—this is a Foundations book, after all; it's intended to teach you the fundamentals of the technology and to take the edge off the learning process.

I hope you have as much fun reading and using it as I had writing it!

Laurence Moroney

■ ■ ■

CHAPTER 1

Introducing WPF

Welcome to *Foundations of WPF: An Introduction to Windows Presentation Foundation.* This book will get you up and running with the framework that is at the heart of the Microsoft Windows Vista experience.

If you haven't yet encountered Windows Presentation Foundation (WPF), don't worry— you soon will. The experience that it gives from the perspective of users, developers, and designers is as compelling as it is powerful, and before long, just about every application you see will have an element of WPF in it.

This chapter will bring you up to date and up to speed on web application and user interface technology from the dawn of computing history to today, give you a context of application architecture and a peek into the future of web application architectures, and show where WPF fits in and how it works alongside its companion technologies of Windows Communication Foundation (WCF) and Windows Workflow Foundation (WWF).

Presentation Layer Architecture: From Yesterday to Tomorrow

The user interface has evolved along a cyclical path from a light footprint to a heavy footprint and back again. Users' requirements and demands for extra functionality drive the heavier footprint, and users' requirements and demands for an easy installation, upgrade, and maintenance drive the lighter footprint. With each iteration, the "lighter" user interfaces gain rich functionality, and the "heavier" user interfaces become easier to install, upgrade, and maintain.

The original user interfaces were probably the lightest clients of all—punch cards that were fed into a central server that in turn printed results. Figure 1-1 shows this simple request/response architecture.

As computers became more sophisticated, the punch card and the printer were replaced by a terminal that fed results into and rendered results from the central server (see Figure 1-2). For basic processing this was useful, but as the requirements for computer applications became more sophisticated—for example, to support e-mail or network news—the terminals had to get smarter. If you remember the old terminal-based e-mail programs such as elm or the network newsreaders, you'll remember needing three or four extra fingers to do anything useful! Architecturally, this wasn't much different from the punch-card request/response architecture, but it unified the point of contact with the mainframe and changed the medium from paper to electrons. So although the architecture did not change, the implementation did—and it was this change in implementation that was a driving factor in improving the overall user experience of applications, a fact that is still true today.

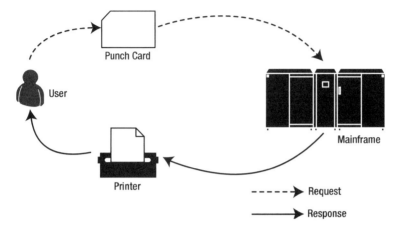

Figure 1-1. *Punch-card request/response architecture*

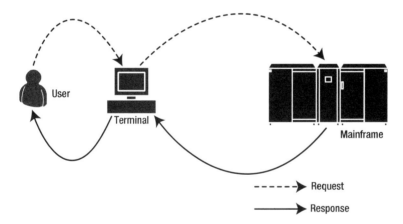

Figure 1-2. *Terminal-based request/response architecture*

With the advent of the personal computer, much of the old server functionality wasn't necessary anymore. This was because the main use of servers at that time was for functions that could easily take place on a personal computer, such as calculations or analyses (see Figure 1-3). Functionality that required connectivity, such as e-mail and network newsreaders, could still be achieved on a personal computer through terminal emulation.

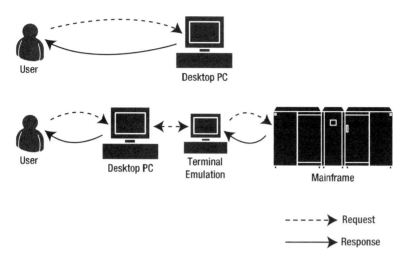

Figure 1-3. *Request/response architecture for personal computer, both online and offline*

Then someone had the bright idea of using the power of the personal computer to enhance the online experience, moving away from the green-and-black terminal toward a user interface that allowed content such as e-mail, news, and graphics to appear in full four-color glory (see Figure 1-4). The personal computer flourished in power, and the early personal computers gave way to much more powerful machines with better graphics, faster processing chips, more memory, and persistent storage through hard drives.

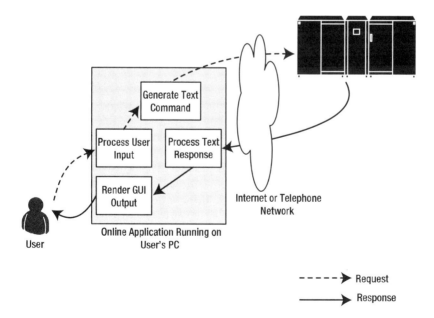

Figure 1-4. *Request/response architecture of user graphical user interface (GUI) application talking to mainframe*

With this exponential increase in computing power at the desktop, applications became more sophisticated, complex, and functional than anything before on centralized mainframe supercomputers. Full GUIs soon became the norm. Apple, Atari, and other GUI-focused computers appeared, followed by the Microsoft Windows operating system, which ran on hardware made by many different companies. Soon after, the popularity of office productivity applications exploded; as people began using these applications daily, they required even faster and more sophisticated platforms, and the client continued to evolve exponentially.

■Note In the past, the more sophisticated applications were *disconnected* applications. Office productivity suites, desktop-publishing applications, games, and the like were all distributed, installed, and run on the client via a fixed medium such as a floppy disk or a CD. In other words, they weren't connected in any way.

The other breed of application, which was evolving much more slowly, was the *connected* application, where a graphical front end wrapped a basic, text-based communication with a back-end server for online applications such as e-mail. CompuServe was one of the largest online providers, and despite an innovative abstraction of its simple back end to make for a more user-centric, graphical experience along the lines of the heavy desktop applications, its underlying old-school model was still apparent. Remember the old Go commands? Despite the buttons on the screen that allowed a user to enter communities, these simply issued a Go <communityname> command behind the scenes on the user's behalf.

Although this approach was excellent and provided a rich online experience, it had to be written and maintained specifically for each platform, so for a multiplatform experience, the vendor had to write a client application for Windows, Unix, Apple, and all the other operating systems and variants.

But then, in the early 1990s, a huge innovation happened: the web browser.

This innovation began the slow merging of the two application types (connected and disconnected)—a merging that continues today. We all know the web browser by now, and it is arguably the most ubiquitous application used on modern computers, displacing solitaire games and the word processor for this storied achievement!

But the web browser ultimately became much more than just a new means for abstracting the textual nature of the client/server network. It became an abstraction on top of the operating system on which applications could be written and executed (see Figure 1-5). This was, and is, important. As long as applications are written to the specification defined by that abstraction, they should be able to run anywhere without further intervention or installation on behalf of the application developer. Of course, the browser has to be present on the system, but the value proposition of having a web browser available to the operating system was extremely important and ultimately launched many well-known legal battles.

The problem, of course, with this abstraction was that it was relatively simple and not originally designed or implemented for anything more complex than laying out and formatting text and graphics. I am, of course, referring to Hypertext Markup Language (HTML). This specification, implemented by a browser, meant that simple text could be placed on a server, transferred from a server, interpreted by a browser, and laid out in a far more pleasing way than simple green-on-black text on a page, giving the user a better experience. More important, it could generate a whole new breed of application developers; all a developer had to do to create an online, connected application with a graphical experience was to generate it as HTML, and the browser would do the rest. You wouldn't need the resources of a CompuServe or an America Online to build an application that rendered the text for you! All you had to do was generate HTML, either by coding it directly or by writing a server-side application (in C) that would generate it for you. Although the Internet had been around for a long time, only at this point was it really being born.

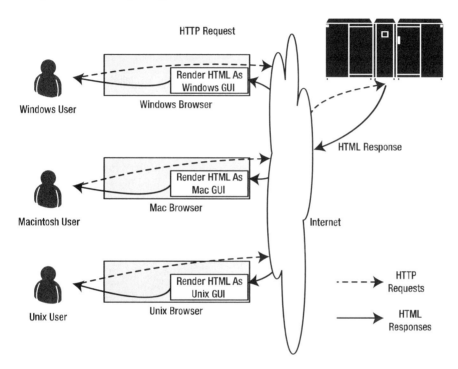

Figure 1-5. *Web browser–based request/response architecture*

And guess what happened? The cycle began again.

Everybody jumped the browser bandwagon, and Common Gateway Interface (CGI) applications, run on a server and delivering content to browsers, were hot. The user experience, with the only interaction being postbacks to the server (in a similar vein to terminals, only prettier), soon became too limiting, and new technologies began to emerge to increase the user experience.

Enter Java and the applet. Java, a virtual machine on top of a virtual machine (the browser) on top of a virtual machine (the operating system) on top of a real machine (the underlying hardware), gave a greater abstraction, and it introduced a new platform that developers could code on and have even richer applications running within the browser. This was important, because it accelerated what could be done within a browser and was delivered using the simple transport mechanisms of the Internet but again without requiring the resources of a huge company writing a GUI platform on which to do it. Of course, it suffered from constraints; namely, to achieve a cross-platform experience, developers had to follow a lowest common denominator approach. The clearest example of this was in its support for the mouse. The Apple operating systems supported one button, the Microsoft Windows–based ones supported two, and many Unix platforms supported three. As such, Java applets could support only one button, and many Unix users found themselves two buttons short!

The Java virtual machine and language evolved to become a server-side implementation and a great replacement for C on the server. In addition to this, HTML continued to evolve, allowing for more flexibility, and its big brother, Dynamic HTML (DHTML), was born. In addition, scripting was added to the platform (at the browser level), with JavaScript (unrelated to Java despite the name) and VBScript being born. To handle these scripting languages, interpreters were bolted on to the browser, and the extensible browser architecture proved to be a powerful addition.

Thanks to extensibility, applications such as Macromedia Flash added a new virtual machine on top of the browser, allowing for even more flexible and intense applications. The extensible browser then brought about ActiveX technology on the Windows platform, whereby native application functionality could be run within the browser when using Microsoft browsers (or alternative ones with a plug-in that supported ActiveX). This was a powerful solution, because it enabled native functionality to be accessible from networked applications (see Figure 1-6). This got around the restrictions imposed by the security sandbox and lowest common denominator approach of the Java virtual machine, but this ultimately led to problems like those when distributing client-only applications; specifically, a heavy configuration of the desktop was necessary to get them to work. Although this configuration could be automated to a certain degree, it produced two show-stopping points for many.

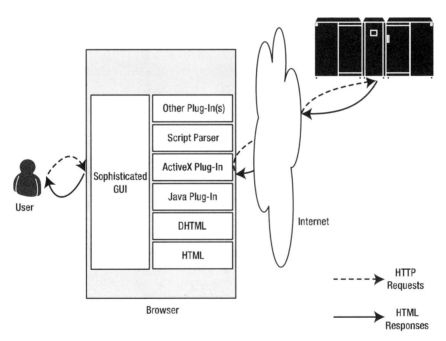

Figure 1-6. *Sophisticated browser architecture*

The first problem was that it didn't always work, and the nature of configuration (changing the Windows registry) often failed; or worse, it broke other applications. ActiveX controls were rarely self-contained and usually installed runtime support files. Different versions of these support files could easily be installed on top of each other, a common occurrence leading to broken applications (called *DLL hell*).

The second problem was security. A user's computer, when connected to the Internet, could effectively allow code to run, written by anybody, and the ActiveX technology was fully native, not restricted by the Java or HTML sandboxes (more about these in a moment); therefore, a user could innocently go to a web page that downloaded an ActiveX control that wrought havoc or stole vital information from their system. As such, many users refused to use them, and many corporate administrators even disallowed them from use within the enterprise. The virtual nature of Java and HTML—where applications and pages were coded to work on a specific virtual machine—offered better security; these machines couldn't do anything malicious, and therefore applications written to run on them couldn't either. The users were effectively safe, though limited in the scope of what they could do.

At the end of the 1990s, Microsoft unveiled the successor to ActiveX (amongst others) in its Java-like .NET Framework. This framework would form Microsoft's strategic positioning for many years. Like Java, it provided a virtual machine—the common language runtime (CLR)—on which applications would run. These applications could do only what the CLR allowed and were called *managed* applications. The .NET Framework was much more sophisticated than the Java virtual machine, allowing for desktop and web applications with differing levels of functionality (depending on which was used). This was part of "managing" the code. With the .NET Framework came a new language, C#, but this wasn't the only language that could be used with .NET—it was a multilanguage, single-runtime platform that provided great flexibility.

The .NET Framework was revolutionary because it united the client-application experience and the connected-application experience across a unified runtime that ActiveX tried but ultimately failed to do. Because the same platform could be written for both, the result was that the user experience would be similar across both (see Figure 1-7). Coupled with the emergence of Extensible Markup Language (XML), a language similar to HTML but specialized for handling data instead of presentation, web application development was finally coming of age.

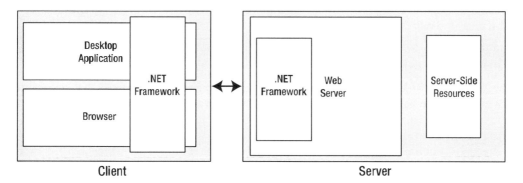

Figure 1-7. *The .NET Framework provides consistent browser, desktop, and server application programming interfaces (APIs).*

Thus, the pendulum has swung back toward the thin client/fat server approach. Ironically, the thin client is probably fatter than the original servers, because it's an operating system that can support a browser that is extended to support XML (through parsers), scripting (through interpreters), and other plug-ins, as well as Java or .NET virtual machines!

With all these runtime elements available to developers and a consistent server-side API (through the .NET Framework or Java server side), rich, high-performing applications built on a client/server model are now fully possible.

And here is where you have to decide how you develop your client applications. One set of technologies—based on HTML, DHTML, Asynchronous JavaScript and XML (Ajax), and Microsoft ASP.NET Atlas—gives you the same level of sophistication that a "heavy" client can give you using "light" technologies. Features such as asynchronous updates, slick user interfaces, handy tooltips, and other embellishments, once the realm of fat clients, are now available to thin, browser-based clients thanks to advances in browser technology.

The other approach, and the one at the core of this book, is an evolutionary step, where the delivery still uses the mechanisms of the thin client, including a declarative XML markup language named Extensible Application Markup Language (XAML) that defines the user interface, but has an incredibly powerful runtime supporting it. This runtime is the basis of WPF. It's a powerful rendering engine that can take the "instructions" passed to it from a server and render them richly. You'll see lots of examples of how to use WPF and XAML in this book. You'll use next-generation APIs for developing Windows applications—version 3.0 of the .NET Framework, sometimes called WinFX or NetFX, as well as the new Windows software development kit (SDK). In the next section, you'll look at the components of this SDK and how they fit together.

The Windows SDK

The Windows SDK contains all the APIs for developing next-generation Windows applications, including those for Windows Vista, and provides the foundation for software development for the Windows server and client platforms for the foreseeable future. It contains content for all the APIs in Windows Vista, including the technology that was formerly available as part of the WinFX API.

The Windows SDK is centered on the .NET Framework 3.0, sometimes called NetFX, which contains the classes you are familiar with from the .NET Framework 2.0 in addition to WPF, WCF, and WWF.

The .NET Framework

The .NET Framework is the core API that contains all the classes and data types that are shared by Windows applications. It is a core Windows component that supports building and running managed applications. It provides a consistent, language-independent, object-oriented programming environment where code is stored and executed in a controlled manner. This code, called Microsoft Intermediate Language (MSIL) code, is byte code compiled from source code that can come from many high-level languages, including C# and Visual Basic 2005, and executes on a virtual machine, the CLR.

It also provides a large suite of classes in the .NET class library, organized and grouped logically into namespaces, commonly called the .NET Framework class library or the .NET SDK.

The CLR is the foundation of the .NET Framework, and it manages how the code executes, providing services such as memory management, thread management, and, in the case of distributed applications, remoting. It enforces type safety and other forms of security services that prevent applications from being exploited by hackers. Because the code runs as byte code on the CLR, backed up by the .NET SDK, it is more distributable, and compiled programs (generally called *assemblies*) do not need to be distributed with a plethora of runtime dependencies, as they did pre-.NET. Of course, if a program uses dependency assemblies that also run on the CLR that are not part of the standard SDK, then these would be distributed alongside your program. So although the .NET Framework architecture has drastically improved the ease in which an application is distributed, it still can have some complications.

Code that targets the CLR and the SDK is called *managed* code, because at runtime it is effectively managed by the CLR and can perform functionality available only in the SDK. This provides inherent security by preventing low-level access to the operating system, memory, and other applications, and thus code that is written to the SDK is more easily trusted.

The framework can also be hosted by other components so that it can be launched to execute managed code, providing an extensible environment. An example of this is the ASP.NET runtime, which is a traditional, unmanaged runtime engine that runs alongside Internet Information Services (IIS). As a result, it is possible to write managed web applications using the set of class libraries supported by the .NET SDK (using ASP.NET). These applications are typically called ASP.NET *web form* applications, where they provide a web user interface, or ASP.NET XML *web service* applications, where they provide service-oriented applications without user interfaces.

Windows Communication Foundation

WCF is the core of service-oriented communications applications for the Windows platform. It is built on top of web service standards and is designed for the needs of service-oriented architecture (SOA) and software as a service (SAAS). The philosophy behind these is that software should be built out of finely grained, loosely coupled components with well-defined interfaces that communicate using standard protocols.

Web services were the beginning of this trend, where business logic is implemented in a technology-agnostic manner, exposing an XML-based interface using a language called Web Services Description Language (WSDL). Developers can then use an XML message in a format called Simple Object Access Protocol (SOAP), which is derived from XML, to communicate with the service.

However, web services are limited and do not support some enterprise-class functionality such as security, reliability, and transactability without complicated add-ons at a minimum.

WCF is designed to allow for all of this and a whole lot more; it provides an API that allows services to be implemented without having to think too much about the underlying plumbing, which allows the developer to concentrate on the business logic.

WCF provides the service-oriented programming model, built on the .NET Framework, and unifies the typically diverse suite of distributed system capabilities, including standard static web services, messaging, transactions, and remoting into a single API. It also supports multiple transport types, messaging patterns, encodings, and hosting models. It subsumes some of the different technologies of .NET that you may already be familiar with, such as ASP.NET web services (ASMX), Web Services Enhancements (WSE), .NET Remoting, Enterprise Services, and System.Messaging.

WCF provides a new namespace, called System.ServiceModel, which provides the tools for a number of distributed application scenarios:

- Messaging, both one-way and duplex

- Remote procedure calls

- Callbacks

- Sessions

- Reliability through queued messaging

- Multiple contract services

- Security

- Ordered delivery of messages

- Transactions

WCF is a huge and drastically important API in its own right and is worthy of several books. I'll be touching on it from time to time in this book, particularly in some of the examples that provide the back end to the WPF front ends that you'll be developing in this book.

Windows Workflow Foundation

WWF, announced at Professional Developers Conference 2005, is a vital part of the three pillars of the WinFX API; it provides a programming model that is used for developing and executing applications that require a long-running, stateful, persistent workflow, as is crucial in many business applications. It takes some of the functionality that was previously available only to users and developers of the BizTalk family of servers and provides it to all servers and their clients.

WWF includes a designer tool that allows developers to design workflows using Visual Studio .NET and automatically generate the source code that compiles these into working applications. Applications built on this framework typically include document management, commercial page flow, and line-of-business applications that require several steps of application, some requiring human input.

Windows Presentation Foundation

WPF, as well as being the subject of this book, is the unified presentation subsystem for Windows. It consists of a display engine and a suite of managed classes, similar in concept to the .NET Framework you saw earlier. This runtime environment and SDK allows developers to create, and users to run, rich visual applications. WPF introduces XAML as the glue that binds everything together. XAML is a rich XML-based document format that allows for the declarative development of WPF applications using the WPF object model.

WPF is based on managed code. When you build an application using XAML, you are putting together a declarative command set for the WPF runtime engine. The runtime manages everything for you.

A great example of a XAML application is Microsoft Codenamed Max, which is available at `http://www.microsoft.com/max/`. This application allows you to manage your digital pictures and turn them into visually attractive slide shows.

You can see Max in action in Figure 1-8.

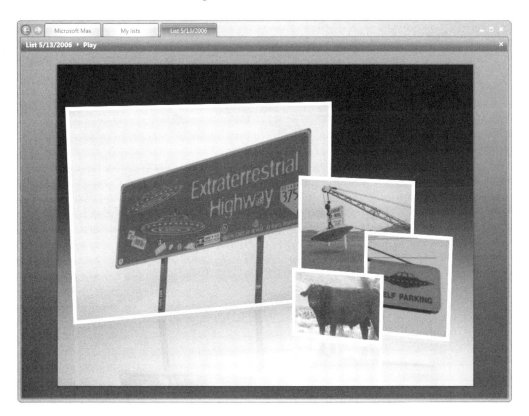

Figure 1-8. *Max in action*

This application uses a number of WPF features. As you can see from Figure 1-8, it is manipulating the images by rotating them in a 3D plane. It also dynamically resizes images and shows a reflection of the image on an imaginary 3D surface.

As you run the application, it animates your images by sliding image collections (called *mantles*) on and off the screen. Images can also be attributed, without changing the underlying image, as shown in Figure 1-9.

In Figure 1-9 you can see where an image has been marked up and attributed. You can do this without affecting the underlying image. Max stores XAML metadata with the image and uses this information to draw on top of the image at render time.

This just touches the surface of what is possible with WPF. Throughout this book, you'll work through this API, learning how to build applications like Max and a lot more besides.

Figure 1-9. *Attributed images*

Tools of the Trade

To build applications on the Windows SDK using WinFX, you can use several tools made available by Microsoft. At the time of writing, these tools were in beta and as such require some work to install and use. If you want to get started developing WPF applications, you'll need to download and install the various tools, runtimes, and SDKs.

Visual Studio 2005

The main tool you'll use is, of course, Visual Studio 2005. This is available in a number of editions:

> *Visual Studio 2005 Team System*: This is the top-of-the-line model that is intended for large teams that are collaborating on Windows-based projects.

> *Visual Studio 2005 Professional Edition*: This version, aimed at a single developer, provides the Visual Studio development environment that allows you to develop all types of applications including web, server, Windows, mobile, and Office-based ones.

Visual Studio 2005 Standard Edition: This version, also aimed at a single developer, provides a scaled-down version of Visual Studio 2005 Professional Edition. It allows you to build web, Windows, and mobile applications.

Visual Studio Express Edition: This is a free edition of the Visual Studio integrated development environment (IDE) that allows you to build simple websites and Windows applications.

You can use any of these editions to build WPF applications utilizing the skills you learn in this book. The choice is yours!

Microsoft Expression

Designers can use the Microsoft Expression family of products to complement the developers who are using Visual Studio. Part of the power of XAML is that it allows for a separation of design and implementation. Designers can build user interfaces in XAML using tools that cater to their skills, and then developers can craft the back-end logic for these using the Visual Studio toolkit that appeals to their skills.

As such, the Expression family has arrived, and it caters to the designer. It comes in three editions:

Expression Graphic Designer: This fully featured toolkit brings together the best of vector and raster graphics to give graphic designers the tools they need to provide the perfect graphical designs for applications or websites.

Expression Web Designer: This gives web designers the tools they need to produce websites the way they want. The websites will be based on standard web technologies such as HTML, Cascading Style Sheets (CSS), and JavaScript so they can be used on any server and any browser.

Expression Interactive Designer: This provides an environment to design fully featured Windows applications using XAML and WPF. You'll be using this application extensively as you work through this book. It is the perfect tool to allow for the separation of design and implementation, and you'll perform much of the user interface design using this tool and the back-end development using Visual Studio 2005.

You can check out the Expression family and download the trial editions from the Expression website at `http://www.microsoft.com/expression`.

The WinFX Runtime Components

The WinFX runtime components are necessary to run WinFX applications that use WCF, WWF, or WPF applications. The WinFX runtime is present on Windows Vista but will need to be installed on Windows XP or Windows Server 2003 if you want to develop and run WinFX applications on these operating systems.

This book's examples will use the February Community Technical Preview (CTP) versions of the runtime. You can download the WinFX runtime components from MSDN.

The Windows Software Development Kit (SDK)

The Windows SDK contains the documentation, samples, and tools necessary to make developing WinFX (and other) applications as straightforward as possible. These are essential tools if you want to develop any applications for the next generations of Windows. In this book, I'll be using the July 2006 CTP versions in the examples.

Even if you are using Windows Vista, you will need to download and install these tools. They are available to download from MSDN.

Visual Studio Development Tools for WinFX

These development tools provide an add-on to Visual Studio .NET that allows you to develop WinFX applications and services. They provide templates that you can use to create these applications, as well as tools such as the XAML designer for Visual Studio (code-named Cider) and XAML IntelliSense for the Visual Studio code editor.

Summary

In this chapter, you took a whirlwind tour of user interface development, up to where it stands today. You are at a fork in the road, with one fork going toward a thin rich client using browsers, XML user interfaces, and Ajax development, and the other going toward a super-rich client that solves many of the problems of distributing rich, or "heavy," client applications by using a managed architecture and an XML delivery and design platform. Microsoft implements the latter methodology using WPF.

WPF, along with WCF and WWF, forms the basis for how next-generation applications will be built and run on Windows.

You also went through the suite of tools and SDKs you'll need and how they all fit together to give you the best development experience possible.

This book will concentrate on WPF and how you can use it to develop rich applications that include graphics, animation, 3D effects, and more. It will also step you through the development process, particularly how you can work closely with professional designers using the Expression toolkits to produce the best applications possible.

In the next chapter, I will go into more detail about how to architect applications in WPF, WWF, and WCF, putting WPF into context by showing how you can use it to build next-generation connected and disconnected applications.

CHAPTER 2

▄▄▄

Programming WPF Applications

One of the key features of Windows Vista (and other versions of Windows that support WinFX) is the ability to differentiate applications by drastically enhancing the user experience using the Windows Presentation Foundation (WPF). WinFX introduces a new graphics driver model that is fault tolerant and designed to use the power of the graphics processor unit (GPU) that is on board most modern desktop computers. Its memory manager and scheduler enable different graphics applications to use the GPU to run simultaneously. Built on top of the GPU and graphics driver is the Windows Graphics Foundation (WGF), also known as Direct3D 10. Applications can use this application programming interface (API) to take direct advantage of the power available in the GPU.

In this chapter, you will get a very high-level overview of the architecture that makes this possible. You'll look at the different types of WPF applications that you can build, as well as the choices you have for distributing them, which of course affects how you build them.

You'll then look at the architecture of WPF and how it all hangs together, including taking a brief tour of some of the underlying classes that do the grunt work for your applications.

Finally, you'll look at the high-level classes such as Application and Window that form the workhorse of your WPF application. Although much of the information is theoretical in this chapter, it will give you the basis for understanding the stuff to come in later chapters, which is where you'll build a real-world application and get into the details of the application-level classes you can use to put together the latest, greatest WPF application.

What Are WPF Applications?

Any application you build using WPF will typically consist of a number of Extensible Application Markup Language (XAML) pages plus their supporting code. However, as you can imagine, the functionality that a collection of independent pages can provide is limited and is not sufficient for meeting most requirements. For example, the processing that occurs on the page level cannot support necessities such as preserving the state of a page as a user navigates, passing data or context between pages, detecting when new pages have loaded, managing global-level variables, and so on.

As such, the application model for WPF supports collecting XAML pages into a single application in the traditional manner. If you think about it in terms of Windows forms applications, a XAML page is analogous to a form file, so where a traditional .NET WinForms application collects a number of forms together into a single executable, a WinFX desktop application does the same—except that instead of WinForms, it collects XAML pages.

XAML applications can run in one of two ways:

XAML browser applications: They can run as XAML browser applications where they are hosted in the browser. They are not run on a user's system and cannot run offline. From a security point of view, they execute in the Internet security zone, which limits their access to system resources. Because of this higher level of safety, they do not require user permission to run.

Installed applications: They can also run as installed applications. These applications will either be hosted in a stand-alone window (like any Windows application, as shown in Figure 2-1) or be hosted in the WPF navigation window (see Figure 2-2). This window contains a navigation band at the top of the client region with forward and backward buttons. This band is overridable by developers who want to build their own navigator, and to that end the navigation window is programmable through the System.Windows.Navigation.NavigationWindow class. This is beyond the scope of this book, but you can check out the Windows software development kit (SDK) documentation for this class for details about how to do this. Each type has full access to system resources.

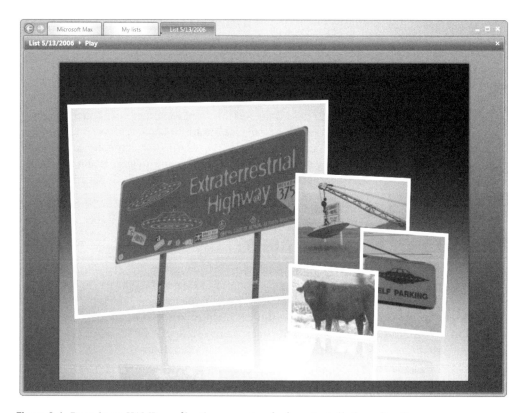

Figure 2-1. *Running a XAML application as a stand-alone installed application*

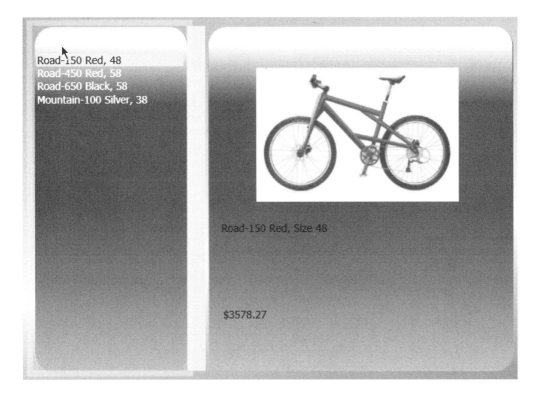

Figure 2-2. *Running a XAML application using the NavigationWindow class*

When using WPF, you can use custom controls or other components, and these behave, from a security point of view, in a similar manner to installed applications, because they are compiled into a DLL file. As such, they are available only to applications and not directly to the user.

In the next section, you will look at these methodologies in a little more detail and learn how you should consider designing your application for hosting or deployment.

Choices in Application Distribution

As you saw earlier, you have two types of application and three types of deployment, with the browser application running only in the browser and the installed application being able to run stand-alone or in the navigation window. Which option you choose will have an impact on security; therefore, it is a good idea to understand each type of application in order to make an informed decision.

Choosing a XAML Browser Application

If you want a web-like experience in your application, you should consider the XAML browser application type. This will allow a user to have a seamless web-like experience, including the ability to navigate to other web pages and then return. Of course, if the application runs in this manner, you have to treat it as a typical web application, and as such it is restricted to the

Internet security zone. Thus, if your application needs to go beyond this—to access the file system or the Windows registry, for example—then this type of application isn't suitable. If you want the user to browse directly to your application and not have to accept installation dialog boxes, this of course is a good approach. Finally, many applications require offline access—when building a XAML browser application, offline access isn't available, so you should consider in this case an installed application.

A XAML browser application is intended to provide a rich experience to a web user. Typically, web applications are quite static in nature, and they require many page refreshes and round-trips to perform processing tasks. Therefore, they don't usually create the most engaging experience, but advances in design and technology with frameworks and methodologies such as Asynchronous JavaScript and XML (Ajax) are driving a more compelling web experience. Microsoft offers the framework code-named Atlas, which provides a consistent server-side programming model that enables ASP.NET developers to quickly and easily build Ajax applications.

Additionally, plug-ins to the browser such as the near-ubiquitous Flash and Shockwave from Adobe offer this rich experience. In many ways, XAML in the browser is a competitor to them, and it is a powerful one offering the same programming model as will be used in the next generation of desktop applications, which could be a decisive factor. In fact, Microsoft is developing an API called Windows Presentation Foundation Everywhere (WPF/E) that provides a browser plug-in that renders XAML and appears to be the basis of a competitor to Flash and Shockwave. This API is in its earliest stages at the moment and as such is not covered in this book.

A XAML browser application is browsed to rather than deployed. The browser makes a request to the server to retrieve the application, which is downloaded and executed within the browser. The rich features of WPF are then available to the browser-based (and hence web) application.

You create and build browser XAML applications in the same way as installed applications. The differentiator happens at compile time where you change compiler settings. Indeed, using this methodology, a single-source code base is available to be shared between a browser and an installed application. Thus, if you are developing an application that needs to run on both (perhaps with an enhanced offline mode), you can use this single-source code base and make the changes at compile time. You'll see more about this in Chapter 9.

When building a XAML browser application, the build process creates three files:

Deployment manifests: These are denoted by the .xbap file extension. ClickOnce uses this file type to deploy the application.

Application manifests: These are denoted by the .exe.manifest extension. This contains the standard .NET metadata that is created for any managed application.

Executable code: This is denoted by the .exe extension. Yes, that's right, this is an EXE file that your users download and execute. It's not too scary, though, because you are still protected by the Internet security zone in the browser.

Deployment occurs when the user navigates to the uniform resource indicator (URI) of the .xbap file. This invokes ClickOnce to download the application. Note that users can deploy XAML browser applications only using ClickOnce. Therefore, Chapter 10 is devoted to this task and how you can create, build, and deploy a XAML browser application. The application cannot later be invoked by launching the .exe file; you have to browse to the .xbap file on the hosting server to run the application again. This also ensures application version consistency because only the server-hosted application version can be run.

Note that if the .xbap file resides on your system (instead of a server as is intended), it will run in the browser with local security zone permissions. This is particularly useful when developing, but of course, you should do your final testing from a server so you can test the application running in Internet security zone permissions.

Because the application runs in the Internet security zone, a number of features are not permitted. This is because the application runs with *partial trust*. This occurs regardless of where the server is hosted, be it the Internet or an intranet. Features that are not allowed in XAML browser applications and that will incur a compiler error are launching new windows, using application-defined dialog boxes, and using the UIAutomation client.

Choosing an Installed Application

A WPF installed application, from the point of view of requirements, behaves similarly to a traditional WinForms application. If your requirements call for access to system resources such as the file system or the registry, you should use an installed application. Of course, if you also need to have an offline experience, then this approach is best.

WPF installed applications are rich client applications that have full access to system resources, and they behave in the same way as any other installed application. They run stand-alone in their own window and not within a browser.

When you build a WPF installed application, you will build three standard files. These are the deployment manifest (an .application extension), which ClickOnce uses to deploy the application; the application manifest (an .exe.manifest extension), which contains the standard application metadata that is created for any managed application; and the executable (an .exe extension), which is the application's executable code.

Additionally, you can create support DLLs as needed.

An installed application is typically deployed from a server using either ClickOnce or Microsoft Windows Installer (MSI). Of course, because it supports these technologies, it can also be deployed from media such as a DVD or a CD.

When it comes to security, take note that the installable application type has the same access to system resources as the logged-on user, in the same manner as any other Windows application. The security gateway comes at deployment time, so you should make sure your application distribution is controlled. Also, your users should be trained to understand that even though they may install WPF applications from a browser, the browser sandbox will not protect them when they *run* the application.

Windows Presentation Foundation Architecture

You'll now look at the WPF architecture from a programmer's viewpoint, taking a tour of the class libraries that a typical WPF application uses. You'll look into the major classes used by a WPF application and how they interact. Although the framework handles much of your work, particularly when using Microsoft Expression Interactive Designer (as you'll see in Chapters 3 and 4), it's still a good idea to have an inkling of what lies beneath.

The primary WPF programming model is exposed as managed code classes that run on top of the common language runtime (CLR). The presentation framework is built on top of the presentation core libraries (also managed code), which then run on the CLR. However, because WPF uses DirectX to interact with the video hardware, it requires a component that runs on top of this. This component is called *milcore*, and Figure 2-3 shows all three components.

Figure 2-3. *WPF architecture*

Now let's start looking into the major classes that WPF uses.

System.Threading.DispatcherObject

Most WPF objects derive from the DispatcherObject object. It provides the basic underlying constructs that deal with concurrency and threading. It handles messages such as mouse movements (a raw input notification), layout, and user commands. When you derive from a DispatcherObject object, you are effectively creating an object that has single-thread affinity execution and will be given a pointer to a dispatcher at the time the object is created.

System.Windows.DependencyObject

A primary design consideration in WPF is to use properties as much as possible and to use, wherever possible, properties instead of methods and events to handle object behaviors. As such, you could achieve a data-driven system for displaying user interface content via properties. For example, you can define much of the behavior of a user interface by binding properties, such as binding to a data source.

So, to beef up the behavior of a system that is driven by properties, the property system should be richer than the classic property model where properties define nonfunctional behavior such as color and size. So, for example, if you want to bind a property to the property of another object, then a change notification on properties needs to be supported; in fact, both sides of the binding need to support this.

This is where you use the DependencyObject type. The classic example of this is in inherited properties where you can have a property that is inheritable (for example, FontSize) and want this property on a *child* object to automatically update when the property on the *parent* object changes.

Property dependency is also nicely demonstrated when using control templates in WPF. You can specify a template for how a control or set of controls should appear and then apply that to a number of control sets to set their properties coherently.

For example, if you look at Figure 2-4, you can see the bicycle application that will be introduced in Chapter 3. This shows how the controls are laid out and how their default physical properties are set. The application has two panes; the left pane contains a list of products, and the right pane contains details for the selected product.

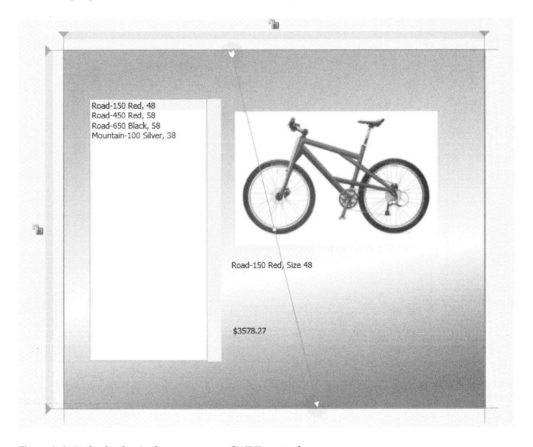

Figure 2-4. *Default physical appearance of WPF controls*

Now consider Figure 2-5. In this case, a *template* has been created for the controls, and each pane of the application derives its styling from this template. This uses the DependencyObject under the hood to pass property information from the template to the controls within the pane, presenting a coherent user interface between the two panes that has to be developed only once.

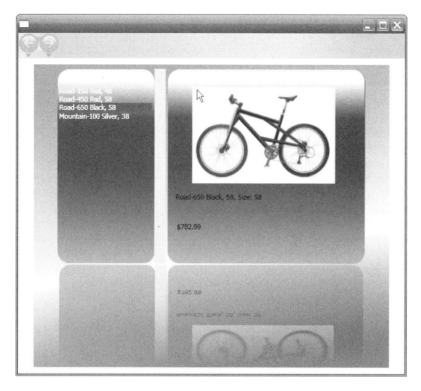

Figure 2-5. *Controls deriving their properties from a template*

System.Windows.Media.Visual

This is the entry point into the WPF composition system. It displays data by traversing the data structures managed by the milcore, and these are represented using a hierarchical display tree with rendering instructions at each node of the tree. When you build a WPF user interface, you are creating elements of this class, which communicate with milcore using an internal messaging protocol.

System.Windows.UIElement

UIElement is at the heart of three major subsystems in WPF—layout, input, and events.

Layout is a core concept in WPF, and UIElement introduces a new concept of how this is achieved differently from the familiar flow, absolute, and table layouts. It does this using two passes, called *measure* and *arrange*.

The measure pass allows a component to specify how much real estate it needs. This allows applications to automatically size their content areas, determining a desired size based on the size of the application.

When a measure phase results in changes to the desired size of controls, the arrange pass may need to change how they are arranged on the screen.

When it comes to input, a user action originates as a signal on a device driver (such as that for the mouse) and gets routed via the kernel and User32 to WPF. At the WPF level, it is converted into a raw WPF message that is sent to the dispatcher. At this level, it can be converted into multiple events; for example, a mouse move event can also spawn a mouse enter event for a specific control. These events can then be captured at the UIElement layer and passed to derived controls for the programmer to handle.

System.Windows.FrameworkElement

The primary features provided by FrameworkElement relate to application layout. FrameworkElement builds on the layout introduced by UIElement (see the previous section) and makes it easier for layout authors to have a consistent set of layout semantics. Effectively, it allows the programmer or designer to override the automatic layout functionality introduced by UIElement by specifying alignment and layout properties for controls. These then use FrameworkElement under the hood.

Two critical elements that FrameworkElement introduces to the WPF platform are data binding and styles. You'll see these used throughout WPF applications.

How to Program WPF Applications

In Chapters 3 and 4, you will use Expression Interactive Designer and Visual Studio 2005 with the Cider designer to build a WPF application. Earlier, you saw the underlying classes that support WPF applications, but before you start developing applications, it's a good idea to know how your higher-level managed code works. You may not directly use many of the classes in the previous sections, but you are likely to use the ones in the following sections extensively. So, before you get down and dirty with development, let's take a tour of these objects.

Using the Application Object

At the core of all WPF applications is the Application object. The class is in the System.Windows namespace and is in the presentationframework.dll assembly.

This object forms the interface between your application and the operating system, allowing you to manage your application as a collection of XAML pages.

It handles message dispatching on your behalf, so you do not need to implement a message loop, and it supports navigation between pages in its collection. It also has an application-level global object that provides a way to share data between pages and a number of application-level events that can be handled by the programmer, such as when the application starts.

This object is global to the application. Every page has access to the *same* Application object. It is created when the executable is launched and runs for the duration of the application. It is also local to the user's system. The application does not communicate with a server to update it.

By providing methods and events that can be overridden and handled respectively, you can customize your Application object because it is extensible.

The WPF creates the Application object at compile time using the application definition file, which is the XAML file, and its (optional) associated code-behind file. The application definition file is distinguished from other XAML files by using an ApplicationDefinition item instead of a Page definition item. Listing 2-1 shows an example of a simple Application definition file.

Listing 2-1. *Application Definition File*

```
<Application
    xmlns="http://schemas.microsoft.com/winfx/2006/xaml/presentation"
    xmlns:x="http://schemas.microsoft.com/winfx/2006/xaml"
    x:Class="UntitledProject1.MainApplication"
    StartupUri="Scene1.xaml"/>
```

Similarly, Listing 2-2 shows a Page definition file.

Listing 2-2. *Page Definition File*

```
<Page
    xmlns="http://schemas.microsoft.com/winfx/2006/xaml/presentation"
    xmlns:x="http://schemas.microsoft.com/winfx/2006/xaml"
    xmlns:mc="http://schemas.openxmlformats.org/markup-compatibility/2006"
    xmlns:d="http://schemas.microsoft.com/expression/interactivedesigner/2006"
    mc:Ignorable="d"
    x:Name="RootPage"
    x:Class="UntitledProject1.Page1"
    WindowTitle="Root Page">

    <Page.Resources>
        <Storyboard x:Key="OnLoaded"/>
    </Page.Resources>

    <Page.Triggers>
        <EventTrigger RoutedEvent="FrameworkElement.Loaded">
            <BeginStoryboard
                                    x:Name="OnLoaded_BeginStoryboard"
                                    Storyboard="{DynamicResource OnLoaded}"/>
        </EventTrigger>
    </Page.Triggers>

    <Grid Background="#FFFFFFFF" x:Name="DocumentRoot" Width="640" Height="480">
        <Grid.ColumnDefinitions>
            <ColumnDefinition/>
        </Grid.ColumnDefinitions>
        <Grid.RowDefinitions>
            <RowDefinition/>
        </Grid.RowDefinitions>
    </Grid>
</Page>
```

When you create an application in Visual Studio 2005 using the WinFX Windows Application template, the application definition file will be created automatically for you. The root tag of this file is the <Application> tag, and it is used to define application-level resources such as styles, which will be inherited by all the pages in your application. Listing 2-3 shows the simple application definition file again.

Listing 2-3. *Application Definition File*

```
<Application
    xmlns="http://schemas.microsoft.com/winfx/2006/xaml/presentation"
    xmlns:x="http://schemas.microsoft.com/winfx/2006/xaml"
    x:Class="UntitledProject1.MainApplication"
    StartupUri="Scene1.xaml"/>
```

The first two tags describe the namespaces that are used to validate the document. They are the presentation and xaml schemas from WinFX 2006 in this example. As the API evolves, these schemas will likely also evolve. The latter of these defines the xaml schema to dictate the x namespace, and you can see this in use in the third attribute.

This attribute, x:Class, determines the underlying class file for which this application XAML defines the Application object.

The StartupUri property specifies the XAML file that initially loads. When this is specified, a NavigationWindow object is automatically created and the page is loaded into it.

When you compile, this information is used to create the Application object for your application. It then sets the StartupUri property as specified. In this case, it has no code-behind page, and you need to use one only when you want to handle an event of the Application object or you do not use the StartupUri property to specify a starting page. You would use such a file in the following scenarios:

Application events: The object supports a number of application-level events such as Startup and Exit that are used to handle some actions upon start-up or shutdown.

Global navigation events: The Application object supports all the events that fire when navigation takes place in any of your application windows. These include events such as Navigated, when navigation is complete; Navigating, while it is in progress; and NavigationStopped, when the user has canceled a navigation action.

Custom properties and methods: You can use these to add data points and functions that you'd like to call from any page in the application.

Accessing Properties

To access your Application object, you use the Application.Current property. This allows you to access properties and other information.

You would set the information like this:

```
MyApp.Current.Properties["UserName"] = txtUserName.Text;
```

To retrieve the information, you should cast the data type before using it like this:

```
string strUserName = (string) MyApp.Current.Properties["UserName"]
```

Handling Events

The Application object provides a number of events as well as methods that can be called to raise these events. I discuss them in the following sections.

Activated Event

You can use the Activated event to handle the application being activated by the system. So if the user activates the already running application by selecting its icon on the Windows taskbar, this event is fired.

So, for example, if you want to implement a handler for Activated, you would have a XAML application definition that looks like Listing 2-4.

Listing 2-4. *Application Definition File Containing Activated Handler*

```
<Application
    xmlns="http://schemas.microsoft.com/winfx/2006/xaml/presentation"
    xmlns:x="http://schemas.microsoft.com/winfx/2006/xaml"
    x:Class="AvalonBook.MyApp"
    StartupUri="Scene1.xaml"/
            Activated="MyApp_Activated">
```

Your associated code-behind file would look like Listing 2-5.

Listing 2-5. *Handling the Activated Event*

```
using System;
using System.Windows;

namespace AvalonBook
{
    public partial class MyApp : Application
    {
        private bool isApplicationActive;

        void MyApp_Activated(object sender, EventArgs e)
        {
            // Activated
            this.isApplicationActive = true;
        }

    }
}
```

Deactivated Event

The Deactivated event handles the response to the window being deactivated, which happens if the user presses Alt+Tab to move to a different application or selects the icon of a different application on the taskbar.

You would configure your application to handle the Deactivated event using the application definition XAML like in Listing 2-6.

Listing 2-6. *Specifying the Deactivated Event*

```
<Application
    xmlns="http://schemas.microsoft.com/winfx/2006/xaml/presentation"
    xmlns:x="http://schemas.microsoft.com/winfx/2006/xaml"
    x:Class="AvalonBook.MyApp"
    StartupUri="Scene1.xaml"/
            Activated="MyApp_Activated"
            Deactivated="MyApp_Deactivated">
```

Your application would be coded to support the event like in Listing 2-7.

Listing 2-7. *Handling the Deactivated Event*

```
using System;
using System.Windows;

namespace AvalonBook
{
    public partial class MyApp : Application
    {
        private bool isApplicationActive;

        void MyApp_Activated(object sender, EventArgs e)
        {
            // Activated
            this.isApplicationActive = true;
        }

        void MyApp_Deactivated(object sender, EventArgs e)
        {
            // Activated
            this.isApplicationActive = false;
        }

    }
}
```

SessionEnding Event

The SessionEnding event handles the situation where the application is being shut down by the operating system. So if the user shuts down the computer while the application is still running, you may need to do some cleanup. Here is a good place to do it!

To use it, you specify it in the application definition file like in Listing 2-8.

Listing 2-8. *Specifying the SessionEnding Event*

```
<Application
    xmlns="http://schemas.microsoft.com/winfx/2006/xaml/presentation"
    xmlns:x="http://schemas.microsoft.com/winfx/2006/xaml"
    x:Class="AvalonBook.MyApp"
    StartupUri="Scene1.xaml"/
                SessionEnding="MyApp_SessionEnding">
```

The associated code-behind file would look like Listing 2-9.

Listing 2-9. *Handling the SessionEnding Event*

```
using System;
using System.Windows;

namespace AvalonBook
{
    public partial class MyApp : Application
    {
        void MyApp_SessionEnding(object sender, SessionEndingCancelEventArgs e)
        {
            // Save data using a helper function
            SaveOpenData();
        }
    }
}
```

Supporting Application-Level Navigation Events

The Application object supports events that are related to navigation events, such as the Navigating event. In the context of the Application object, they are raised on the application rather than on a particular window.

The supported events are as follows:

Navigating: The navigation has been initiated. It is still possible for the user to cancel the event and prevent navigation from taking place.

NavigationProgress: This tracks the progress of the navigation. It is raised periodically to provide information about the progress of the navigation action.

Navigated: The target has been found, and the page download of the target document has begun. Part of its user interface tree has been parsed, and at least its root has been attached to the window.

LoadCompleted: The target page has been loaded and fully parsed.

Using the Application Object to Manage Your Windows

The Application object provides two properties that can help to manage the windows in your application.

The Windows property is a reference to a collection of open windows in your application. You can iterate through this collection to find and activate (or perform another action) on the window of your choice.

The MainWindow property contains a reference to the main window of your application. This is, by default, the first window to open when you run your application.

Managing the Shutdown of Your Application

After the application calls the Shutdown method, the system raises the Exit event. To run code that performs a final cleanup, you can write code in its event handler or in an override of its corresponding method OnExit.

You can also control how and when your application shuts down using the Shutdown-Mode property. This can contain any of the following values (which have an enumeration type within the API). Each of these can trigger the shutdown in addition to the explicit call to Shutdown.

OnLastWindowClose: As its name suggests, the application shuts down when the last window closes.

OnMainWindowClose: This shuts down the application when the main window is closed.

OnExplicitShutdown: This shuts down the application only on an explicit call to the Shutdown function.

Another instance of when the application can be shut down is when the operating system attempts to shut it down when, for example, the user logs off or shuts down the system while your application is still running. In this case, the Application object raises the SessionEnding event, which you can handle to tidy up the application state. If the user does not cancel this event (if given a choice to in your code), the system then calls the Shutdown function, which as described earlier raises the Exit event.

Window Management

Most applications have more than one window. WPF offers three types of window you can use, each with its own strengths and associated costs. You build them using the Window class, the NavigationWindow class, and the Page class. I discuss them in the next sections.

Using the Window Object

The Window object supports basic window functionality. If your application does not use navigation, it is good to use this type of object as opposed to NavigationWindow (see the next section) because it has less overhead and uses fewer system resources than a navigation window. However, your application can use both, so an application that uses NavigationWindows can still use Window objects for secondary windows or dialog boxes that don't require navigation support.

The API of the Window object supports properties, events, and methods that you can use to control how the window appears and how it responds to user interaction.

Some of these actions control creating, closing, showing, and hiding the window. You can also control its size and position through properties. Many of the window's adornments, including the style, caption, status bar, and taskbar icon, are available via the Window object API. Additionally, changes in window state and location can trigger custom code through event handlers associated with them.

Using the NavigationWindow Object

The NavigationWindow object is an extension of the Window object and thus supports its API. However, it adds support to allow for navigating between XAML pages. This includes a Navigate method that allows for programmatic navigation from one page to another. It also implements a default navigation user interface that supports forward and backward navigation that can be customized by the developer. You can see these in Figure 2-6.

Figure 2-6. *The navigation buttons from the NavigationWindow object*

Using the Page Object

The Page object provides an alternative way to access the NavigationWindow object. However, the NavigationWindow object does not allow (despite its name) navigation to a page that has Window or NavigationWindow as its root element. To get around this restriction, WPF also provides a page element. When using this element, you can freely navigate between windows that use Window or NavigationWindow as their root elements.

Managing Windows

Your application will have a window that is designated as the *main* window. When your application starts, the first window that is created will become this main window. A reference to this window is available from the Application object by accessing its MainWindow property. This is a read/write property, so you can change your main window should you like by assigning another window to it. Note that it contains a reference to a Window object, so if you want access to methods, events, or properties that may be used for navigation, you'll have to cast it to a NavigationWindow object.

Additionally, the Application object has a collection of references to all the open windows in your application. They appear in the order in which they were created. Thus, as you create and close windows, their indexes can change. Although the main window is the first one opened and will typically have the index of 0 under this scheme, this may not always be the case; therefore, if you use the MainWindow property to change, for example, MainWindow to another window, then the Window that was formerly the main window will still have index 0, and the MainWindow will have a different index in the Windows collection. This is why it is always good practice to use the MainWindow property to establish the main window, not Windows[0].

The events in Table 2-1 can be handled to manage the behavior of your application upon changes of state to your windows.

Table 2-1. *Window Management Events*

Event	Occurs When
Activated	The window has been activated programmatically or by user action.
Closed	The window is about to close.
Closing	The window is in the process of closing. Occurs directly after closed and can be used to reverse the process of closing.
ContentRendered	The content of the window has finished rendering.
Deactivated	The window has been deactivated by activating another window with Alt+Tab or by selecting another application on the taskbar.
LocationChanged	The location of the window has changed.
StateChanged	The state of the window has changed between Minimized, Maximized, and Normal.

Summary

In this chapter, you were introduced to the framework that WPF offers. You first looked into the types of applications you can build, exploring the differences between browser-based and Windows-based installed applications and the impact on security, and thus functionality, that each offers.

Next, you looked into the architecture of WPF and how all the parts hang together, including a look at the underlying classes that help everything to work. You may never need to use these classes explicitly, but you will always use them implicitly, so it's nice to have an idea of what they are doing!

Finally, you learned about some of the objects that are global to your application such as the Application, Window, and NavigationWindow objects and how they work together. This may all seem pretty theoretical at the moment, but don't worry—just put the information away in your toolbox, and when you start getting into application creation, they'll become useful.

In the next couple of chapters, you'll start putting this theory into practice, first using Expression Interactive Designer to build a simple application that uses a localized data store and then expanding it into one that connects with a live data service using the Windows Communication Foundation; through these examples you'll see how the different aspects of WinFX can work together seamlessly.

CHAPTER 3

███

Building Your First WPF Application

In the first two chapters of this book, you looked at the overall architecture of the next generation of Windows development, focusing on the core of user interface development through the Windows Presentation Foundation (WPF).

In this chapter, you'll get your hands dirty by building your first WPF application. Specifically, you'll build a heavy client application that uses a local Extensible Markup Language (XML) file as the data store for a proof of concept of how an online store could present a slick user interface in WPF using the Microsoft Expression Interactive Designer. In the next chapter, you'll build an application using Visual Studio .NET end to end to create a Windows Communication Foundation (WCF) service that fronts a SQL Server database and exposes it to a WPF front end—built using Cider, the Extensible Application Markup Language (XAML) add-in for Visual Studio 2005.

Getting Started

You'll build this application exclusively using the Expression Interactive Designer. This tool, formerly known as Sparkle, is a new addition to your developer toolbox. It is a fully featured XAML designer that is targeted to professional graphics and user experience designers. It allows them to work in an environment with which they are familiar (instead of using Visual Studio 2005) and allows the developers who implement the application to work in their familiar coding, debugging, and deployment environment. Both use the same project file format and structure, both use XAML to define the user interface, and both can write C# or Visual Basic 2005 code; therefore, the Interactive Designer allows the designer and developer to work closer together than ever before.

█Note You can learn more about the Interactive Designer at http://www.microsoft.com/expression.

It is good, as a developer, to get some familiarity with the Expression Interactive Designer because you can use it for coding and developing "live" applications. That's why you'll be using the Interactive Designer exclusively in this chapter. In the next chapter, as you tie the application to live data, delivered via WCF, you'll get back into Visual Studio and use Cider to develop the XAML.

The Application

The application in question uses data from the AdventureWorks sample database in SQL Server 2005. To start simple, you'll use a snapshot of data from this database that is stored in a flat XML file. The file format is straightforward, as shown in Listing 3-1.

Listing 3-1. *XML Format for Sample Data*

```xml
<?xml version="1.0" encoding="UTF-8"?>
<Catalog>
 <Products>
  <Product>
    <PCode>BK-R93R-48</PCode>
    <Name>Road-150 Red, 48</Name>
    <Image>c:\bikecatalog\1.GIF</Image>
    <Description>Road-150 Red, Size 48
    </Description>
    <Rating>***</Rating>
    <Price>$3578.27</Price>
  </Product>
  <Product>
    <PCode>BK-R68R-58</PCode>
    <Name>Road-450 Red, 58</Name>
    <Image>c:\bikecatalog\2.gif</Image>
    <Description>Road-450 Red, 58 Size 58
    </Description>
    <Rating>****</Rating>
    <Price>$1457.99</Price>
  </Product>
  <Product>
    <PCode>BK-R50B-58</PCode>
    <Name>Road-650 Black, 58</Name>
    <Image>c:\bikecatalog\3.gif</Image>
    <Description>Road-650 Black, 58, Size: 58
    </Description>
    <Rating>**</Rating>
    <Price>$782.99</Price>
  </Product>
  <Product>
    <PCode>BK-M82S-38</PCode>
    <Name>Mountain-100 Silver, 38</Name>
    <Image>c:\bikecatalog\4.gif</Image>
    <Description>Mountain 100 Silver, Size 38
    </Description>
```

```
    <Rating>*****</Rating>
    <Price>$3399.99</Price>
   </Product>
  </Products>
</Catalog>
```

As you can see, this is a pretty straightforward format. The <Products> node contains each <Product>, and in turn each of these contains child nodes with the associated data for a specific product such as its product code, its name, its price, and the path to the product image. The paths are hard-coded to the c:\bikecatalog directory.

Expression Interactive Designer allows you to bind to an object data source or a flat XML file. You'll be using the latter of these as you create this application.

You'll first create a basic application that uses XAML controls to create a bound list of products, and when each product is selected, details about that product and a product picture will load into other controls on the page. You can see the application in action in Figure 3-1.

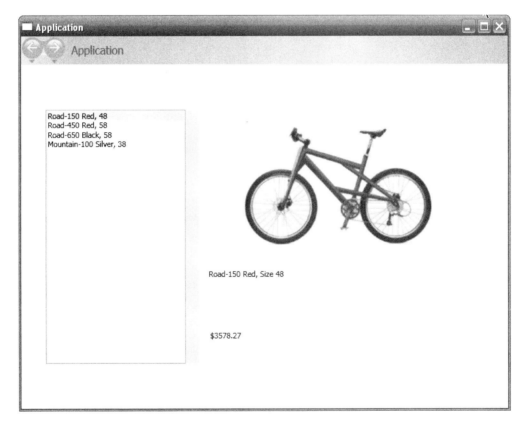

Figure 3-1. *The basic version of the AdventureWorks browser application*

Once you've built this, you'll next use Expression Interactive Designer and XAML to dress up the application with some nice graphical effects.

But let's walk before we run—you'll now get started building the basic application.

Building an Application in Expression Interactive Designer

The following sections will take you through how to use Expression Interactive Designer to build a basic application. You'll add window dressing, including gradients, reflections, 3D, and gel effects, later. Expression Interactive Designer is a straightforward tool to use, although some features are a bit different from what you may be used to using in Visual Studio. It's a good idea to take a step-by-step approach to using Expression Interactive Designer to build a simple application, and that's what these sections will provide. By the time you're done with this chapter, you'll be much more confident in how to build applications like Microsoft Codenamed Max using XAML.

Creating the Basic Application Layout

With Expression Interactive Designer, you can start a new project of type Windows EXE. This creates a Visual Studio 2005–compatible project file that contains the XAML and other project files necessary to compile and run the application. You can see the Create New Project dialog box in Figure 3-2.

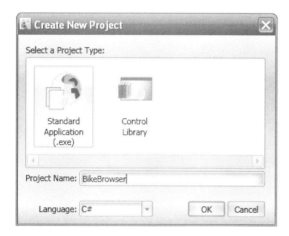

Figure 3-2. *Creating a new Windows application*

The application is based on the Master/Details pattern. It lists the products on the left side, and when you select a product, it shows its details on the right.

A splitter down the middle breaks the scene into two independent panes that can be resized relative to each other. To get the splitter, you place a Grid control on the scene and then place a splitter inside the grid.

If you look at the Library palette, you'll see the Grid control in it, as shown in Figure 3-3; simply select it, and draw the area you want the grid to occupy on the scene.

Figure 3-3. *The Library palette containing the Grid control*

At the bottom of the screen you'll see a Timeline panel containing all the elements. Note that a new grid has been added. Rename it to ProductGrid. Figure 3-4 shows the Timeline panel.

Figure 3-4. *The Expression Interactive Designer Timeline panel*

When you select the grid by double-clicking it in the Timeline panel, Expression Interactive Designer draws a yellow border around it in the designer, with an additional blue border to the top and to the left. Figure 3-5 shows this in the context of the completed user interface.

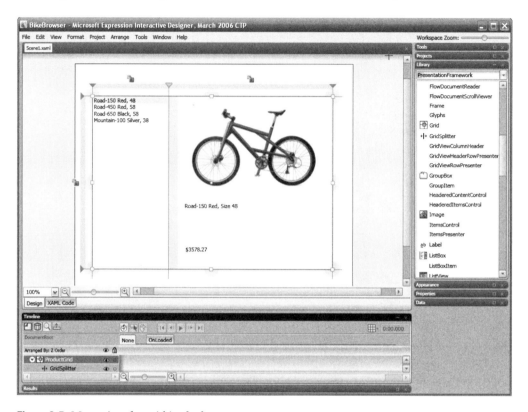

Figure 3-5. *Managing the grid in the browser*

Make sure you are using the Selection tool in the Tools palette, and then hover over the blue border with your mouse pointer. A red bar will appear. This bar, called a *grid line*, will be the location of your splitter. Set it to a place you are happy with, and click it to split the grid into two columns. See Figure 3-6 for an example.

When you want to place content on a grid, you use ContentControl. This acts as a parent to store a *single* control within the grid. If you want to store more than one control within a grid, you use a Panel control. You simply place a ContentControl on the grid, put a Panel control within ContentControl, and store as many child controls within the panel as you would like.

The left side of the screen will contain a List control within the grid. This has to be contained within a ContentControl, so drag a ContentControl onto the left pane of the grid.

This ContentControl will form the container for the master list of products you saw earlier. As such, it needs to fill its complete pane. At this point, it's good to rename it to something such as Master.

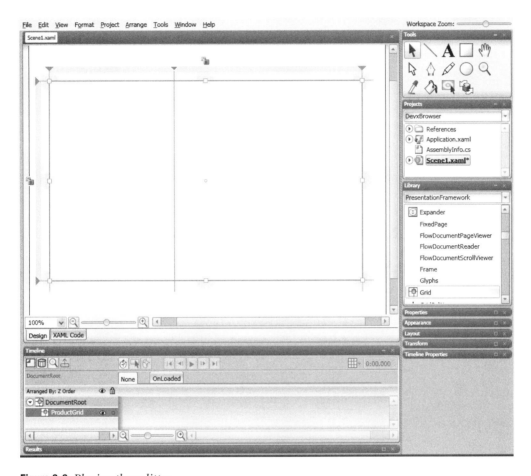

Figure 3-6. *Placing the splitter*

Next, you'll need to resize the ContentControl to fit completely within its pane. Doing this is a little different in Expression Interactive Designer/XAML than in Visual Studio 2005. You'll first need to select the ContentControl and edit its layout properties. If you don't see a Layout panel near the tools on the right side of the screen, open the View drop-down list, and select Layout. To make the ContentControl fill its parent column, set the Width and Height properties to NaN (which means "Not a Number"), its alignments to Stretch, and its margins all to 0 pixels. See Figures 3-7 and 3-8 for more details.

Figure 3-7. *Editing the size of a control*

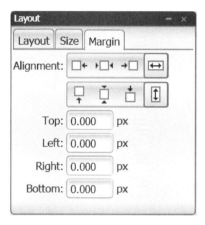

Figure 3-8. *Editing the margins and alignments for a control*

The right side of the screen will contain the details for the product selected on the left. To achieve this, you put a ContentControl control on the grid and then place a Grid control into this. The Grid control can then contain multiple child controls.

Therefore, the next step is to draw another ContentControl control anywhere in the right side of the grid. Name this control Details.

Your screen should look something like Figure 3-9.

This controls the layout details for Size, and you should set Margin in the same way that you did for the first ContentControl except in this case, give it a small left margin (20 pixels should do the trick). This will create a space between the two panes into which you'll put a splitter control. This will handle all split and window resizing automatically for you at runtime. If you're lost, don't worry—all will become clear later when you run the application.

To get a splitter, find the GridSplitter control in the Toolbox, and draw it in the small space that you left between the Master and Details panes. It should fill in with a rectangle. If you are having difficulty placing it, you can use the Zoom tool at the bottom of the scene to zoom in and get more precision when drawing the splitter.

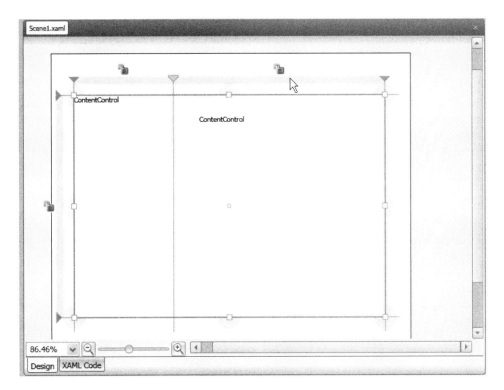

Figure 3-9. *Placing the second ContentControl control*

Performing the Basic Data Binding

As you saw earlier in this chapter, the data source you'll use is a flat XML file containing the product details as well as the hard-coded path to the picture file.

Expression Interactive Designer and XAML support data binding, which you can achieve through a data source connection to the XML file. If you cannot already view the Data palette, select View ➤ Data. You'll then see it (see Figure 3-10).

Figure 3-10. *The Data palette*

Because this is an XML data source, click the Add XML Data Source link.

In the ensuing dialog box, browse to the XML file containing the catalog information, and give it a friendly name such as BikeSource. This XML file will be an exact copy of Listing 3-1; alternatively, you can get the file and relevant pictures from the Source Code/Downloads section of the Apress website (http://www.apress.com/).

Next you will tie this to your application by selecting the base grid (called ProductGrid) and then viewing the Properties palette. On this palette, you can see the DataContext property. If you select it, a menu pops up. From this menu, you can click DataBind, as shown in Figure 3-11, to open the Create Data Binding dialog box.

Figure 3-11. *Using the DataContext property*

Your aim in this step is to set the application's data context, namely, the root part of the overall data structure that contains the part in which you are interested. In this case, several Product elements appear in the file (denoted by Product[n] in the field browser on the right side of Figure 3-12), and this is what you want the data context of the application to be—after all, it will be a product browser.

Next, you'll want to start adding some of the individual controls and map them to fields within this context. Naturally, you'll want a list that displays the names of the products.

Add a List control to the Master pane (remember, Master is the name of the ContentControl you placed on the left side of the grid earlier). The easiest way to do this is to select Master in the Timeline panel by double-clicking it. After you select it, you can then find the ListBox control in the Library panel and double-click it to add it to the page. You'll see the ListBox fill the Master pane, which will appear as a child control to Master in the Timeline, as shown in Figure 3-13.

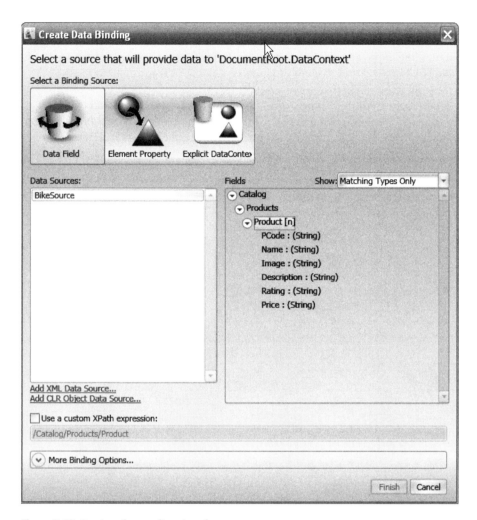

Figure 3-12. *Setting the application data context*

Figure 3-13. *ProductList is a child of Master.*

A ListBox is bound to its data using its ItemsSource property, which you can find in the Properties palette. When you're happy with the layout of the ListBox, select the ItemsSource property, and from the menu that pops up, select DataBind. You'll be presented with the Create Data Binding dialog box. Remember to expand the nodes as in Figure 3-13 to see the elements in the Product[n] node.

This time, as you are binding a control to an explicit data context, you should click the Explicit DataContext binding source button. Remember that the parent grid was bound to the Catalog data source, and the ListBox control should bind to a field within this context. See Figure 3-14.

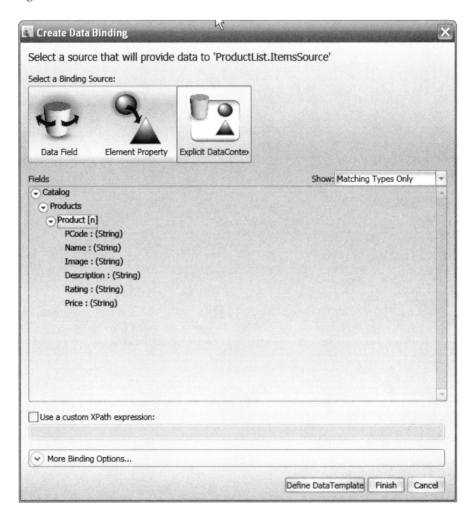

Figure 3-14. *Binding the list to an explicit data source*

You're not done with this dialog box yet. When binding the list, you need to create a data template for the binding. At the bottom of the dialog box you'll see the Define Data Template button, which allows you to create one of these. You use the data template to specify the fields of the Product record to which you want to bind the list.

If you click the Define Data Template button, you'll see the dialog box shown in Figure 3-15. It will have all the fields under Product already checked. Remove the checks from all but the Name field. This will populate the list with the contents of the Name field for each record.

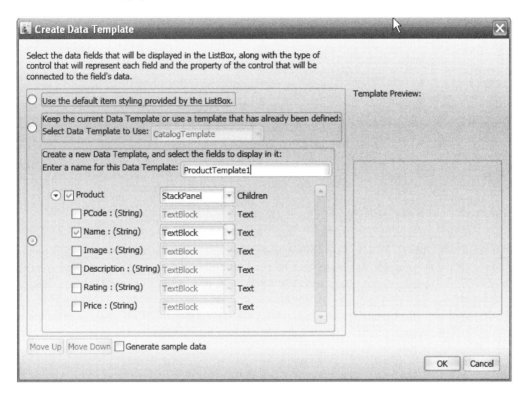

Figure 3-15. *Defining the data template for the list*

Click OK; you should be returned to your designer view, and the contents of the list box will already be filled. Data binding occurs at design as well as runtime in Expression Interactive Designer, helping you make sure your presentation is perfect. You can see this in Figure 3-16.

Before running the application, you should pick and set a default item to be selected so that the Details pane will have something to show. To do this, set the ListBox's SelectedIndex property to 0, ensuring that the top item in the list is selected by default. You should also set the IsSynchronizedWithCurrentItem property to true to ensure that the list stays synchronized with the current context of the data.

Next, you'll add the fields that show the data related to the current selected item, such as its picture, its product code, and its price. These will get added to the Details pane.

Road-150 Red, 48
Road-450 Red, 58
Road-650 Black, 58
Mountain-100 Silver, 38

Figure 3-16. *The list data is loaded through the binding—even at design time.*

Remember, the Details area is a content pane that can hold only one control, so you have to put a Grid control inside it, which can hold many children. Make sure the Details pane (and only the Details pane) is selected. It will have a yellow border around it when it is properly selected. If you have trouble with this, double-click it in the Timeline panel to select it. Next, double-click the Grid control in the Library. That will add a new grid, sized to fit perfectly within the Details pane.

To this Grid control you should add two new TextBlock controls and an Image control. Size and place them anyway you'd like. When you are working on it, your screen should look something like Figure 3-17.

You can bind the TextBlock controls by selecting their Text property and clicking Data-Bind. This will take you to the Create Data Binding dialog box.

Because you are binding to something on an already well-known context, click the Explicit DataContext button, and then navigate to the relevant field—in this case, bind the TextBlock controls to the Description and Price properties of the data. You don't need to set a template for them, because they are a simple mapping of a property on the control to a field in the data context. See Figure 3-18 for an example of binding the Description field to the Description text block.

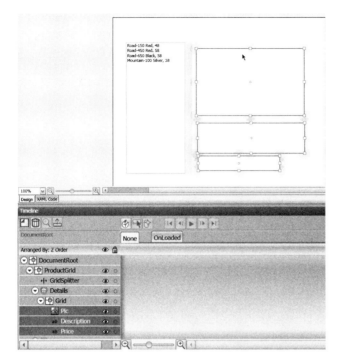

Figure 3-17. *Building the Details pane*

Figure 3-18. *Binding the Description text block to the appropriate field*

Binding the picture box is particularly clever. In this case, the path to the image is stored in the data context as a text string. If you bind this string to the Source property of the image, WPF will then load that image and render it in the picture box. You don't need to write any code to handle loading from the file system. You can see its binding dialog box in Figure 3-19. As you can see, it works in the same way as binding the TextBlock from Figure 3-18.

Figure 3-19. *Binding the image to the data context*

Running the Application

As in Visual Studio, pressing F5 will execute the application. This runs it within the XAML browser, as shown in Figure 3-20.

You'll notice in Figure 3-20 that there is a large gray bar down the middle of the screen. This is the splitter you added earlier. If you drag this to the left or right of the screen, not only will the list adjust its width to fit but also the controls on the right side will automatically scale themselves to fit the available space. Figure 3-21 shows the effect of the splitter being shifted a long way to the right, leaving less screen space for the image, description, and price fields.

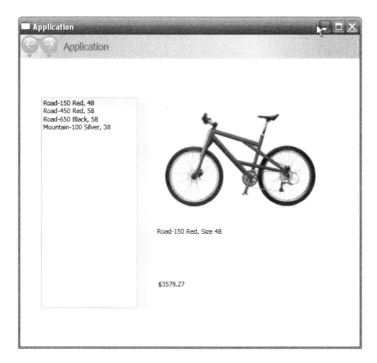

Figure 3-20. *Running the bike browser application*

Figure 3-21. *Automatic elastic features when using the splitter*

All this has been handled for you *automatically* when using WPF. In addition to the fields dynamically allocating their sizes based on the splitter, they'll also automatically resize if you resize the application window. Figure 3-22 shows how the details interior grid resizes itself if the right half of the base grid is made larger.

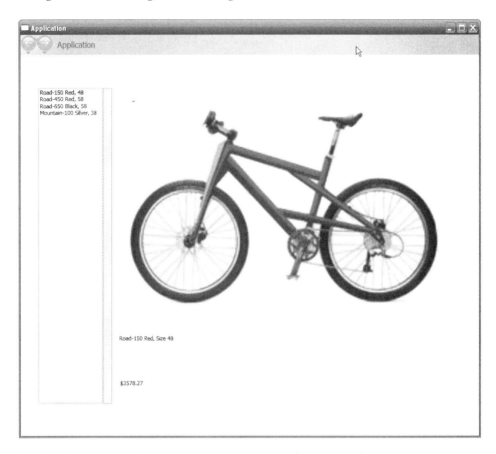

Figure 3-22. *Behavior of the application when the window is resized*

So, there you have it—your first, basic WPF application, built using Expression Interactive Designer. It's pretty dull, but it's functional. In the "A More Advanced WPF User Interface" section of this chapter, you'll learn how you can dress up this application with fancy shading, reflection, and other effects. But first, because this is a XAML application, let's take a short breather from playing with Expression Interactive Designer and look at what has been going on under the hood.

Exploring the XAML for the Bike Browser

When using Expression Interactive Designer, you can hand-code XAML for your application if you prefer by selecting the XAML Code tab at the bottom of the designer window. Alternatively, you can use this to do some fine-tuning or editing.

Document Root: The Grid

The base level of definition on an Expression Interactive Designer XAML page is the *grid*. You can see this as the root node of the document, as shown in Listing 3-2.

Listing 3-2. *The Root <Grid> Node*

```
<Grid
  xmlns="http://schemas.microsoft.com/winfx/2006/xaml/presentation"
  xmlns:x="http://schemas.microsoft.com/winfx/2006/xaml"
  xmlns:mc="http://schemas.openxmlformats.org/markup-compatibility/2006"
  xmlns:d="http://schemas.microsoft.com/expression/interactivedesigner/2006"
  mc:Ignorable="d"
  Background="#FFFFFFFF"
  x:Name="DocumentRoot"
  x:Class="BikeBrowser.Scene1"
  Width="579.68" Height="480">
```

This defines the base node for the XAML document, specifying the namespaces that contain the definitions for the different nodes used by the designer and the WPF runtime. It specifies the background color, the document root name, the code-behind class of the scene, and the class representing the present scene. In this case, you are looking at BikeBrowser.Scene1. A *scene* is analogous to a form in Windows development parlance. Scenes are more complex because they are timeline based instead of being purely static, like forms, leading to the possibility of animation effects. In fact, you'll see some of these animation effects later in the "A More Advanced WPF User Interface" section.

Scene Resources

Next will come the <Grid.Resources> node, which contains the definitions of all the resources that will be used by this scene. Examples of such a resource are the data-binding definition and the data template that was used to map the Name field to the list. You can see snippets from the XAML that defines these in Listings 3-3 and 3-4.

Listing 3-3. *Data Binding Definition in Grid.Resources*

```
<XmlDataProvider x:Key="BikeSource"
                 d:IsDataSource="True"
                 Source="C:\bikecatalog\bikecatalog.xml"/>
```

Listing 3-4. *The Data Template for the List Control*

```
<DataTemplate x:Key="ProductTemplate1">
  <StackPanel x:Name="StackPanel">
    <TextBlock x:Name="TextBlock" Text="{Binding Mode=OneWay, XPath=Name}"/>
  </StackPanel>
</DataTemplate>
```

The data template for the List control is given a key, called ProductTemplate1. You'll return to this in a moment, when you see the definition of the ListBox control in XAML and see where it gets mapped back to this template.

Triggers

Next up is the <Grid.Triggers> node where you would define triggers to actions. By default, a XAML scene has a trigger associated with the scene being loaded. This is defined in the <BeginStoryBoard> node, which specifies the resource to execute. In this case, there is no action to perform, so the resource node (under <Grid.Resources>) for the OnLoaded action is empty. Listing 3-5 contains the trigger definitions.

Listing 3-5. *Specifying Triggers*

```
<Grid.Triggers>
  <EventTrigger RoutedEvent="FrameworkElement.Loaded">
    <BeginStoryboard x:Name="OnLoaded_BeginStoryboard"
                     Storyboard="{DynamicResource OnLoaded}"/>
  </EventTrigger>
</Grid.Triggers>
```

And this indicates the OnLoaded dynamic storyboard resource, which is currently empty:

```
<Storyboard x:Key="OnLoaded"/>
```

User Interface Definition

The main part of the application is defined within a <Grid> node at the bottom of the document. This <Grid> node contains the columns and the ContentControls you placed within the columns, as well as the ListBox, Picture, and TextBlock controls.

You can see this in Listing 3-6.

Listing 3-6. *The User Interface Definition XAML*

```
<Grid Margin="36,65,41,64" x:Name="ProductGrid"
        RenderTransformOrigin="0.5,0.5"
        DataContext="{Binding Mode=OneWay,
                      Source={StaticResource BikeSource},
                      XPath=/Catalog/Products/Product}">
  <Grid.ColumnDefinitions>
    <ColumnDefinition Width="0.321492007104796*"/>
    <ColumnDefinition Width="0.678507992895204*"/>
  </Grid.ColumnDefinitions>
  <Grid.RowDefinitions>
    <RowDefinition/>
  </Grid.RowDefinitions>
  <ContentControl HorizontalAlignment="Stretch"
                  VerticalAlignment="Stretch"
```

```
                         x:Name="Master"
                         RenderTransformOrigin="0.5,0.5">
         <ListBox x:Name="ProductList" RenderTransformOrigin="0.5,0.5"
                         IsSynchronizedWithCurrentItem="True"
                         ItemsSource="{Binding Mode=OneWay}"
                         ItemTemplate="{DynamicResource ProductTemplate1}"
                         SelectedIndex="0"/>
    </ContentControl>
    <ContentControl HorizontalAlignment="Stretch" VerticalAlignment="Stretch"
                         Margin="20,0,0,0" Width="Auto" Height="Auto"
                         Grid.Column="1" x:Name="Details"
                         RenderTransformOrigin="0.5,0.5">
      <Grid x:Name="Grid" RenderTransformOrigin="0.5,0.5">
      <Grid.ColumnDefinitions>
        <ColumnDefinition/>
      </Grid.ColumnDefinitions>
      <Grid.RowDefinitions>
        <RowDefinition/>
      </Grid.RowDefinitions>
      <TextBlock VerticalAlignment="Bottom" Margin="15.3923978685612,0,82.68,8"
                 Height="39" x:Name="Price" RenderTransformOrigin="0.5,0.5"
                 Text="{Binding Mode=OneWay, XPath=Price}" TextWrapping="Wrap"/>
      <TextBlock VerticalAlignment="Bottom" Margin="13.3923978685612,0,14.68,54"
                 Height="81" x:Name="Description" RenderTransformOrigin="0.5,0.5"
                 Text="{Binding Mode=OneWay, XPath=Description}"
                 TextWrapping="Wrap"/>
      <Image Margin="10.3923978685612,17,15.68,155" x:Name="Pic"
                 Source="{Binding Mode=OneWay, XPath=Image}"
                 RenderTransformOrigin="0.5,0.5"/>
      </Grid>
    </ContentControl>
    <GridSplitter HorizontalAlignment="Left"
         Margin="0.392397868561062,0.333333333333314,0,-0.666666666666686"
         Width="18.6666666666667" Grid.Column="1" x:Name="GridSplitter"
         RenderTransformOrigin="0.5,0.5"/>
</Grid>
```

ListBox Definition

To understand your application better, take a look at the declarations for each of the controls, starting with the ListBox:

```
<ListBox x:Name="ProductList" RenderTransformOrigin="0.5,0.5"
             IsSynchronizedWithCurrentItem="True"
             ItemsSource="{Binding Mode=OneWay}"
             ItemTemplate="{DynamicResource ProductTemplate1}"
             SelectedIndex="0"/>
```

Here you can see that the ListBox is called ProductList and has its selected index set to 0, indicating that the first item on the list will be selected by default. The specification for the binding is defined in the ItemTemplate attribute, and this is set to {DynamicResource ProductTemplate1}, indicating that this should be taken from the resources section and is defined using the key ProductTemplate1. Refer to Listing 3-4, and you'll see this code.

Within the template, the Name field is defined as the point of interest using its XPath within the current data context. You can see that here:

```
<TextBlock x:Name="TextBlock" Text="{Binding Mode=OneWay, XPath=Name}"/>
```

The interesting part of this is the Text attribute. It shows that the binding is one-way, meaning the list will be reading values from the database and not writing new ones to it. The XPath indicates where the data should be taken from in the current data context. Although the XPath of the Name data isn't simply Name when taken from the document root, it is when taken from the current Data context, which is the Product level, so you simply specify Name to access the Name data.

TextBlock Definitions

You define the TextBlock controls using the <TextBlock> node in XAML. You can see them here:

```
<TextBlock VerticalAlignment="Bottom" Margin="15.3923978685612,0,82.68,8"
               Height="39" x:Name="Price" RenderTransformOrigin="0.5,0.5"
               Text="{Binding Mode=OneWay, XPath=Price}" TextWrapping="Wrap"/>
<TextBlock VerticalAlignment="Bottom" Margin="13.3923978685612,0,14.68,54"
               Height="81" x:Name="Description" RenderTransformOrigin="0.5,0.5"
               Text="{Binding Mode=OneWay, XPath=Description}"
               TextWrapping="Wrap"/>
```

These are straightforward, containing attributes for the layout of the control. The interesting attribute is for the Text property of each control. These contain a {Binding} string that specifies Mode (OneWay, meaning the controls are bound to the data in a read-only manner) and the XPath that indicates the data location within the current context. Because the context is currently on the Product[n] level, the XPath of Price will show the price for the currently selected product.

Image Definition

You define the picture box that contains the images of the bicycles using the <Image> tag in XAML:

```
<Image Margin="10.3923978685612,17,15.68,155" x:Name="Pic"
           Source="{Binding Mode=OneWay, XPath=Image}"
           RenderTransformOrigin="0.5,0.5"/>
```

The interesting attribute here is Source. An image control can load an image from a specified source on the file system, and because in this case the images are stored on the file system and their locations are stored in the XML data document, then when binding the source property to the correct Node, the image will automatically get loaded into the control. In this case, the XPath of the node containing this data, within the current data context, is Image, and when you used the data binding dialog box to indicate this earlier, you were setting up this attribute.

A More Advanced WPF User Interface

Now that you've built the basic application, the next step is to have a little bit more fun with it and to enhance it to look like other WPF applications such as Max by adding some gradient backgrounds, some animations, some gel effects, and more.

You can see the finished version in Figure 3-23. Compare this to the look and feel of the basic version shown in Figure 3-22. In the next few sections, you'll learn how you can achieve the fancy version.

Figure 3-23. *The finished application*

Setting the Background Gradient

The first step is to set the background gradient and lighting effects. You do this on the DocumentRoot element. The easiest way to select this is to find it in the Timeline panel and double-click it. When it is selected properly, you'll see a yellow border around it in the Timeline panel. Figure 3-24 shows what the screen should look like once it is selected.

Figure 3-24. *Selecting the document root in the Timeline*

You will be using the Appearance palette to edit the background of the document root. If it isn't already visible, then open it by selecting View ➤ Appearance. You can see what the Appearance palette looks like in Figure 3-25.

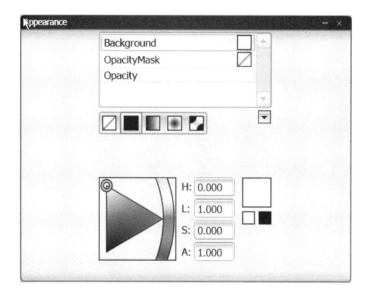

Figure 3-25. *The Appearance palette*

The five squares you see in the Appearance palette are different types of brushes—effectively, they're transforms for how pixels get rendered on the screen. Their names are, from left to right, as follows:

No Brush: The selected area will not get filled.

Solid Brush: The selected area will get filled using a solid color.

Linear Gradient Brush: The selected area will get filled using a gradient that goes from one color to the other by phasing between them in a straight line.

Radial Gradient Brush: The selected area will get filled using a gradient that goes from one color to another with a circular arc between them; specifically, the center of the circle will be one color, the outside will be the other, and the gradient will blur the circle between them.

Tile Brush: This fills the selected area with a tiled image that you specify.

In this case, you'll be using a gradient brush to fill the background of the selected item. As you can see in Figure 3-25, the background is currently set to be a white solid brush, and that is why it appears as a plain white background. With Background still selected, choose Linear Gradient Brush. You'll see that the background of the application instantly changes to a black-to-white, left-to-right linear gradient and that the gradient designer appears on the Appearance palette, as shown in Figure 3-26.

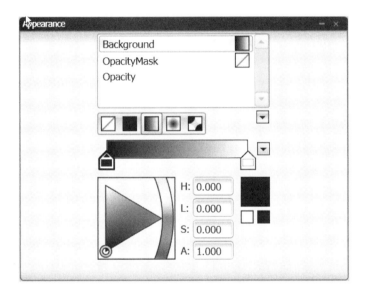

Figure 3-26. *The Appearance palette with Linear Gradient Brush*

You'll see on the gradient designer that there are two color stops: the black on the left and the white on the right. This gives a simple gradient from black to white. You can add new color stops by clicking the gradient tool. You can then change their colors by using the color palette immediately below the tool. See Figure 3-27 for an example of a three-stop linear gradient, from blue to white and then to red.

Now, it would be boring if the gradient were just from left to right, even if you have a number of stops along the way. Fortunately, you can adorn the gradient to make it interesting, such as a top-to-bottom gradient or one at any angle you like. To do this, you need to return to the Tools palette and select the Brush Transform tool, as shown in Figure 3-28.

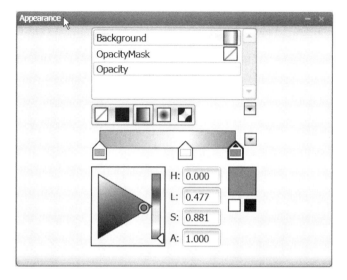

Figure 3-27. *Configuring a three-stop linear gradient*

Figure 3-28. *The Brush Transform tool*

Once you've selected this, you'll notice an arrow appearing on the gradient in the background. This arrow is called the *transform adorner*. You can change the location and direction of this arrow by dragging it. This in turn changes the direction and size of the gradient. Figure 3-29 shows a diagonal gradient made with the adorner.

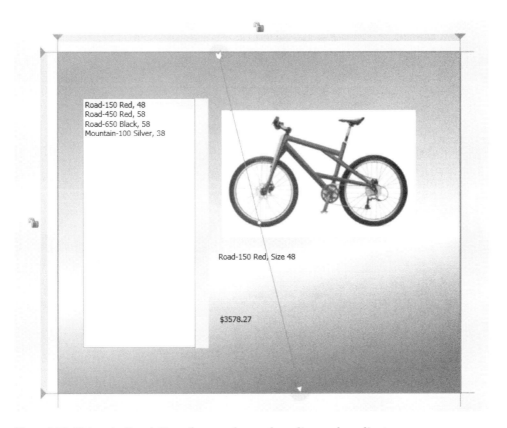

Road-150 Red, 48
Road-450 Red, 58
Road-650 Black, 58
Mountain-100 Silver, 38

Road-150 Red, Size 48

$3578.27

Figure 3-29. *Using the Brush Transform tool to make a diagonal gradient*

Creating the 3D "Gel" Effect

You can achieve the nice 3D gel effects you saw in Figure 3-23 using *control templates*. These are templates for how a grid may appear on a scene. Because you want the left and right sides to have the same 3D effect, it makes sense to create a single template and derive their presentation from it, instead of managing their appearance explicitly twice.

In the Timeline panel, double-click the Master pane, then right-click, and finally select Edit Template. In the ensuing menu, select Edit a Copy of the Template, as shown in Figure 3-30.

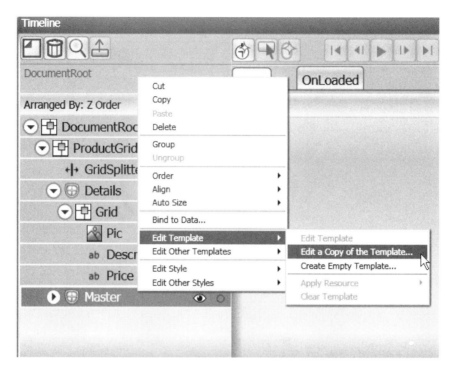

Figure 3-30. *Editing a copy of the template*

When you select this menu entry, the Create ControlTemplate Resource dialog box will appear. You can see it in Figure 3-31.

Figure 3-31. *The Create ControlTemplate Resource dialog box*

You use this dialog box to create the control template. You need to give it a name (for example, ListTemplate) and specify where in the document it is defined and its target type. The former setting allows you to centralize templates in a multidocument application; for now you don't need to do anything, so just leave it as Grid: DocumentRoot. The Target type is important, because it sets the type of control on which the template should be applied. In this case, you are using ContentControls, so you should set this to ContentControl.

When you click OK, you'll notice that the Timeline panel changes—your controls are now gone, as shown in Figure 3-32. Don't worry, it is now just in template-editing mode. You'll return to the main document once you're done here.

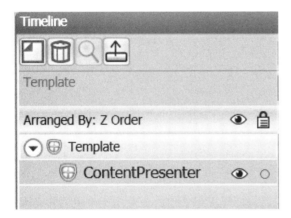

Figure 3-32. *The Timeline panel now shows template material.*

Because the ContentControl you based this template on already had a control in it (the List control), the template has a child ContentPresenter item. Delete this item, and you will see the List control disappear from the designer. Note that you are not deleting the control from your application, just from the template, because it isn't necessary.

When you finish the template and apply it to the application, the List control will acquire the template styling, because it's still present in the content panel that is being templated. Don't worry if this is all a little confusing at the moment—all will become clear as you work with Expression Interactive Designer more.

With the template still selected, double-click the Grid entry in the Toolbox to add a Grid control that completely fills the templated area.

Make sure the grid is selected (double-click it in the Timeline panel), and draw a rectangle inside the grid (the Rectangle tool is in the Tools palette) so that it completely fills the grid. Use the Appearance palette to fill the rectangle with a gradient color. Figure 3-33 shows an example using a vertical gradient.

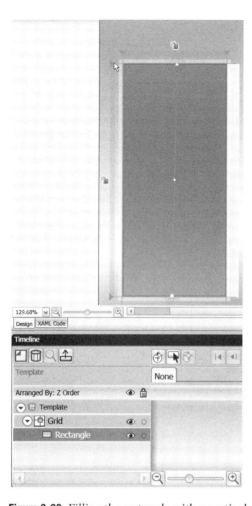

Figure 3-33. *Filling the rectangle with a vertical gradient*

The next step is to round the corners of the rectangle. On the design surface you'll see the corner adorners for the rectangle, as shown in Figure 3-34.

You add the gel highlight using another, smaller rectangle (with a gradient brush fill and white as its color) on top of the existing one. You'll be using an Alpha gradient where the transparency of the rectangle is graded also, leading to the highlight effect.

First, draw a smaller rectangle on the first, and round its corners to match the rounding of the existing rectangle, as shown in Figure 3-35.

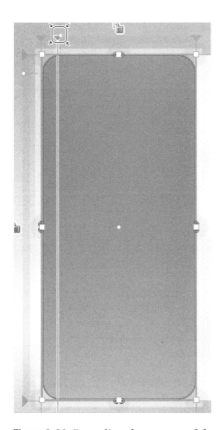

Figure 3-34. *Rounding the corners of the rectangle*

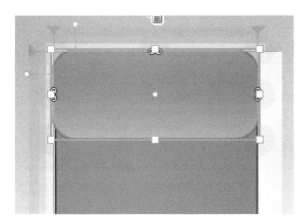

Figure 3-35. *Drawing a second rectangle inside the first*

For this rectangle, set the fill to be a linear gradient and the colors of each side of the gradient to be white. However, the left color on the gradient tool should have an Alpha setting of 0, and the right tool should have an Alpha setting of 0.5. You specify the Alpha setting in the A text box on the Appearance palette, as shown in Figure 3-36.

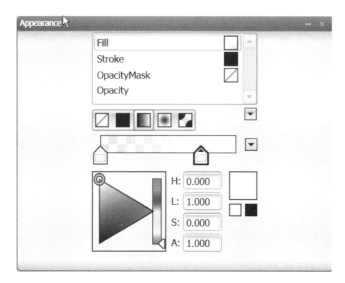

Figure 3-36. *Setting the appearance of the smaller rectangle*

Now you are ready to add the content elements onto the template to try them. Make sure the grid is selected in the Timeline panel, and then double-click ContentPresenter in the Library palette. You'll see the list reappear on top of the rectangles. Resize the list to fit the template area according to your desires underneath the new gel header. Remember that you aren't really laying out a list box here (despite appearances); you are configuring the content presenter so all other controls that derive from this template will know to lay out their controls in the same way. This pane uses the list within its content presenter, and as such, for convenience, Expression Interactive Designer shows the list here.

You are now done with editing the template to get the gel effect. In the Timeline panel, click the Return Scope to Root button to bring you out of template-editing mode and back into designing your application.

Your list is in its nice new gel background, but it is opaque against it and doesn't look too good. You can make it transparent by setting its BackGround and BorderBrush properties to No Brush using the Appearance palette. Figure 3-37 shows how the list should appear.

■**Note** The March Community Technical Preview (CTP) of Expression Interactive Designer has a small bug. Sometimes the settings of the list may appear to be No Brush while the list is still opaque. Explicitly unset and set them again, and it should appear properly.

Figure 3-37. *The transparent list*

Now that you have a template, it's easy to apply it to other controls. On the Details pane, for example, you can get the same effect easily. Find Details in the Timeline pane, and select Edit Template. Then, select Apply Resource, and pick the template. If you've followed along and used the same names as I did, it will be called List Template. The Details pane will now have the gel effect, as shown in Figure 3-38.

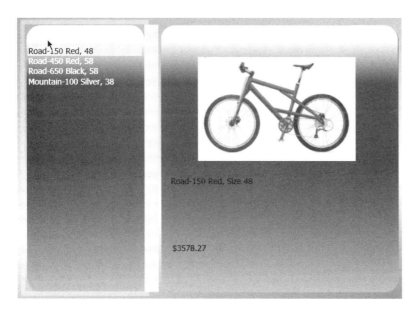

Figure 3-38. *Applying the template to the Details pane*

Creating a Reflection Effect

A reflection effect shows a reflected image of existing content. This is straightforward to create in Expression Interactive Designer but will require you to write some code. In fact, it requires one line of C# code to be written, which you will see in a moment!

The first step is to draw a new rectangle on the document root and call it Reflection. You may need to rearrange your screen a little make room for it. You can see an example of it in Figure 3-39.

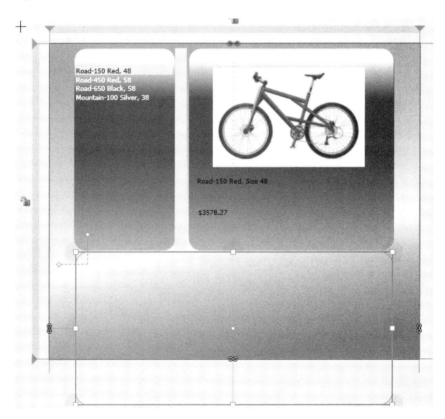

Figure 3-39. *Placing the reflection rectangle on the screen*

This rectangle should have its Fill and Stroke brushes set to No Brush, and its OpacityMask should be an all-white linear gradient. The linear gradient should be white on both sides, with the left having an Alpha setting of 0.7 and the right having an Alpha setting of 0.0, as shown in Figure 3-40.

You'll next need to apply a flip transform to the rectangle. If you don't already see the Transform palette, select View ➤ Transform. Then, on the Flip tab of the Transform palette, select Flip Y, as shown in Figure 3-41.

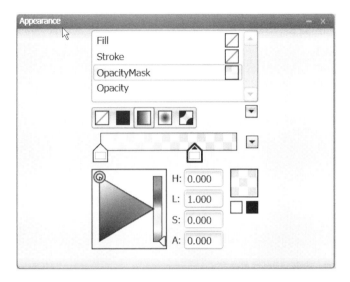

Figure 3-40. *Appearance settings for the reflection rectangle*

Figure 3-41. *Using the flip transform*

Now comes the small amount of code you need to write. This handles copying the contents of the screen into the new rectangle, and the flip transform and opacity will handle the rest.

In the Projects palette, find Scene1.xaml, and expand it. This will reveal Scene1.xaml.cs, as shown in Figure 3-42.

Figure 3-42. *Editing the source code*

Double-click Scene1.xaml.cs, and you'll enter the code editor.

You'll need to add a handler for OnInitialized (which is already being called as a result of a trigger but is being ignored because there is no handler in the code) and add the code to handle copying from the ProductGrid to the reflection rectangle. The code looks like this:

```
protected override void OnInitialized(EventArgs e)
{
    Reflection.Fill = new VisualBrush(ProductGrid);
}
```

Simple, right? Now when you run your application, you should see the reflection.

And that's all there is to it—using simple layout tools that give complex-looking effects, you've been able to almost "codelessly" put together a simple application!

Figure 3-43 shows the final application running, complete with the reflection.

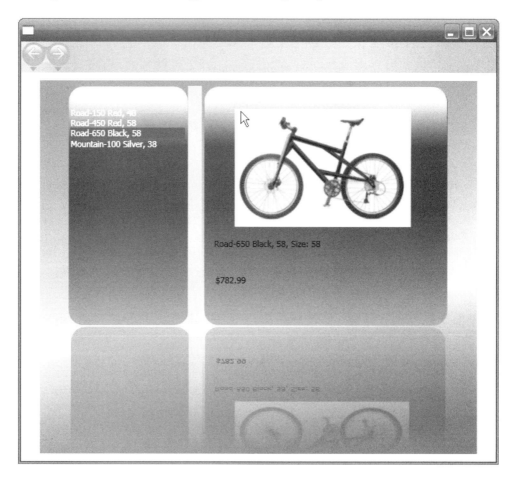

Figure 3-43. *The final application—what an improvement!*

Summary

In this chapter, you built your first XAML-based application using the Expression Interactive Designer. It is a simple data-binding application that binds to a local data store in a flat-file XML.

You also took a good tour of Expression Interactive Designer and its power in user interface design and modeling. You saw that it is more than just a design tool; it is able to bind to data and to write code within a code editor. You used the Appearance palette extensively and learned how straightforward it makes gradients and other visual adorners; these make your user interface far more sophisticated than the standard Windows forms approach.

In Chapter 4, you'll bring Visual Studio back into the application design picture. You'll continue building the bike browser application, but you'll start using live data from a SQL Server 2005 database, which will be exposed via WCF services. You'll first use Cider to build a simple user interface that can be used for testing the connection between a XAML-based WPF front end and the WCF service-oriented back end, and then you'll bind the rich client you've built in this chapter to the live data.

CHAPTER 4

■■■

Building a Connected WPF Application

In the first two chapters of this book, you looked at the overall architecture of the next generation of Windows development, focusing on the core of user interface development through the Windows Presentation Foundation (WPF). Then, you started building an application that took you step by step through how to use Microsoft Expression Interactive Designer to put together a client application.

In this chapter, you will continue that work and build the back-end service that the WPF front end will use for a "live" experience.

Figure 4-1 shows the finished application from Chapter 3. It is a simple product browser that allows you to peruse a catalog of bicycles that is stored on the file system as an Extensible Markup Language (XML) file. A more realistic scenario for a real-world application would be that this is a deployed client that runs on your desktop and communicates with the store's catalog service in a secure, reliable, and transactable manner.

When it comes to security, reliability, and transactability in a hosted service, Microsoft offers a one-stop shop that gives it all: the Windows Communication Foundation (WCF). This framework is the core of all the next-generation communications applications built on the .NET platform. It subsumes web services, remoting, and messaging for synchronous and asynchronous application development. It incorporates all recent relevant standards and builds on a model of declarative configuration of services through XML configuration files, instead of C# coding (though you can do it all in code too if you like). The design philosophy is that developers should concentrate on developing the required business logic and not the "plumbing" that makes it work. WCF will handle this for you and make it as easy as possible through the use of external configuration files.

This is a WPF, and not a WCF book, so I won't go into too much depth, but for you to be able to get the most out of WPF for building distributable applications that can be connected to services, it's good to go through something of a primer. So for the next couple of sections, you'll dive into WCF, learning enough to start building simple services, and you'll later connect to these services from your WPF application. In Chapters 9 and 10, you'll take these skills to the next level, using technologies that will allow you to enable trust and security when deploying your application to your customers and using WPF to integrate tightly with Windows Vista.

Figure 4-1. *The basic "disconnected" product browser*

Getting Started with WCF

WCF is an incremental technology that is designed to bring many of the distinct connectivity technologies into a single programming namespace, called the System.ServiceModel namespace. When formerly you had to learn lots of different application programming interfaces (APIs) and methodologies to handle web services (ASMX), Web Services Enhancements (WSE), Microsoft Message Queuing (MSMQ), Enterprise Services, COM+, and .NET Remoting, you now have a single programming model that handles the functionality that is inherent in all of them.

WPF without WCF will allow you to create pretty but likely meaningless applications. In this distributed-model world, having a good grip on WCF is necessary to get the most out of your WPF applications.

WCF follows the software as a service (SAAS) philosophy where all the units of functionality (or at least back-end functionality) in an application are defined as services. These services are generally abstract and technology independent. They are accessible via well-defined interfaces.

Using the SAAS model, developers take on the role of assemblers by tying services together, many times chaining and orchestrating them into workflows (which is the reason for the existence of the Windows Workflow Foundation), and fronting these composite service applications with a user interface.

To access a service, you need to remember the ABCs of service development:

- *A* is for the service *address*. This defines where the service resides. Is it on the Internet? Is it on a machine on your network or even on the same machine as the client?

- *B* is for the service *binding*. Once you've found my service, how do you talk to it? Can you use Simple Object Access Protocol (SOAP)? Do you need a shared object? Can you talk with a messaging protocol?

- *C* is for the service *contract*. What does this service do for you? What do you pass to it, and what can you expect in return?

If you're familiar with web services, it's useful to think of these three aspects in terms of web services and Web Services Description Language (WSDL). The location of the service, the binding for the service, and the contract for the service are all available as part of a WSDL document. With WCF, you'll extend this to work with the aforementioned communications methodologies. If you aren't familiar with the technology or are still not clear, don't worry—all will become clear as you work through it, and it will eventually become second nature.

But enough theory; let's look at actually building something in WCF. You'll first build a simple stateless synchronous web service that converts a unit from feet to meters, and vice versa.

Creating the Service

If you've configured Visual Studio 2005 for WinFX, you're good to go. If not, return to Chapter 1, and follow the process that it outlines to install the requisite components. From Visual Studio 2005, you should then issue a File ➤ New Web Site command; you'll see the dialog box shown in Figure 4-2.

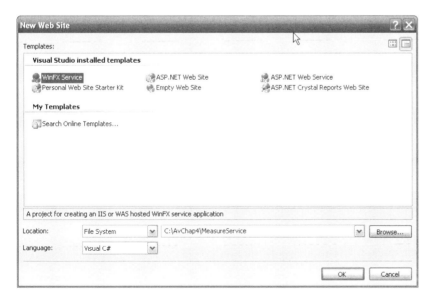

Figure 4-2. *Creating a new web-based WinFX service*

In this dialog box, you can select the location and language of your service. The location can be your file system or can be on an HTTP or FTP server. The language can be any supported .NET language. For this example, the service will be put on the file system, and will, as a result, be managed by the Cassini web server.

If you fill out your dialog box like that in Figure 4-2, entering the address of where you would like the service to be located, Visual Studio will create the service and all the requisite configuration files.

You'll see three files in your Solution Explorer (see Figure 4-3).

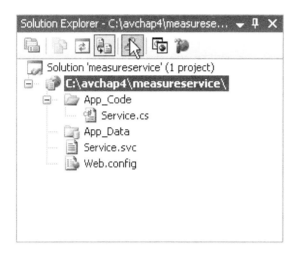

Figure 4-3. *Solution Explorer for a new WCF service*

These files are as follows:

Service.svc: The endpoint of a WCF service. This is roughly analogous to the ASMX of a .NET web service.

Service.cs: The code behind the Service.svc file that implements the business logic of the service.

Web.config: The familiar configuration file from .NET web applications and web services. However, when using WCF, it is likely to be more widely used because you will configure the serviceModel at the heart of WCF using entries in this file.

Your C# code behind the service will look something like Listing 4-1.

Listing 4-1. *Simple WinFX Web Service*

```
using System;
using System.ServiceModel;

// A WinFX service consists of a contract (defined below as IMyService),
// a class that implements that interface (see MyService),
// and configuration entries that specify behaviors associated with
// that implementation (see <system.serviceModel> in Web.config)
```

```
[ServiceContract()]
public interface IMyService
{
    [OperationContract]
    string MyOperation1(string myValue1);
}

public class MyService : IMyService
{
    public string MyOperation1(string myValue1)
    {
        return "Hello: " + myValue1;
    }
}
```

This is a basic "Hello, World!" service that returns the passed-in value, prefixed by Hello. This looks similar to a typical pre-WCF C# web service, but it has a couple of additions.

First, if you want to have a service, you declare its interface and use the [ServiceContract()] attribute. Within the interface, each method you want to have exposed (analogous to web methods) should have the [OperationContract] attribute. The theory behind this is that the interface should have the associated complexity necessary to define the service contract details, and the underlying code that implements the business logic should be "pure" code that implements this interface. As you can see from the class definition, MyService implements the IMyService interface and is coded normally. The operation MyOperation as a result is not *uniquely* a web-accessible operation. Other classes and objects within the same application can access it in the usual object-oriented manner, without going through a web interface.

So, to implement a two-operation service that handles conversion between feet and meters, you can use the service shown in Listing 4-2. It handles the conversion by assuming a meter is 3.3 feet. (This isn't a precision conversion and is used only for demonstration purposes.)

Listing 4-2. *WinFX Service for Simple Metric to Imperial Conversion: [ServiceContract()]*

```
public interface IMetricImperial
{
    [OperationContract]
    double ftom(double f);

    [OperationContract]
    double mtof(double m);

}

public class MetricImperial : IMetricImperial
{
    public double ftom(double f)
    {
        return f / 3.3;
    }
```

```
    public double mtof(double m)
    {
        return m * 3.3;
    }
}
```

Before you can use this code as a WCF service, you also need to configure the service-Model to tell .NET it is a WCF service, and you can achieve this using Web.config. Listing 4-3 shows the entire Web.config file for this service. The important parts are in bold.

Listing 4-3. *Web.config for the Service*

```
<?xml version="1.0"?>

<configuration xmlns="http://schemas.microsoft.com/.NetConfiguration/v2.0">
  <system.serviceModel>
    <services>
      <service name="MetricImperial"
               behaviorConfiguration="returnFaults">
        <endpoint contract="IMetricImperial" binding="wsHttpBinding"/>
      </service>
    </services>
    <behaviors>
      <behavior name="returnFaults"
                returnUnknownExceptionsAsFaults="true" />
    </behaviors>
  </system.serviceModel>

  <system.web>
    <compilation debug="true"/>
  </system.web>

</configuration>
```

You can see that this uses the <system.serviceModel> configuration. This instructs .NET to configure WCF with the specified settings. The <services> node contains the definitions for each service, and because only one service is being used, they only have one child node. This takes the name of the service (in this case MetricImperial) and the endpoint details. These contain the contract and the method of binding that is desired. The contract is the interface that describes the service, in this case IMetricImperial. The binding specifies the binding type, and we will be using HTTP binding à la web services, and to do this, you set the attribute to wsHttpBinding.

Before running the application, you also need to edit the Service.svc file, which is configured to use the default MyService class.

Here's what it should look like:

```
<% @ServiceHost Language=C# Debug="true"
    Service="MetricImperial" CodeBehind="~/App_Code/Service.cs" %>
```

Note that Service should be set to MetricImperial. When you run the application, you'll get the screen in Figure 4-4—you may get some errors because of unsupported attributes when you are compiling, but don't worry about these for now. Because the application doesn't have any default page set (the application doesn't have any pages at all), you'll see a file listing. In a production environment, this would be disabled, and you'd use the uniform resource locator (URL) to Service.svc instead of the web application root.

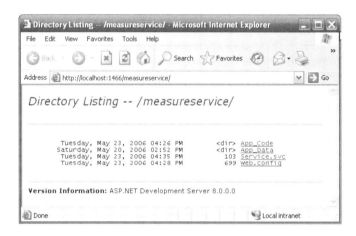

Figure 4-4. *Directory listing for the service*

If you click Service.svc on this screen, you'll be taken to the default page for the service, as shown in Figure 4-5.

Unlike web services, WCF services do not have a test page accessible via the browser. Clients to these services have to be generated using the svcutil tool as instructed on this page. This page also outlines a skeleton client application that will call the service.

You can find the svcutil tool in the C:\Program Files\Microsoft SDKs\Windows\v1.0\Bin directory. It's recommended that you add this directory to your path so you can call it from anywhere. Make sure your service is running before you go through the following steps. Also, the port that your service runs on may be different because the Cassini web server assigns the port at runtime. Note the address of your WSDL, and use that in the svcutil command as follows.

Open a DOS box, and issue this command:

```
svcutil http://localhost:1466/measureservice/Service.svc?wsdl
```

This will generate two files—these are the proxy class and the configuration files to access your service. If you create a new web or Windows forms application, you can import these files to it and use them to call the measuring service.

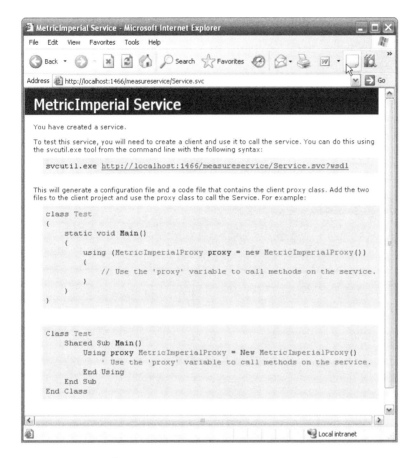

Figure 4-5. *Service home page*

To do this, first create a Windows forms application using Visual Studio 2005. Figure 4-6 shows the dialog box with the Windows Application template listed.

This will create a new Windows application containing a single form. To get this application to talk to the WinFX service, you will need to make a few minor changes. First, you'll have to import the two files you created with the svcutil utility a little earlier. You can do this by right-clicking the project and selecting Add ➤ Existing Item.

Second, you'll browse to the directory containing the two files and add them.

Next, you should rename the output.config you created to App.config. A Windows forms application will read this as the application configuration file automatically.

Finally, in order to use WCF and the proxy classes, you'll need a couple of references to the appropriate assemblies. The ones to reference are System.ServiceModel and System.Runtime.Serialization.

Once you've done this, your application should be good to go. Sometimes when compiling WCF applications, you'll get errors that some attributes are not supported. This seems to be a moving target of a problem, and you can blame it on that the software is not yet production ready. Feel free to delete the offending attributes. Because this book is a WPF and not a WCF book, I won't go into any more detail on these configuration files nor how to use them.

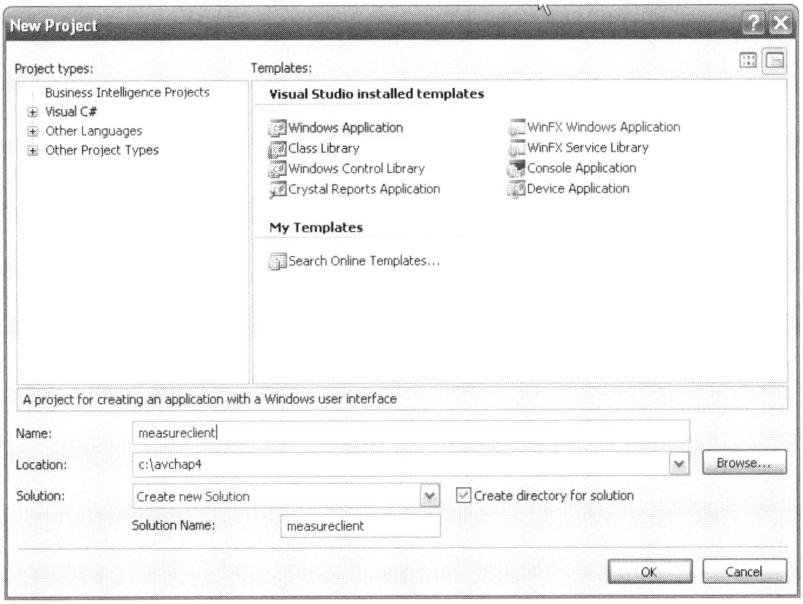

Figure 4-6. *Creating a new Windows application*

To test your connection to your service, drag a button onto the form. Double-click it, and the code editor will open with the button's click event handler active. Change this click event handler so it looks like the following:

```
private void button1_Click(object sender, EventArgs e)
{
  using (MetricImperialProxy proxy =
           new MetricImperialProxy())
  {
    double f = proxy.mtof(6);
    MessageBox.Show(f.ToString());
  }
}
```

This creates an instance of the MetricImperialProxy called *proxy*. This proxy class is defined in a .cs file that was generated by the svcutil tool.

It then makes a simple call to the mtof method of the proxy, passing it the value 6 and displaying the returned value in a message box. Make sure your service is running first—if all is right, when you run the application, you'll see something like Figure 4-7.

Figure 4-7. *Running the test client*

Now that you've looked into what it takes to build a WinFX service and connect to it from a client, the next step is to build the real service application that fronts the AdventureWorks database. Once that is done, you'll hook it up to a WPF front end, and you'll be back on the Extensible Application Markup Language (XAML) train once more!

Creating the WCF Service Application

This application will front the AdventureWorks database, exposing a number of products from it to the WPF-based front end. You'll build this service in the following sections, and in the "Connecting the User Interface to the Service" section you'll import the XAML you produced earlier in Expression Interactive Designer and tie it to the service.

The service will interact with the front end in the following manner: It will expose a service call that the interface will use to build the overall list of products, and it will also expose a service call that provides the details of a single, specified product to the interface. The interface will call the first of these methods to build its list of products, and then whenever the user selects a product, it will call the service and download the details for that product, including pricing and a picture.

You'll first step through creating the service project and the first service method, and you will then import the XAML from the front end created in Chapter 3 and tie that to the "live" data from this service call. Next, you'll add the second service method and tie that to the user interactions on the client.

Creating the WCF Service Project

To begin, you'll create a simple WinFX service project that includes the basic necessities for a WCF service application. You do this using the File ➤ New Web Site command in Visual Studio 2005. This will show you the New Web Site dialog box, as shown in Figure 4-8. Fill it out with the directory and project name, and click OK. If you are following along with the example, use the same directory and filename as in Figure 4-8 to minimize any changes you need to make for your application to work correctly.

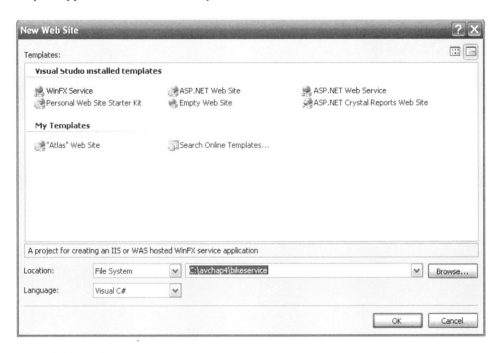

Figure 4-8. *Creating a new WinFX service application*

This will create a new service application called BikeService. This will contain the boiler-plate service information that was discussed in the previous section. You'll be making a lot of edits to this as you progress.

Adding the Database Wrapper

This service will expose data from the AdventureWorks database, so some form of data access will be necessary. It is a huge database with many products, most of which aren't applicable for a simple browser like the one you are building here. As such, you'll use a query to filter out what is appropriate to use.

To get started, add a new DataSet to the project. You do this by right-clicking the project file and selecting Add New Item (as shown in Figure 4-9).

This will open the Add New Item dialog box. In this dialog box, you can select the DataSet item and call it Bikes.xsd, as shown in Figure 4-10.

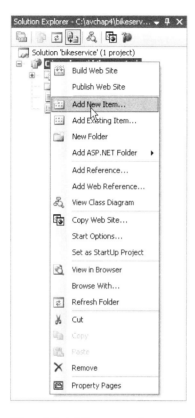

Figure 4-9. *Adding a new item*

Figure 4-10. *Creating the DataSet*

When you select Add, you will see a warning asking whether you would like the code to be placed in the App_code folder of your project (as shown in Figure 4-11). Click Yes in this dialog box.

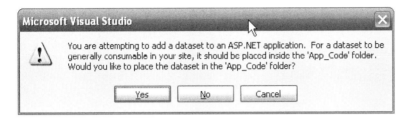

Figure 4-11. *Visual Studio warning*

The integrated development environment (IDE) will now create the DataSet and its designer within your solution, and then it will launch the TableAdapter Configuration Wizard. This will allow you to configure your connection and the query you'll use to filter the data to a reasonable subset.

The first step in this wizard is to configure the connection to the database. From this it will generate the connection string that will be stored in the Web.config file within the project. Note that if you are using the downloaded code for this book, you'll have to edit the Web.config file to use the connection string appropriate for your database location. You can see this dialog box in Figure 4-12.

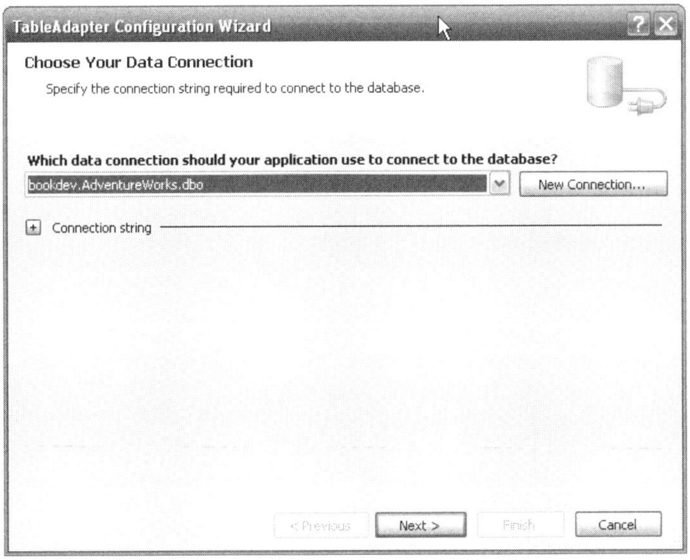

Figure 4-12. *TableAdapter Configuration Wizard, step 1*

You'll notice in Figure 4-12 that the connection name begins with *bookdev*. This is because the development machine that was being used to create this dialog box bore that name. In your case, you should see the name of your development machine. Please also make sure that SQL Server 2005 is installed and running and that the AdventureWorks sample database is installed with it.

Clicking Next takes you to the Save the Connection String to the Application Configuration File screen (see Figure 4-13). You'll want to do this, so make sure the Yes checkbox is selected, and click Next.

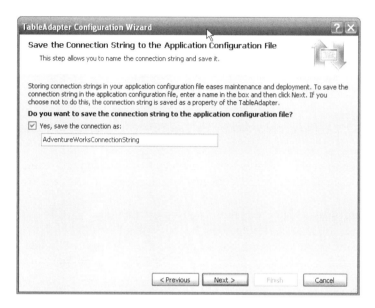

Figure 4-13. *TableAdapter Configuration Wizard, step 2: saving the configuration file*

The next step in the wizard is for specifying how you will access the database. The options are as follows:

Use SQL Statements: This will take you into a query designer flow where you can specify the SELECT statement to retrieve the TableAdapter Configuration Wizard data you want to access. You'll be selecting this option.

Create New Stored Procedures: This will take you into a flow where you can provide a single table SELECT statement. The Insert, Update, and Delete stored procedures associated with this will automatically be generated. Because the query you need to run is across three tables (more on this later), you cannot select this option.

Use an Existing Stored Procedure: If you have existing stored procedures in your database and want to expose their results to your application, you would select this option.

You can see this dialog box in Figure 4-14. Make sure that Use SQL Statements is selected, and click Next.

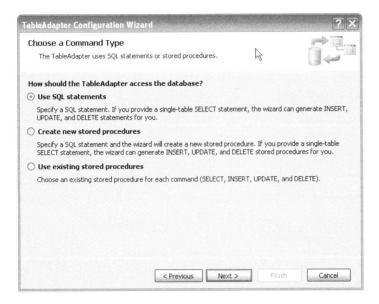

Figure 4-14. *Selecting the command type for your data connection*

The next step in the wizard allows you to enter a SQL statement that represents your data (as shown in Figure 4-15). If you have a SQL statement already that you would like to use, you can enter it here. For example, if you used SQL Server Management Studio to create a query on your data, you can export the results to a text file and then cut and paste that content here. Alternatively, you can use hbfnd to design a query that will automatically get added.

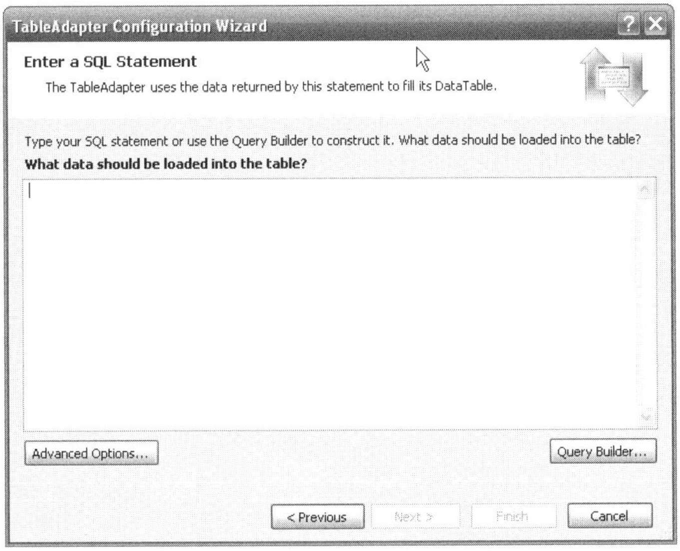

Figure 4-15. *The wizard's Enter a SQL Statement screen*

To access the Query Builder, you click the Query Builder button (surprise, surprise) on this screen. This launches the Query Builder that starts with an empty query that reads SELECT FROM. It will launch the Add Table dialog box. You will use this dialog box to add tables to your query (as shown in Figure 4-16).

Figure 4-16. *Adding a new table to the query*

For this query, you'll need only a single table: Product. Add that and then click Close, and you'll be taken to the Query Builder. From here, select the ProductID, ListPrice, and Name fields. On the Output column, make sure ListPrice is not selected. In the Filter column, the text should look like >2000, as shown in Figure 4-17.

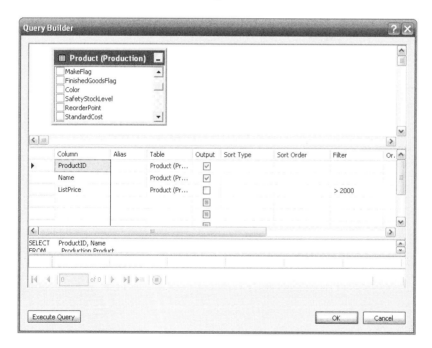

Figure 4-17. *Designing the query*

When you're done, click OK, and you'll be taken to the TableAdapter Configuration Wizard (as shown in Figure 4-18). This will be filled out with the SQL for your retrieval query, which should look something like this:

```
SELECT     ProductID, Name
FROM         Production.Product
WHERE      (ListPrice > 2000)
```

This is a simple query that just pulls the name and the product ID of all bicycles costing more than $2,000. This is done to limit the results for the purpose of demonstration.

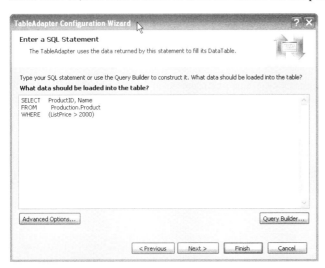

Figure 4-18. *The SQL statement is now filled in.*

Click Next on the wizard, and you will be taken to the Choose Methods to Generate step, as shown in Figure 4-19.

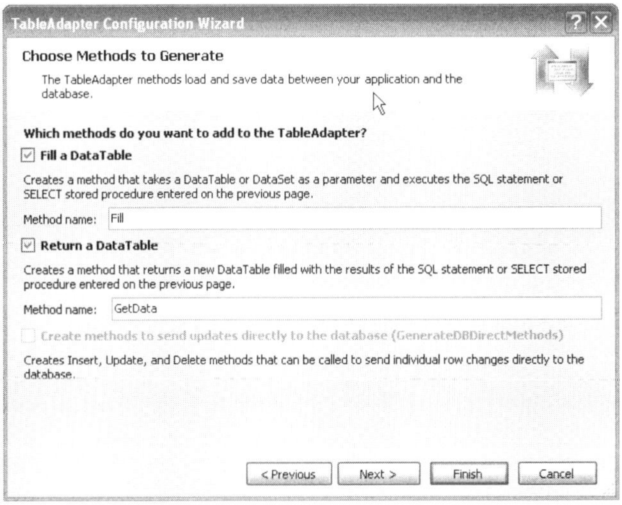

Figure 4-19. *Choosing the methods to generate*

The wizard will automatically generate the necessary code to connect to the database, execute the query, and fill up a data table with the results. You can specify the method names that the generated source code will expose here. The defaults are Fill to fill the DataTable and GetData to return it. Accept the defaults here, and click Next. You don't need the methods to send updates directly to the database, so if this option is available to you, make sure it is unselected.

You'll see the wizard's results. This should show the successful configuration of the DataTable and DataAdapter as well as details of the statements, mappings, and methods that were automatically generated for you, as shown in Figure 4-20.

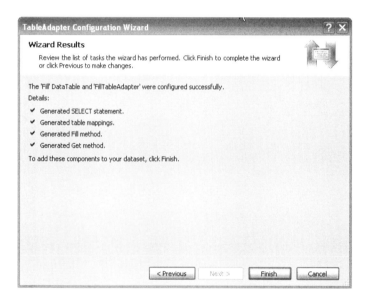

Figure 4-20. *Final step of the wizard*

The Visual Studio IDE will now have a new Bikes.xsd in your project and a designer show-ing the DataTable and its DataAdapter. You will use these from your code to expose the results of this query to the service caller, as shown in Figure 4-21.

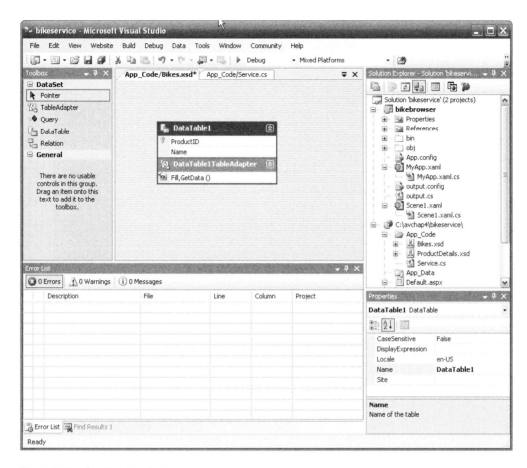

Figure 4-21. *The DataSet designer*

Adding the Service Interface

Now that you have the database connection set up, adding the service interface is a snap. The service is defined in the Service.cs file within your App_Code folder. Open this, and you will see the default service stubs discussed earlier in this chapter.

Use the code in Listing 4-4 instead.

Listing 4-4. *The Bike Service Code*

```
using System;
using System.Data;
using System.ServiceModel;
using System.Data.SqlClient;
using System.IO;
using System.Xml;
using System.Text;

[ServiceContract()]
public interface IBikeService
{
    [OperationContract]
    string GetData();
}

public class BikeService : IBikeService
{
    public string GetData()
    {
        BikesTableAdapters.DataTable1TableAdapter da =
            new BikesTableAdapters.DataTable1TableAdapter();
        Bikes.DataTable1DataTable dt = da.GetData();
        string st = ConvertDataTableToXML(dt);
        return st;
    }
    // Function to convert passed DataSet to XML data
    private string ConvertDataTableToXML(DataTable xmlDS)
    {
        MemoryStream stream = null;
        XmlTextWriter writer = null;
        try
        {
            stream = new MemoryStream();
            // Load the XmlTextReader from the stream
            writer = new XmlTextWriter(stream, Encoding.Unicode);
            // Write to the file with the WriteXml method
            xmlDS.WriteXml(writer);
            int count = (int)stream.Length;
            byte[] arr = new byte[count];
            stream.Seek(0, SeekOrigin.Begin);
            stream.Read(arr, 0, count);
            UnicodeEncoding utf = new UnicodeEncoding();
            return utf.GetString(arr).Trim();
        }
        catch
        {
```

```
            return String.Empty;
        }
        finally
        {
            if (writer != null) writer.Close();
        }
    }
}
```

Several things are going on in this code, so let's go through it step by step so that you can understand it.

First, because this is a service, you have to define the service contract. You do this using the following code:

```
[ServiceContract()]
public interface IBikeService
{
    [OperationContract]
    string GetData();
}
```

This sets up an interface that exposes a single operation, called GetData(), which returns a string. The service will serialize DataTable information into XML, which gets passed across the wire as a string, because this will ease any interoperability issues should you want to consume this service from a different client later.

Second, now that you have your service contract interface set up, the next step is to implement this interface in a class that provides your service:

```
public class BikeService : IBikeService
{
    public string GetData()
    {
        BikesTableAdapters.DataTable1TableAdapter da =
            new BikesTableAdapters.DataTable1TableAdapter();
        Bikes.DataTable1DataTable dt = da.GetData();
        string st = ConvertDataTableToXML(dt);
        return st;
    }
}
```

This provides a class, BikeService, that implements the interface that was defined previously. The data set you configured earlier is then used to pull the data from the database and store it in a DataTable. This DataTable is then serialized into an XML string and returned to the caller. The ConvertDataTableToXML helper function achieves this.

You should then run this application in the manner described earlier and use the svcutil tool to create the proxy and configuration information. Note that when you create the configuration information, it is a good idea to look at the maxReceivedMessageSize property. This is usually set for 65,536 (64Kb). If your images are greater than 64Kb in size, you may have some trouble. In that case, it is good to set this to a higher number.

Creating the Front End

To create a WinFX-based front end for this service in Visual Studio, you should right-click your solution and select Add ➤ New Project. This will open the Add New Project dialog box, from which you should select the WinFX Windows Application template. Call this application *bikebrowser*, as shown in Figure 4-22.

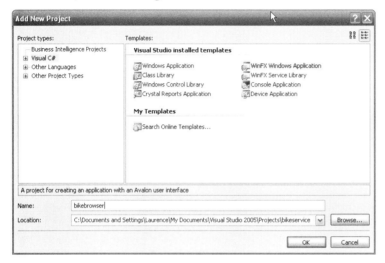

Figure 4-22. *Creating a new WinFX Windows application*

   This will create a new WinFX Windows application, which uses the Cider editor for creating XAML-based WinFX applications in Visual Studio .NET. You will notice that you have two XAML files here: MyApp.xaml and Window1.xaml. You should delete Window1.xaml because you will replace that with the Scene1.xaml file created in Chapter 3.

   It is recommended that you make a copy of Scene1.xaml and Scene1.xaml.cs in the working directory for BikeBrowser and then import them into the project. Additionally, you should import the output.config and output.cs files that were generated by the svcutil tool.

   Finally, you should use the Add ➤ New Item dialog box to specify an application configuration file called App.config.

   When you're done, your project should look something like Figure 4-23.

Figure 4-23. *Solution Explorer for bikebrowser*

The first step you'll need to take is to use the MyApp.xaml file to configure which XAML to launch when the application first runs.

If you view this XAML, it will look like this:

```
<Application x:Class="bikebrowser.MyApp"
    xmlns="http://schemas.microsoft.com/winfx/2006/xaml/presentation"
    xmlns:x="http://schemas.microsoft.com/winfx/2006/xaml"
    StartupUri-"Window1.xaml">
    <Application.Resources>

    </Application.Resources>
</Application>
```

You should change this so StartupUri points to Scene1.xaml, and thus the MyApp.xaml file will look like this:

```
<Application x:Class="bikebrowser.MyApp"
    xmlns="http://schemas.microsoft.com/winfx/2006/xaml/presentation"
    xmlns:x="http://schemas.microsoft.com/winfx/2006/xaml"
    StartupUri="Scene1.xaml">
    <Application.Resources>

    </Application.Resources>
</Application>
```

If you now run the application, you'll get the same results as you did in Chapter 3—a static browser for the bicycles that is driven from a local XML configuration file. When working in an online-connected mode, the data source should be the hosted service, and this user interface should be built from calls to this service.

Connecting the User Interface to the Service

To do this, you should first configure the application to use the service model and set up the App.config file accordingly. The application template has already added all the necessary references, and the svcutil tool generated an output.config file that contains the information for App.config. Cut and paste this into your App.config file. You'll also find it useful to rename the endpoint to a different name. By default, the name of the endpoint and the name of the binding configuration are the same. I have found that this doesn't always run properly in the prerelease bits of WCF, but changing the name of the endpoint seems to fix this. Listing 4-5 shows an example of App.config with the endpoint renamed to *default*.

Listing 4-5. *App.config for the User Interface*

```
<?xml version="1.0" encoding="utf-8"?>
<configuration>
  <system.serviceModel>
    <bindings>
      <wsHttpBinding>
        <binding name-"WSHttpBinding_IBikeService"
```

```
                    bypassProxyOnLocal="false"
                    transactionFlow="false"
                    hostNameComparisonMode="StrongWildcard"
                    maxBufferPoolSize="524288"
                    maxReceivedMessageSize="65536"
                    messageEncoding="Text"
                    textEncoding="utf-8"
                    useDefaultWebProxy="true">
          <readerQuotas maxDepth="2147483647"
                    maxStringContentLength="2147483647"
                    maxArrayLength="2147483647"
                    maxBytesPerRead="2147483647"
                    maxNameTableCharCount="2147483647" />
          <reliableSession ordered="true"
                    inactivityTimeout="00:10:00"
                    enabled="false" />
          <security mode="Message">
            <transport clientCredentialType="None"
                    proxyCredentialType="None"
                    realm="" />
            <message clientCredentialType="Windows"
                    negotiateServiceCredential="true"
                    establishSecurityContext="true" />
          </security>
        </binding>
      </wsHttpBinding>
    </bindings>
    <client>
      <endpoint address="http://localhost:4865/bikeservice/Service.svc"
                    binding="wsHttpBinding"
                    bindingConfiguration="WSHttpBinding_IBikeService"
                    contract="IBikeService"
                    name="default" />
    </client>
  </system.serviceModel>
</configuration>
```

You should expect the endpoint address to be different in your case.

Next, you'll write the code to call the service and get the results of the query as an XML string. This XML string will then be used to construct a DataSet, from which you can get a DataTable. You cannot get a DataTable directly because this class cannot infer a schema, where the DataSet can, and it contains one or more DataTables.

You'll update Scene1.xaml.cs to look like Listing 4-6.

Listing 4-6. *Scene1.xaml.cs Code*

```
using System;
using System.IO;
using System.Net;
using System.Windows;
using System.Windows.Controls;
using System.Windows.Data;
using System.Windows.Media;
using System.Windows.Media.Animation;
using System.Windows.Navigation;
using System.Data;
using System.Text;
using System.Xml;

namespace BikeBrowser
{
  public partial class Scene1
  {
    public Scene1()
    {
            InitializeComponent();
            using (BikeServiceProxy proxy = new BikeServiceProxy("default"))
            {
                string s1 = proxy.GetData();
                DataSet d = ConvertXMLToDataSet(s1);
                DataTable t = d.Tables[0];
                DataContext = t;
            }
    }

    protected override void OnInitialized(EventArgs e)
    {
        Reflection.Fill = new VisualBrush(ProductGrid);
    }

    public DataSet ConvertXMLToDataSet(string xmlData)
    {
        StringReader stream = null;
        XmlTextReader reader = null;
        try
        {
            DataSet xmlDS = new DataSet();
            stream = new StringReader(xmlData);
```

```
            // Load the XmlTextReader from the stream
            reader = new XmlTextReader(stream);
            xmlDS.ReadXml(reader);
            return xmlDS;
        }
        catch (Exception ex)
        {
            string strTest = ex.Message;
            return null;
        }
        finally
        {
            if (reader != null)
                reader.Close();
        }
    }
  }
}
```

Within the constructor, you see this code:

```
using (BikeServiceProxy proxy = new BikeServiceProxy("default"))
{
    string s1 = proxy.GetData();
    DataSet d = ConvertXMLToDataSet(s1);
    DataTable t = d.Tables[0];
    DataContext = t;
}
```

This creates a BikeServiceProxy called *proxy*, based on the endpoint configuration called *default*. See the App.config definition in Listing 4-5 where this naming is taking place. This then called the GetData() service operation on the proxy returning a string. This string contains serialized XML data, which is then converted to a DataSet using the helper function. From this, the first DataTable is extracted (there is only one), and the DataContext is set to it.

When using WPF, you can set the DataContext for the scene programmatically like this. You can then configure (using the XAML markup) the binding to this data context for each of your page elements. If you run the application now, you'll be surprised to see that nothing happens—it is still using the XML you configured in Chapter 3.

Now, let's start looking at the XAML in a little more depth and configuring the application to use the live data. Remember, the use case here is that the designer has used Expression Interactive Designer to put together a working prototype of the application. It is your job as a developer to tie this to the service. The ideal model is to work on the source code directly and to change the binding. And that's exactly what you are going to do.

Within the XAML from Expression Interactive Designer, you'll see the definition of the XMLDataProvider. It looks like this:

```
<XmlDataProvider x:Key="BikeSource"
    d:IsDataSource="True"
    Source="C:\bikecatalog\bikecatalog.xml"/>
```

You should comment this out by putting the standard Hypertext Markup Language (HTML) comment markup in front of and behind it (<! - - and - - >).

Also, the ProductGrid was defined to bind to this. Find the line of XAML where this is set up. It will look like this:

```
<Grid Margin="36,6.62313396736548,41,166.182837337067"
    x:Name="ProductGrid"
    RenderTransformOrigin="0.5,0.5"
    DataContext="{Binding Mode=OneWay,
                        Source={StaticResource BikeSource},
                        XPath=/Catalog/Products/Product}">
```

From here you should remove the DataContext definition, because the DataContext was set up in the code, as you saw earlier. It should now look like this:

```
<Grid Margin="36,6.62313396736548,41,166.182837337067"
    x:Name="ProductGrid"
    RenderTransformOrigin="0.5,0.5">
```

Now, the list that contains the product should be built from the DataContext you set up earlier, and this contains the DataTable of items that were returned from the database. This table, as you may recall, contains the ID and the name for every product in the database that costs more than $2,000. To configure the user interface to use this information, you'll have to perform two steps.

First, you'll need to create a DataTemplate that contains this information in XAML. On the list, you aren't simply displaying the Name information; you also want the ID to be embedded in the list so that when you click it, you have this information, which you can then pass to the service to get the detailed information.

Here is the DataTemplate:

```
<DataTemplate x:Key="ProductListTemplate">
  <StackPanel Orientation="Horizontal">
  <TextBlock Text="{Binding Path=ID}" />
  <TextBlock Text=" " />
  <TextBlock Text="{Binding Path=Name}" />
  </StackPanel>
</DataTemplate>
```

Second, you'll need to bind the ProductList to the data using this DataTemplate. Its present XAML declaration will look like this:

```
<ListBox x:Name="ProductList"
    RenderTransformOrigin="0.5,0.5"
    IsSynchronizedWithCurrentItem="True"
    ItemsSource="{Binding Mode=OneWay}"
    ItemTemplate="{DynamicResource ProductTemplate1}"
    SelectedIndex="-1"
    Background="{x:Null}"
    BorderBrush="{x:Null}"
    Foreground="#FFFFFFFF" />
```

To update it to use the new binding, you would change the ItemTemplate property to point at the new context. After the change, it would look like this:

```
<ListBox x:Name="ProductList"
    RenderTransformOrigin="0.5,0.5"
    IsSynchronizedWithCurrentItem="True"
    ItemsSource="{Binding Mode=OneWay}"
    ItemTemplate="{DynamicResource ProductListTemplate}"
    SelectedIndex="-1"
    Background="{x:Null}"
    BorderBrush="{x:Null}"
    Foreground="#FFFFFFFF" />
```

As you can see, the only change you needed to make was to update the ItemTemplate to point at the new template you created. Indeed, if you wanted to change as little as possible, you could have replaced the existing ProductTemplate1 with the new one, and then you wouldn't need to change anything.

Let's see how the application looks now. If you run it, you should see something like Figure 4-24.

Figure 4-24. *Running the application with the new binding*

The desired functionality is to then update the right pane with the product details when the user selects an item on the list. Next, you'll implement this on the service and then will switch back to the graphical user interface to hook it up.

Implementing the Product Detail Service Method

The first step is to add a new DataSet to the service as you did earlier. Select File ➤ Add New Item to open the Add New Item dialog box, and then select a DataSet and use the wizard to generate a new query. In this case, the DataSet is called ProductDetails.

The query you'll want to use will use three tables, so when you reach the Add Table stage in the query designer, make sure you add them in the correct order:

1. First, add the table called ProductProductPhoto (Production).

2. Second, add the table called ProductPhoto (Production).

3. Finally, add the table called Product (Production).

Once you've done this, your Query Builder will be populated with the three tables and the joins between them.

Right now the query doesn't do much because it isn't selecting anything, but the joins between the tables are good.

To add some selection criteria, check the following boxes:

- LargePhoto on the ProductPhoto table

- ProductID on the ProductProductPhoto table

- Name on the Product table

- ListPrice on the Product table

Click the Execute Query button. You'll have several hundred responses (504 in the default AdventureWorks database).

In this case, you want only one record, and it is the one that is specified when the user clicks the product list. This is a parameter that will be passed to the service method and then passed by the method to the query. To do this, go to the Filter column on the Query Designer, and on the ProductID row, enter =@ID.

Now if you execute the query, you'll receive the Query Parameters dialog box (see Figure 4-25).

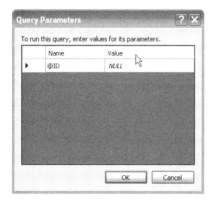

Figure 4-25. *Query Parameters dialog box*

Enter a value such as **726** in the Value column, and click OK. If the number you entered has an associated product, you'll see it in the results list.

Your SQL should now look something like this:

```
SELECT  Production.Product.ProductID,
        Production.Product.Name,
        Production.Product.ListPrice,
        Production.ProductPhoto.LargePhoto

FROM    Production.ProductProductPhoto

INNER JOIN Production.ProductPhoto
ON  Production.ProductProductPhoto.ProductPhotoID =
    Production.ProductPhoto.ProductPhotoID

INNER JOIN Production.Product
ON  Production.ProductProductPhoto.ProductID =
    Production.Product.ProductID

WHERE
    (Production.Product.ProductID = @ID)
```

Now that you have this, you can implement the service method. Because you are returning a number of fields, you'll need a data type that encapsulates them. This needs a data contract associated with it so that the client can understand and consume it.

You implement a data contract quite simply; attribute the class using the [DataContract()] attribute and each member you want exposed in the contract using [DataMember]. You will need to add a reference to System.Runtime.Serialization to get this to compile if you don't have one already.

Here is the data contract for ProductRecord:

```
[DataContract()]
public class ProductRecord
{
```

```
    [DataMember]
    public int ID;
    [DataMember]
    public string Name;
    [DataMember]
    public string ListPrice;
    [DataMember]
    public byte[] Photo;
}
```

If the DataSet (XSD) you added earlier was called ProductDetails, your service call will look like this:

```
public ProductRecord GetProductDetails(string strID)
{
    ProductDetailsTableAdapters.DataTable1TableAdapter da =
            new ProductDetailsTableAdapters.DataTable1TableAdapter();
    ProductDetails.DataTable1DataTable dt =
            da.GetData(Convert.ToInt16(strID));
    ProductRecord pReturn = new ProductRecord();
    ProductDetails.DataTable1Row theRow =
            (ProductDetails.DataTable1Row) dt.Rows[0];
    pReturn.ID = theRow.ProductID;
    pReturn.ListPrice = theRow.ListPrice.ToString();
    pReturn.Name = theRow.Name;
    pReturn.Photo = theRow.LargePhoto;
    return pReturn;

}
```

You will, of course, also need to add the operation as a contract on the interface. It will look like this:

```
[ServiceContract()]
public interface IBikeService
{
    [OperationContract]
    string GetData();
    [OperationContract]
    ProductRecord GetProductDetails(string strID);
}
```

Before editing the interface, you will need to use the svcutil tool once again and add the output to your client application. You'll also need to update your App.config file with the contents from output.config generated by this tool, and if you edited the binding name, you'll have to edit it again.

You now have a service that is capable of returning the description, price, and picture of the selected item. The next step is to knit that into your application workflow.

Implementing the User Interface for the Product Service Call

Once you've updated your proxy and App.config files correctly, the next step is to set up the selection handler for the product list. You do this by adding the SelectionChanged attribute and setting it to the name of the function you want to use in code. You can see how the ListBox declaration should look here:

```
<ListBox
    SelectionChanged="ProductList_Click"
    x:Name="ProductList"
    RenderTransformOrigin="0.5,0.5"
    IsSynchronizedWithCurrentItem="True"
    ItemsSource="{Binding Mode=OneWay}"
    ItemTemplate="{DynamicResource ProductListTemplate}"
    SelectedIndex="-1"
    Background="{x:Null}"
    BorderBrush="{x:Null}"
    Foreground="#FFFFFFFF" />
```

You now implement the ProductList_Click handler. This pulls the selected item from the list and loads it into a DataRowView. From this it can get the ProductID column and establish the ID of the selected item from that.

Then it creates an instance of the service proxy and uses it to call GetProductDetails, passing it this ID. Because the ProductRecord class was defined using a data contract, it is available to the caller; thus, an instance of ProductRecord is created, and it gets returned from the call to the service. Then, the details of the product are parsed from the ProductRecord and written directly to the screen by setting the properties of the TextBlock controls.

For the bitmap handling, you'll need to use the following using statement:

```
using System.Windows.Media.Imaging;
```

Here's the code:

```
private void ProductList_Click(object sender,
            SelectionChangedEventArgs e)
{

  try
  {
    DataRowView d = (DataRowView)ProductList.SelectedItem;
    string strID = d.Row["ProductID"].ToString();
    using (BikeServiceProxy proxy = new BikeServiceProxy("default"))
    {
      ProductRecord r = proxy.GetProductDetails(strID);
      Price.Text = r.ListPrice;
      Description.Text = r.Name;
      BitmapImage myBitmapImage = new BitmapImage();
      myBitmapImage.BeginInit();
      myBitmapImage.StreamSource =
          new System.IO.MemoryStream(r.Photo);
```

```
      myBitmapImage.EndInit();
      Pic.Source = myBitmapImage;
    }
  }
  catch (Exception ex)
  {
  }
}
```

When you run the application, you'll see the results in Figure 4-26. Remember, if you get errors about the byte stream exceeding the maximum size of a byte array, change the maxReceivedMessageSize attribute in the .config file to something larger.

Figure 4-26. *Running the application with live data*

Tidying Up the XAML

You can further tidy up the XAML by removing a number of the artifacts used by the prototype, such as the templates that were used to bind to the XML data source, the XML data source declaration, and others. Listing 4-7 shows the complete XAML for this application.

Listing 4-7. *The Complete XAML for the Application*

```
<Grid x:Class="bikebrowser.Scene1"
    xmlns="http://schemas.microsoft.com/winfx/2006/xaml/presentation"
    xmlns:x="http://schemas.microsoft.com/winfx/2006/xaml"
    Height="538" Width="709">
    <Grid.Resources>
      <DataTemplate x:Key="ProductListTemplate">
        <StackPanel Orientation="Horizontal">
          <TextBlock Text="{Binding Path=ID}" />
          <TextBlock Text=" " />
          <TextBlock Text="{Binding Path=Name}" />
        </StackPanel>
      </DataTemplate>
      <ControlTemplate x:Key="ListTemplate"
        TargetType="{x:Type ContentControl}">
        <Grid x:Name="Grid" RenderTransformOrigin="0.5,0.5">
          <Grid.ColumnDefinitions>
            <ColumnDefinition />
          </Grid.ColumnDefinitions>
          <Grid.RowDefinitions>
            <RowDefinition />
          </Grid.RowDefinitions>
          <Rectangle Stroke="{x:Null}"
              RadiusX="18.7776353175993"
              RadiusY="18.7776353175993"
              HorizontalAlignment="Stretch"
              VerticalAlignment="Stretch"
              Margin="2.55527063519848,2.08617090524538,
                  -1.3375943461854,-1.16802827284738"
              Width="Auto"
              Height="Auto"
              x:Name="Rectangle"
              RenderTransformOrigin="0.5,0.5">
           <Rectangle.Fill>
             <LinearGradientBrush
                 StartPoint="0,0.5"
                 EndPoint="1,0.5">
               <LinearGradientBrush.RelativeTransform>
                 <TransformGroup>
                   <TranslateTransform
                       X="-0.5" Y="-0.5" />
                   <ScaleTransform
                       ScaleX="1" ScaleY="1" />
                   <SkewTransform
                       AngleX="0" AngleY="0" />
                   <RotateTransform
                       Angle="631.401376641438" />
```

```xml
            <TranslateTransform
                X="0.5" Y="0.5" />
            <TranslateTransform
                X="-1.1102230246251565E-16"
                Y="-1.1102230246251565E-16" />
          </TransformGroup>
        </LinearGradientBrush.RelativeTransform>
        <LinearGradientBrush.GradientStops>
          <GradientStopCollection>
            <GradientStop
              Color="sc#1, 0.954263,
                  0.30914855, 0.35360992"
              Offset="0" />
            <GradientStop
              Color="sc#1, 0.04024682,
                  0.06393177, 0.284197628"
              Offset="0.49145299145299121" />
          </GradientStopCollection>
        </LinearGradientBrush.GradientStops>
      </LinearGradientBrush>
    </Rectangle.Fill>
  </Rectangle>
  <Rectangle Stroke="{x:Null}"
      RadiusX="18.7776353175993"
      RadiusY="18.7776353175993"
      HorizontalAlignment="Stretch"
      VerticalAlignment="Top"
      Margin="2.55527063519873,
              1.31506549254158,
              -0.566488933483129,0"
      Width="Auto"
      Height="128.774603921563"
      x:Name="Rectangle1"
      RenderTransformOrigin="0.5,0.5">
    <Rectangle.Fill>
      <LinearGradientBrush
          StartPoint="0,0.5"
          EndPoint="1,0.5">
        <LinearGradientBrush.RelativeTransform>
          <TransformGroup>
            <TranslateTransform X="-0.5" Y="-0.5" />
            <ScaleTransform ScaleX="1" ScaleY="1" />
            <SkewTransform AngleX="0" AngleY="0" />
            <RotateTransform Angle="270.50646021872143" />
            <TranslateTransform X="0.5" Y="0.5" />
            <TranslateTransform X="0" Y="0" />
          </TransformGroup>
```

```xml
                </LinearGradientBrush.RelativeTransform>
                <LinearGradientBrush.GradientStops>
                  <GradientStopCollection>
                    <GradientStop
                        Color="sc#0, 1, 1, 1"
                        Offset="0.40170940170940145" />
                    <GradientStop
                        Color="sc#1, 1, 1, 1"
                        Offset="0.863247863247863" />
                  </GradientStopCollection>
                </LinearGradientBrush.GradientStops>
              </LinearGradientBrush>
            </Rectangle.Fill>
          </Rectangle>
          <ContentPresenter
              VerticalAlignment="Stretch"
              Margin="2.07136184102533,
                      26.1279146178311,
                      1.17593257642784,
                      16.6005128566424"
              Height="Auto"
              x:Name="ContentPresenter"
              RenderTransformOrigin="0.5,0.5"
              Content="{TemplateBinding Content}"
              ContentTemplate="{TemplateBinding ContentTemplate}"
              ContentTemplateSelector=
                "{TemplateBinding ContentTemplateSelector}" />
        </Grid>
      </ControlTemplate>
    </Grid.Resources>
    <Grid.ColumnDefinitions>
      <ColumnDefinition />
    </Grid.ColumnDefinitions>
    <Grid.RowDefinitions>
      <RowDefinition />
    </Grid.RowDefinitions>
    <Grid.Background>
      <LinearGradientBrush StartPoint="0,0.5" EndPoint="1,0.5">
        <LinearGradientBrush.RelativeTransform>
          <TransformGroup>
            <TranslateTransform X="-0.5" Y="-0.5" />
            <ScaleTransform ScaleX="1" ScaleY="1" />
            <SkewTransform AngleX="0" AngleY="0" />
            <RotateTransform Angle="78.483689233447421" />
            <TranslateTransform X="0.5" Y="0.5" />
            <TranslateTransform X="0" Y="0" />
          </TransformGroup>
```

```xml
          </LinearGradientBrush.RelativeTransform>
        <LinearGradientBrush.GradientStops>
        <GradientStopCollection>
          <GradientStop
              Color="sc#1, 0.0537335165,
                    0.413330764, 0.9373776"
              Offset="0" />
          <GradientStop
              Color="sc#1, 0.8969137,
                    0.0566387065, 0.0566387065"
              Offset="1" />
          <GradientStop Color="sc#1, 0.9840131,
                    0.9460652, 0.9460652"
              Offset="0.63247863247863223" />
        </GradientStopCollection>
      </LinearGradientBrush.GradientStops>
     </LinearGradientBrush>
  </Grid.Background>
  <Grid
    Margin="36,6.62313396736548,41,
            166.182837337067"
    x:Name="ProductGrid" RenderTransformOrigin="0.5,0.5">
    <Grid.ColumnDefinitions>
      <ColumnDefinition Width="0.321492007104796*" />
      <ColumnDefinition Width="0.678507992895204*" />
    </Grid.ColumnDefinitions>
    <Grid.RowDefinitions>
      <RowDefinition />
    </Grid.RowDefinitions>
    <ContentControl
        HorizontalAlignment="Stretch"
        VerticalAlignment="Stretch"
        x:Name="Master"
        RenderTransformOrigin="0.5,0.5"
        Template="{DynamicResource ListTemplate}">
      <ListBox
          SelectionChanged="ProductList_Click"
          x:Name="ProductList"
          RenderTransformOrigin="0.5,0.5"
          IsSynchronizedWithCurrentItem="True"
          ItemsSource="{Binding Mode=OneWay}"
          ItemTemplate="{DynamicResource ProductListTemplate}"
          SelectedIndex="-1"
          Background="{x:Null}"
          BorderBrush="{x:Null}"
          Foreground="#FFFFFFFF" />
    </ContentControl>
```

```xml
<ContentControl
    HorizontalAlignment="Stretch"
    VerticalAlignment="Stretch"
    Margin="20,0,0,0"
    Width="Auto"
    Height="Auto"
    Grid.Column="1"
    x:Name="Details"
    RenderTransformOrigin="0.5,0.5"
    Template="{DynamicResource ListTemplate}">
    <Grid
        x:Name="Grid"
        RenderTransformOrigin="0.5,0.5">
        <Grid.ColumnDefinitions>
          <ColumnDefinition />
        </Grid.ColumnDefinitions>
        <Grid.RowDefinitions>
          <RowDefinition />
        </Grid.RowDefinitions>
        <TextBlock
            VerticalAlignment="Bottom"
            Margin="15.3923978685612,0,82.68,8"
            Height="39"
            Name="Price"
            RenderTransformOrigin="0.5,0.5" />
        <TextBlock
            VerticalAlignment="Bottom"
            Margin="13.3923978685612,0,14.68,53.9999999999998"
            Height="40.6180054009367"
            x:Name="Description"
            RenderTransformOrigin="0.5,0.5"
            Text="Description"
            TextWrapping="Wrap" />
      <Image
        Margin="10.3923978685612,3.5204047434711,
                15.68,109.171526781706"
        x:Name="Pic"
        RenderTransformOrigin="0.5,0.5" />
  </Grid>
</ContentControl>
<GridSplitter
    HorizontalAlignment="Left"
    Margin="0.392397868561062,0.333333333333314,
            0,-0.666666666666686"
    Width="18.6666666666667"
    Grid.Column="1"
    x:Name="GridSplitter"
```

```xml
            RenderTransformOrigin="0.5,0.5" />
</Grid>
<Rectangle
  Stroke="{x:Null}"
  Fill="{x:Null}"
  RadiusX="18.7776353175993"
  RadiusY="18.7776353175993"
  HorizontalAlignment-"Stretch"
  VerticalAlignment="Bottom"
  Margin="41.365746699413,0,
          41.9252929076306,-69.4219689819472"
  Width="Auto" Height="232.284577619781" x:Name="Reflection"
  RenderTransformOrigin="0.5,0.5">
  <Rectangle.RenderTransform>
    <TransformGroup>
      <TranslateTransform X="0" Y="0"/>
      <ScaleTransform ScaleX="1" ScaleY="-1"/>
      <SkewTransform AngleX="0" AngleY="0"/>
      <RotateTransform Angle="0"/>
        <TranslateTransform X="0" Y="0"/>
        <TranslateTransform X="0" Y="0"/>
    </TransformGroup>
  </Rectangle.RenderTransform>
  <Rectangle.OpacityMask>
    <LinearGradientBrush StartPoint="0,0.5" EndPoint="1,0.5">
    <LinearGradientBrush.RelativeTransform>
     <TransformGroup>
      <TranslateTransform X="-0.5" Y="-0.5"/>
      <ScaleTransform ScaleX="1" ScaleY="1"/>
      <SkewTransform AngleX="0" AngleY="0"/>
      <RotateTransform Angle="270.50646021872143"/>
      <TranslateTransform X="0.5" Y="0.5"/>
      <TranslateTransform X="0" Y="0"/>
     </TransformGroup>
    </LinearGradientBrush.RelativeTransform>
    <LinearGradientBrush.GradientStops>
     <GradientStopCollection>
     <GradientStop
        Color="sc#0.7, 1, 1, 1" Offset="0"/>
     <GradientStop
        Color="sc#0, 1, 1, 1" Offset="0.68803418803418825"/>
    </GradientStopCollection>
   </LinearGradientBrush.GradientStops>
  </LinearGradientBrush>
 </Rectangle.OpacityMask>
</Rectangle>
</Grid>
```

Summary

In this chapter, you built a real-world application using Visual Studio 2005 that ties the XAML-based design that you would have implemented, or received, to a live back end. It communicates with this back end using the sister technology of WPF—the WCF. You learned how to construct an application that data binds to a distant service written in this technology and how to evolve a prototype application that uses a local XML cache and bindings into one that uses the WCF and shared data types. This is a pretty typical use case for applications that will be built using the next-generation Windows technologies, but it is only scratching the surface of what is possible with WPF.

In the next chapter of this book, you will explore the technology of WPF in more detail; you'll start with the basics of layout, looking at what a lot of the XAML that you used in this application does, and then you'll move onto data binding. After that, you'll get into one of the more important aspects of WPF—the rich integration of graphics and media that allow you to build applications that make the most of the multimedia features of WPF and Windows Vista. Finally, you'll look at the animation functionality offered by WPF so you can bring life to your applications.

CHAPTER 5

■ ■ ■

Exploring the Layout Controls

Presenting information to your users is of paramount importance. *Effective* presentation is harder than you may think, and you need a set of tools that give you the flexibility to do it properly. Fortunately, the Windows Presentation Foundation (WPF) comes with a wide variety of tools that allow you to lay out and present your user interface (UI). Part of the theme of this book, and WPF in general, is to allow close interaction between designer and developer, and a common frustration between the two is that the technology can limit what the developer can implement, frustrating the dreams of the designer for how the application should look and how it should function. WPF's designer-friendly approach, including tools such as Microsoft Expression Interactive Designer as well as Visual Studio 2005, intends to ease this tension and allow you to work more effectively to deliver world-class applications.

Layout tools are a huge part of the designer trade, and as a developer, it is useful to get to know them well. In this chapter, you will learn about the different tools and controls that are available to WPF, including the different types of layout, panel, grid, and canvas controls. By the end of this chapter, you'll understand more about how to render and display your UI.

Understanding Layout Basics

At the root of WPF layout is the concept of a panel. A *panel* is an area of the screen that can contain a number of controls and handle their layout. The type of panel you choose to use will determine how your UI is designed. The different panel types are as follows—take note that although an element's position is always controlled by its parent panel, some panels will also manage the *size* of their children:

- A *StackPanel* will lay out its children in a vertical or horizontal stack. It can be useful, powerful, and effective in simple UI applications.

- A *DockPanel* allocates the entire edge of its client area to each child. If you think in terms of dockable areas within Visual Studio or Microsoft Office, you'll get the idea of a DockPanel.

- A *Grid* arranges its child controls in rows and columns, aligning them without forcing you to set fixed sizes and positions.

- A *Canvas* allows you to lay out children freely, using absolute positioning, by setting their top, left, width, and height properties. You don't need to resort to fixed sizes and positions.

- A *WrapPanel* lays out the child elements in a sequential position from left to right, breaking content onto the next line when it reaches the edge of the containing box, giving a wrapping effect.

In the next sections, you'll look at each of these in detail and learn how you can use them to lay out your UI using Cider, the Extensible Application Markup Language (XAML) designer in Visual Studio 2005.

Using the StackPanel Control

When building a WinFX Windows application in Visual Studio 2005, you will use the Cider designer, and the Toolbox that contains the XAML controls. Here you can find the StackPanel control (see Figure 5-1).

Figure 5-1. *The StackPanel Toolbox control*

Double-clicking this tool will place it on your application canvas in the Cider designer. The Cider designer is a little different from what you may be used to; you can see it in Figure 5-2.

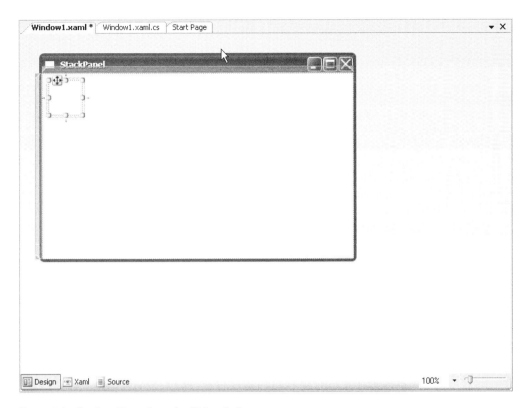

Figure 5-2. *The StackPanel on the Cider designer*

At the bottom of the screen, you'll see three tabs. The first tab, Design, gives you the Cider designer, which you use to lay out your controls. It is similar to the Windows forms designer, allowing you to drag, drop, and arrange your controls and use the Properties window for fine-tuning.

The second tab, Xaml, allows you to view the XAML code underlying your UI. So, as you are dragging and dropping controls and tuning them using their properties, you are really generating XAML code under the hood, displayed on the Source tab, that will be used to render your application at runtime.

So, for example, the simple UI you see in Figure 5-2 has a StackPanel on the screen. When you look at its XAML, it will look something like Listing 5-1.

Listing 5-1. *StackPanel XAML*

```
<Window x:Class="StackPanel.Window1"
    xmlns="http://schemas.microsoft.com/winfx/2006/xaml/presentation"
    xmlns:x="http://schemas.microsoft.com/winfx/2006/xaml"
    Title="StackPanel" Height="300" Width="469">
    <Grid>
    <StackPanel MinHeight="50" MinWidth="50" VerticalAlignment="Top"
                HorizontalAlignment="Left" Grid.Column="0" Grid.ColumnSpan="1"
                Grid.Row="0" Grid.RowSpan="1" Margin="10,10,0,0"
```

```
                    Width="50" Height="50" Name="stackPanel1" />
    </Grid>
</Window>
```

Because the StackPanel is a layout controller, it can contain other components. When using the designer, you'll find that when you create a StackPanel and drag and drop buttons onto it, the buttons don't become children of the StackPanel. To achieve this, create a closing tag for the StackPanel (in other words, </StackPanel>) after the declarations of the child controls. You can see the XAML for this in Listing 5-2.

Figure 5-3 shows a StackPanel that has had some buttons and text boxes placed in it.

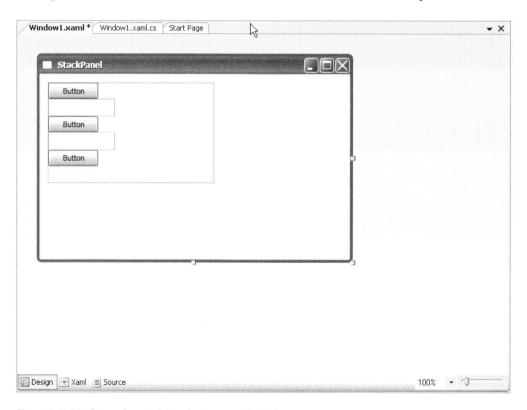

Figure 5-3. *StackPanel containing buttons and text boxes*

Because XAML is an XML derivative, you would expect that the declaration for the StackPanel would then have the declarations for the child controls as child nodes within its node. And you'd be right, as you can see from the XAML underlying the previous UI.

Listing 5-2. *XAML for UI Containing StackPanel, Buttons, and TextBoxes*

```
<Window x:Class="StackPanel.Window1"
    xmlns="http://schemas.microsoft.com/winfx/2006/xaml/presentation"
    xmlns:x="http://schemas.microsoft.com/winfx/2006/xaml"
```

```
        Title="StackPanel" Height="300" Width="469">
        <Grid>
        <StackPanel MinHeight="50" MinWidth="50" VerticalAlignment="Stretch"
                    HorizontalAlignment="Stretch" Grid.Column="0"
                    Grid.ColumnSpan="1" Grid.Row="0"
                    Grid.RowSpan="1" Margin="13,13,201,110.446666666667"
                    Width="NaN" Height="Auto" Name="stackPanel1">
          <Button VerticalAlignment="Top"
                  HorizontalAlignment="Left"
                  Width="75" Height="23"
                  Name="button1">Button
          </Button>
          <TextBox VerticalAlignment="Top"
                   HorizontalAlignment="Left"
                   Width="100" Height="25.276666666666667"
                   Name="textBox1">
           </TextBox>
          <Button VerticalAlignment="Top"
                  HorizontalAlignment="Left"
                  Width="75" Height="23"
                  Name="button2">Button
          </Button>
          <TextBox VerticalAlignment="Top"
                   HorizontalAlignment="Left"
                   Width="100" Height="25.276666666666667"
                   Name="textBox2">
          </TextBox>
          <Button VerticalAlignment="Top"
                  HorizontalAlignment="Left"
                  Width="75" Height="23"
                  Name="button3">Button
          </Button>
        </StackPanel>
      </Grid>
</Window>
```

Getting a StackPanel Orientation

The StackPanel isn't limited to a vertical orientation as you saw in Figure 5-3. It has an Orientation property you can use to stack the child components horizontally. You can set this in the Properties window or directly in the XAML. You can see the effect of making this StackPanel have a Horizontal orientation in Figure 5-4.

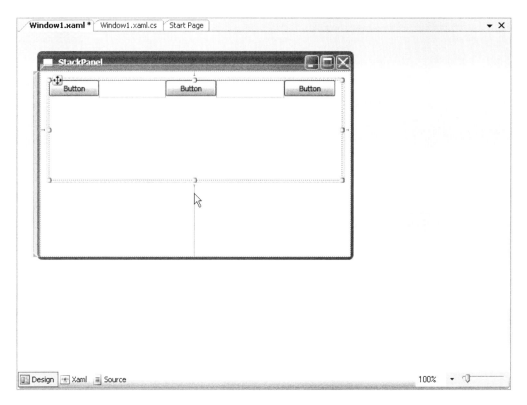

Figure 5-4. *StackPanel with Horizontal orientation*

The XAML for the StackPanel (with the child nodes edited out for brevity) will then look like this:

```
<StackPanel MinHeight="50" MinWidth="50"
        VerticalAlignment="Stretch"
        HorizontalAlignment="Left"
        Margin="13,13,0,110.446666666667"
        Width="435" Height="Auto"
        Name="stackPanel1"
        Orientation="Horizontal">
...
</StackPanel>
```

Docking a StackPanel

You can dock a StackPanel by making it the child of DockPanel and then setting its DockPanel.Dock property accordingly. You'll see more details about DockPanel in the "Using the DockPanel Control" section later in this chapter.

You can add a DockPanel to your window by using the DockPanel control in the Toolbox (see Figure 5-5) or by editing the XAML directly to place a <DockPanel> tag outside the <StackPancl> tag, making it its parent.

Figure 5-5. *The DockPanel control*

Once you've placed the DockPanel and put a StackPanel inside it, you can use the DockPanel.Dock property (of the StackPanel) by setting it to left, right, top, or bottom. Generally, if you are using top and bottom, it is a good idea to have your StackPanel orientation set to Horizontal; if using left and right, you should set it to Vertical.

Figure 5-6 shows the StackPanel within a DockPanel and its DockPanel.Dock property set to the right side.

Figure 5-6. *Setting the StackPanel to dock on the right side*

Listing 5-3 shows the XAML for this.

Listing 5-3. *XAML for Docked StackPanel*

```
<Window x:Class="StackPanelDemo.Window1"
    xmlns="http://schemas.microsoft.com/winfx/2006/xaml/presentation"
    xmlns:x="http://schemas.microsoft.com/winfx/2006/xaml"
    Title="StackPanelDemo"
    Height="300" Width="661">
    <Grid>
      <DockPanel MinHeight="50"
                MinWidth="50"
                LastChildFill="False"
                VerticalAlignment="Stretch"
                HorizontalAlignment="Stretch"
                Grid.Column="0"
                Grid.ColumnSpan="1"
                Grid.Row="0"
                Grid.RowSpan="1"
                Margin="10,10,92,14"
                Width="Auto"
                Height="Auto"
```

```xml
                  Name="dockPanel1">
        <StackPanel DockPanel.Dock="Right"
                    MinHeight="50"
                    MinWidth="50"
                    VerticalAlignment="Stretch"
                    HorizontalAlignment="Left"
                    Grid.Column="2"
                    Grid.ColumnSpan="3"
                    Grid.Row="2"
                    Grid.RowSpan="4"
                    Margin="13,13,0,110.446666666667"
                    Width="115"
                    Height="123.553333333333"
                    Name="stackPanel1"
                    Orientation="Vertical"
                    Grid.IsSharedSizeScope="True"
                    ForceCursor="False">
          <Button VerticalAlignment="Top"
                  HorizontalAlignment="Left"
                  Width="75" Height="23"
                  Name="button1">Button
          </Button>
          <TextBox VerticalAlignment="Top"
                   HorizontalAlignment="Left"
                   Width="100"
                   Height="25.276666666666667"
                   Name="textBox1">
          </TextBox>
          <Button VerticalAlignment="Top"
                  HorizontalAlignment="Left"
                  Width="75" Height="23"
                  Name="button2">Button
          </Button>
          <TextBox VerticalAlignment="Top"
                   HorizontalAlignment="Left"
                   Width="100"
                   Height="25.276666666666667"
                   Name="textBox2">
          </TextBox>
          <Button VerticalAlignment="Top"
                  HorizontalAlignment="Left"
                  Width="75" Height="23"
                  Name="button3">Button
          </Button>
        </StackPanel>
      </DockPanel>
  </Grid>
</Window>
```

Docking the StackPanel at the top with Horizontal orientation will look like Figure 5-7. As you can see, this type of layout and functionality is useful for toolbars.

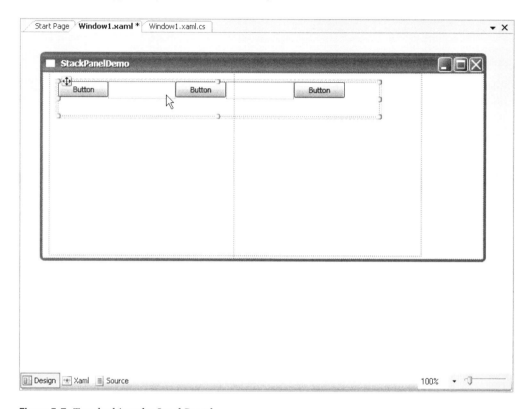

Figure 5-7. *Top docking the StackPanel*

Using Margins in a StackPanel

As you can see in the previous examples, the controls are stuck to the top and left of the StackPanel and to each other. You will likely want to put some spacing between them and also between them and the edge of the screen. You use the Margin property to do this. The Margin property of the StackPanel dictates its margins with respect to its parent, and the Margin property of each child of the StackPanel dictates their margins with respect to the StackPanel.

The Margin property is a comma-separated list of four values: top, bottom, left, and right. So, for example, if you set the StackPanel Margin property to 0,0,0,0 and each of the controls within it to have margins of 5,5,0,0, you get the results in Figure 5-8. A nice shortcut is that if you set only one number, then all margins will be set to that value. So, for example, if you set a margin to 5, then the top, bottom, left, and right margins will all be set to 5.

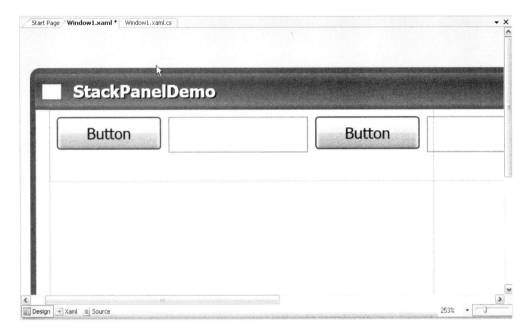

Figure 5-8. *Setting the margins for the child controls*

As you can see, the child controls are now spaced a little more nicely relative to the container and relative to each other.

Understanding When You Would Use a StackPanel

As you can see from the previous sections, the StackPanel is a useful layout tool when you have controls that are organized together in a horizontal or vertical layout. Consider, for example, the Windows XP Search Companion (see Figure 5-9).

Now although this isn't a WPF StackPanel (it's not implemented using WPF), it is a common example of where a user interface uses the same functionality. When viewed in a full-screen context, the Search Companion forms a vertical self-contained set of controls on the left side of the screen. The overall interface is composed of this plus the *client area* to the right where the search results are displayed in addition to the common Explorer toolbar (which could be seen as a horizontal StackPanel) across the top of the screen.

Thus, when building a UI, a good design concept is to think of grouping controls in logical groups to be displayed horizontally or vertically (as toolbars or control stacks) and to implement these groupings using StackPanels.

Figure 5-9. *The Windows XP Search Companion*

Using the DockPanel Control

Now, if you are thinking of organizing your UI into different vertical and horizontal StackPanels, you need to organize each of your StackPanels relative to each other. Earlier you saw how you can use the DockPanel to set the alignment of the StackPanel on the screen, but DockPanel can do a whole lot more besides!

DockPanel is useful for defining the overall layout of your user interface, as a parent to multiple StackPanels, other containers, and individual controls. The DockPanel arranges its children for you, so you can lay out the structure of your UI using a DockPanel and then use other panels within it to handle the details at the individual control level.

The DockPanel arranges its children so each fills up an edge of the panel. If you have multiple children on the same edge, they get stacked up. The order of rendering is simply the order in which the children are declared in the XAML.

To understand the DockPanel a little better, create a new WinFX window using Visual Studio and the Cider designer, and drag a DockPanel control onto it. Next, drag a button onto the designer, and edit the XAML to look like Listing 5-4.

Listing 5-4. *XAML for Button in DockPanel*

```
<Window x:Class="StackPanelDemo.DockPanel"
    xmlns="http://schemas.microsoft.com/winfx/2006/xaml/presentation"
    xmlns:x="http://schemas.microsoft.com/winfx/2006/xaml"
    Title="StackPanelDemo"
    Height="300" Width="300">
    <Grid>
    <DockPanel MinHeight="50" MinWidth="50"
                LastChildFill="False"
                VerticalAlignment="Stretch"
                HorizontalAlignment="Stretch"
                Grid.Column="0"
                Grid.ColumnSpan="1"
                Grid.Row="0"
                Grid.RowSpan="1"
                Margin="10,10,22,21"
                Width="NaN" Height="NaN"
                Name="dockPanel1">
        <Button Name="button1">Button</Button>
    </DockPanel>
  </Grid>
</Window>
```

The button will dock to the left of the DockPanel and take the full height of it, as shown in Figure 5-10.

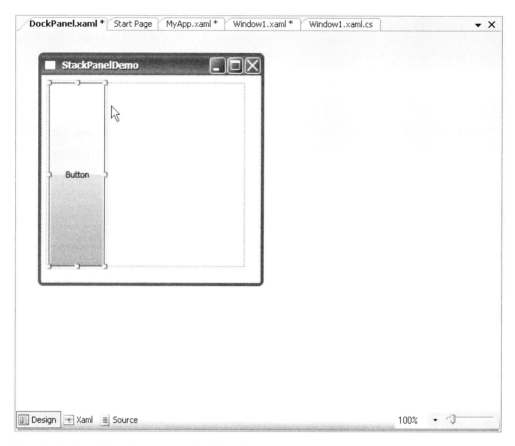

Figure 5-10. *Attaching a button to a DockPanel*

You'll notice that the button does not have its DockPanel.Dock property set. When this isn't set, the alignment of the button within the DockPanel will default to the left. Now if you add three more buttons to the DockPanel (for a total of four), you will see that each is docked to the left, and they are stacked upon each other in the order of declaration. In other words, the first one you dragged is the leftmost, the second is the second from the left, and so on. You can see this in Figure 5-11.

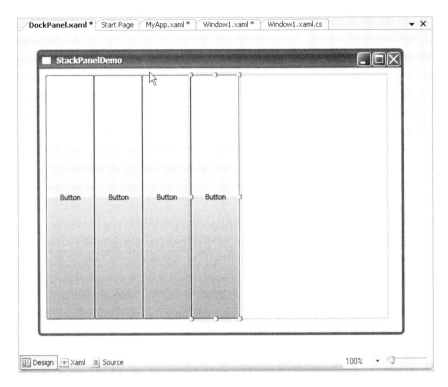

Figure 5-11. *Four buttons stacked within a DockPanel*

Listing 5-5 shows the associated XAML code.

Listing 5-5. *XAML for DockPanel with Four Child Buttons*

```
<Window x:Class="StackPanelDemo.DockPanel"
    xmlns="http://schemas.microsoft.com/winfx/2006/xaml/presentation"
    xmlns:x="http://schemas.microsoft.com/winfx/2006/xaml"
    Title="StackPanelDemo"
    Height="432" Width="569">
<Grid>
<DockPanel MinHeight="50" MinWidth="50"
    LastChildFill="False"
    VerticalAlignment="Stretch"
    HorizontalAlignment="Stretch"
    Grid.Column="0"
    Grid.ColumnSpan="1"
    Grid.Row="0"
```

```
        Grid.RowSpan="1"
        Margin="10,10,22,21"
        Width="NaN" Height="NaN"
        Name="dockPanel1">
    <Button Name="button1">Button</Button>
    <Button Name="button2">Button</Button>
    <Button Name="button3">Button</Button>
    <Button Name="button4">Button</Button>
  </DockPanel>
 </Grid>
</Window>
```

To align these controls, you use their DockPanel.Dock properties; for example, if you set this property for the four buttons to top, left, bottom, right (respectively), your UI will look like Figure 5-12.

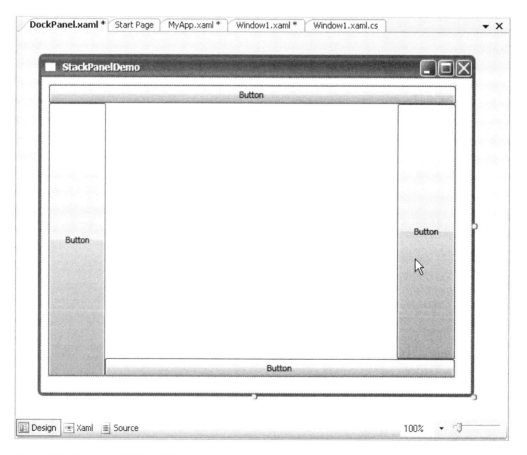

Figure 5-12. *Buttons with DockPanel.Dock set*

Now this looks unusual; the leftmost button is taller than the rightmost, and as a result, the bottom button isn't aligned with the top one. To see why this is the case, take a look at the XAML code in Listing 5-6.

Listing 5-6. *XAML for DockPanel with Children Docked in Different Places*

```
<Window x:Class="StackPanelDemo.DockPanel"
    xmlns="http://schemas.microsoft.com/winfx/2006/xaml/presentation"
    xmlns:x="http://schemas.microsoft.com/winfx/2006/xaml"
    Title="StackPanelDemo"
    Height="432" Width="569">
    <Grid>
    <DockPanel MinHeight="50" MinWidth="50"
               LastChildFill="False"
               VerticalAlignment="Stretch"
               HorizontalAlignment="Stretch"
               Grid.Column="0" Grid.ColumnSpan="1"
               Grid.Row="0" Grid.RowSpan="1"
               Margin="10,10,22,21"
               Width="NaN" Height="NaN"
               Name="dockPanel1">
      <Button Name="button1" DockPanel.Dock="Top">Button</Button>
      <Button Name="button2">Button</Button>
      <Button Name="button3" DockPanel.Dock="Bottom">Button</Button>
      <Button Name="button4" DockPanel.Dock="Right">Button</Button>
    </DockPanel>
  </Grid>
</Window>
```

Remember, the DockPanel doesn't figure out the optimal layout for your controls. It just draws and docks them in the order they are declared. Therefore, as you can see here, the top button is drawn first, and as such, it is docked at the top of the panel and takes up the full width of the panel. Next to be drawn is Button2, and this doesn't have its DockPanel.Dock property set. As such, it is docked to the left and is drawn using the full *available* height on the left side. There is a button already at the top, which means it gets drawn *underneath it*. Next up is Button3, which is docked at the bottom of the panel, but because Button2 is already taking up some of the space on the left, then it gets placed to the right of Button2. Finally, Button4 is docked to the right of the panel and squeezed between Button1 and Button3. This, at render time, will then appear as in Figure 5-12.

For a more traditional look, with a toolbar and status bar at the top and bottom and controls available on the left and right of the screen, such as what you get with the Visual Studio integrated development environment (IDE), you would define your children to dock in top, bottom, left, right order with XAML like shown in Listing 5-7.

Listing 5-7. *Reordering Your XAML*

```xaml
<Window x:Class="StackPanelDemo.DockPanel"
    xmlns="http://schemas.microsoft.com/winfx/2006/xaml/presentation"
    xmlns:x="http://schemas.microsoft.com/winfx/2006/xaml"
    Title="StackPanelDemo"
    Height="432" Width="569">
    <Grid>
    <DockPanel MinHeight="50" MinWidth="50"
            LastChildFill="False"
            VerticalAlignment="Stretch"
            HorizontalAlignment="Stretch"
            Grid.Column="0"
            Grid.ColumnSpan="1"
            Grid.Row="0"
            Grid.RowSpan="1"
            Margin="10,10,22,21"
            Width="NaN" Height="NaN"
            Name="dockPanel1">
      <Button Name="button1" DockPanel.Dock="Top">
          I am the toolbar</Button>
      <Button Name="button2" DockPanel.Dock="Bottom">
          I am the status bar</Button>
      <Button Name="button3">
          I am the left toolbox</Button>
      <Button Name="button4" DockPanel.Dock="Right">
          I am the right toolbox</Button>
    </DockPanel>
  </Grid>
</Window>
```

When rendered, the window will appear as in Figure 5-13, which is more like what you would want to see in your UI.

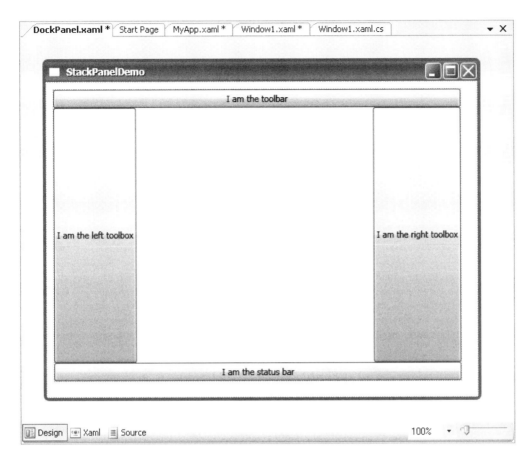

Figure 5-13. *Layout with neater docking*

Of course, if you want to have the left toolbox and right toolbox at the full height of the screen and the toolbar and status bar nestled between them, you would simply order the child controls as left, right, top, bottom instead of top, bottom, left, right.

Using Child Fills

Consider the neat docking layout in Figure 5-13. You have a big white area in the middle where you would like the meat of your application to appear. But how do you put content there? You would expect to be able to put another control onto the panel and not set its DockPanel.Dock property. But if you do this, the DockPanel.Dock will default to the left, and the control will get stacked against the left button. You can see this in Figure 5-14.

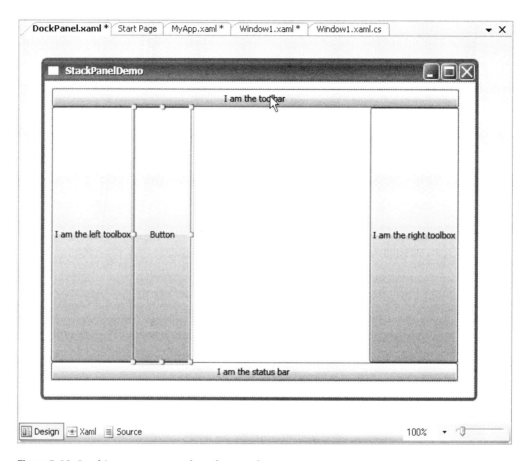

Figure 5-14. *Stacking a new control on the panel*

Of course, this will not work, and the control will not fill the total client area. You can resize it in the designer to fill the whitespace, but at runtime if you resize the window, it will not match. So, in order to fill this area with a control, you use a property called LastChildFill on the DockPanel.

If you look at the XAML you've been using thus far, you'll see the DockPanel declaration. It looks like this:

```
<DockPanel MinHeight="50" MinWidth="50"
           LastChildFill="False"
           VerticalAlignment="Stretch"
           HorizontalAlignment="Stretch"
```

```
        Grid.Column="0"
        Grid.ColumnSpan="1"
        Grid.Row="0"
        Grid.RowSpan="1"
        Margin="10,10,22,21"
        Width="NaN" Height="NaN"
        Name="dockPanel1">
...
</DockPanel>
```

The LastChildFill property is set to False. Change this to True, and take a look at the difference. You'll see that the button automatically fills the client area. And, if you run the application and change the size of the window, it will continue to fill it. See Figure 5-15 where it has been stretched to be wide and short.

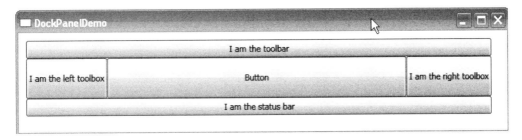

Figure 5-15. *The LastChildFill property is True, and the window has been resized.*

You can see that the last button fills neatly into the area. No code has been written to achieve this; the DockPanel does everything for you. Also, take a look at the window when resized to be tall and thin, as in Figure 5-16.

In this simple example, you placed buttons within the DockPanel to demonstrate how the DockPanel can lay out the areas of your window. In a real UI, you generally wouldn't place controls like this directly on the window surface but would instead use StackPanels containing controls or other panels.

However, because the StackPanel is one dimensional in nature (it can stack controls horizontally or vertically), it may not be able to handle all scenarios for you. For more free-form layout of controls, you can use the Grid layout control, which you'll learn more about in the next section.

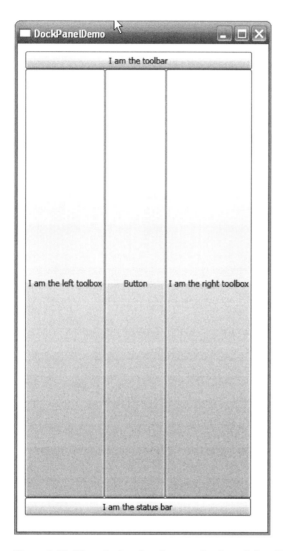

Figure 5-16. *The window has been resized, and the client area still fits.*

Using the Grid Control

In Figure 5-16, you saw an application layout using the DockPanel to lay out controls on the screen, and in earlier examples you saw how to use StackPanels to lay out controls vertically or horizontally. In many cases, these will work nicely to help you lay out your controls neatly and control how they behave when the screen resizes. However, they are restrictive and force you to think in terms of organizing your controls in one-dimensional groups.

If you want something more free-form, you can use the Grid control. This allows you to specify your child controls' locations more freely. Take a look at Figure 5-17. Here, I changed the last child of the DockPanel from a Button control to a Grid control. Then, I placed children on the Grid control and dragged them around freely.

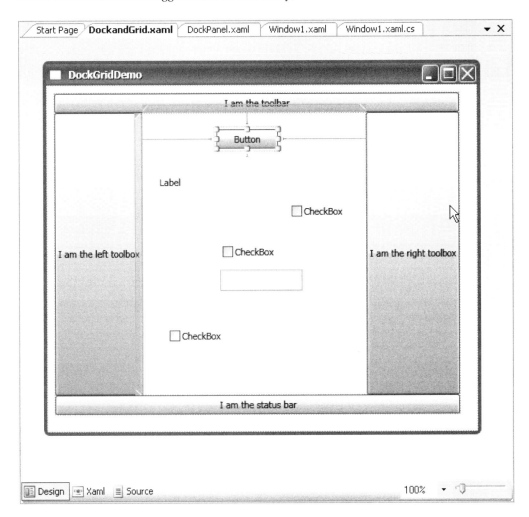

Figure 5-17. *Using the Grid control in the designer*

As you can see, you have full control over the location of the controls within the client area. Additionally, as you resize the window, the controls will reorient themselves automatically.

Now let's look at the XAML for this Grid control, as shown in Listing 5-8, which is a snippet of the overall XAML for the window. To see the DockPanel and Button controls' code, take a look at Listings 5-3 to 5-7 earlier.

Listing 5-8. *XAML for Grid Containing Child Controls*

```
<Grid>
        <Button VerticalAlignment="Top"
                HorizontalAlignment="Stretch"
                Grid.Column="0" Grid.ColumnSpan="1"
                Grid.Row="0" Grid.RowSpan="1"
                Margin="90.41,20,107.526666666667,0"
                Width="NaN" Height="23"
                Name="button5">Button</Button>
        <Label VerticalAlignment="Top"
                HorizontalAlignment="Left"
                Grid.Column="0" Grid.ColumnSpan="1"
                Grid.Row="0" Grid.RowSpan="1"
                Margin="15.78,70.7233333333333,0,0"
                Width="35.63" Height="23.276666666666667"
                Name="label1">Label</Label>
        <CheckBox VerticalAlignment="Stretch"
                HorizontalAlignment="Stretch"
                Grid.Column="0" Grid.ColumnSpan="1"
                Grid.Row="0" Grid.RowSpan="1"
                Margin="97.42,158.72,113.52,164"
                Width="NaN" Height="NaN"
                Name="checkBox1">CheckBox</CheckBox>
        <CheckBox VerticalAlignment="Top"
                HorizontalAlignment="Right"
                Grid.Column="0" Grid.ColumnSpan="1"
                Grid.Row="0" Grid.RowSpan="1"
                Margin="0,110.72,29.52,0"
                Width="61.99" Height="13.27"
                Name="checkBox2">CheckBox</CheckBox>
        <CheckBox VerticalAlignment="Bottom"
                HorizontalAlignment="Left"
                Grid.Column="0" Grid.ColumnSpan="1"
                Grid.Row="0" Grid.RowSpan="1"
                Margin="32.42,0,0,64"
                Width="61.99"
                Height="13.27"
                Name="checkBox3">CheckBox</CheckBox>
        <TextBox VerticalAlignment="Bottom"
                HorizontalAlignment="Stretch"
                Grid.Column="0" Grid.ColumnSpan="1"
                Grid.Row="0" Grid.RowSpan="1"
                Margin="94.41,0,78.52,124" Width="NaN"
                Height="25.27"
                Name="textBox1">
        </TextBox>
</Grid>
```

As you can see, you achieve the absolute location positioning of the components by setting their Margin properties, which, when you think about it, makes sense. Instead of having separate properties for top and left (which you may be accustomed to using Windows forms) and an additional margin that may cause conflicts, you instead just use the Margin property, which allows you to specify the top, left, bottom, and right spacing.

Now, this does have a drawback; because you are specifying a margin—in other words, how far the control will appear off the four edges—you can end up with a scenario where controls overwrite each other upon application resize. Figure 5-17 shows the controls laid out as you may desire them, but look at what happens when the application is resized (see Figure 5-18).

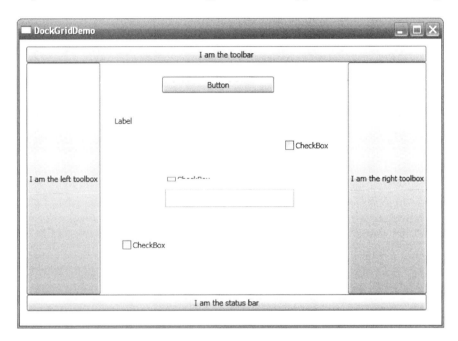

Figure 5-18. *Using margins to set control locations can have undesired effects.*

As you can see, the text box has cropped off the bottom of one of the check boxes. This has happened because the text box is keeping its location based on its margin, and that happens to cause it to need to be written to the same area of the screen as the check box. If you look at the XAML for the application, you can see that the text box is defined last, and this gives it precedence in writing, effectively Z-ordering it above the check box and causing it to be overwritten.

It is with this functionality in mind that the layout properties of the Grid control are available. Using them, you have powerful tools to lay out and organize your controls in a two-dimensional manner, without needing to use margins to specify their locations.

Using Columns and Rows in the Grid

For you to be able to use the two-dimensional properties of the Grid control, you first have to define your grid in terms of rows and columns. If you've ever built web pages using Hypertext Markup Language (HTML) tables to lay out your UI, this will be familiar to you.

You specify your columns and rows in your grid using the ColumnDefinitions and RowDefinitions properties, respectively.

You can use the Properties window in Visual Studio 2005 to create and configure rows and definitions using these properties. So, for example, to add columns to your grid, you click the caret on the ColumnDefinitions property in the editor (see Figure 5-19).

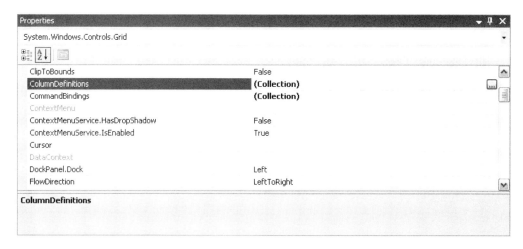

Figure 5-19. *Setting the ColumnDefinitions property*

This will open the Collection Editor where you can add new ColumnDefinitions and configure each one independently, as shown in Figure 5-20.

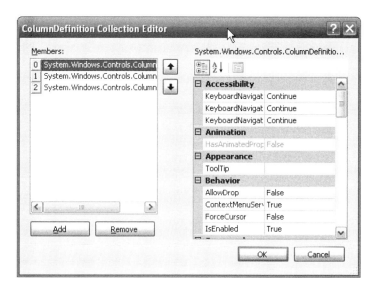

Figure 5-20. *Using the Collection Editor to manage columns*

In a similar manner, you can use the RowDefinition property to open the Collection Editor to add rows. Here is an example of the XAML that is created when adding three columns and three rows to a Grid control:

```
<Grid>
<Grid.RowDefinitions>
  <RowDefinition />
  <RowDefinition />
  <RowDefinition />
</Grid.RowDefinitions>
<Grid.ColumnDefinitions>
  <ColumnDefinition />
  <ColumnDefinition />
  <ColumnDefinition />
</Grid.ColumnDefinitions>
</Grid>
```

As you can see, the <Grid> node has a child node for each of the properties, and these contain a definition tag for each column and row you added. Had you configured these, the configuration would appear as attributes within the RowDefinition and ColumnDefinition tags.

Now, to organize controls within the grid, you simply specify which column and row you want the control to appear in. So, for example, consider the XAML shown in Listing 5-9, which places nine buttons on the grid, one in each row/column combination.

Listing 5-9. *XAML for Grid*

```
<Grid>
    <Grid.RowDefinitions>
      <RowDefinition />
      <RowDefinition />
      <RowDefinition />
    </Grid.RowDefinitions>
    <Grid.ColumnDefinitions>
      <ColumnDefinition />
      <ColumnDefinition />
      <ColumnDefinition />
    </Grid.ColumnDefinitions>
    <Button Grid.Column="0" Grid.Row="0">1</Button>
    <Button Grid.Column="1" Grid.Row="0">2</Button>
    <Button Grid.Column="2" Grid.Row="0">3</Button>
    <Button Grid.Column="0" Grid.Row="1">4</Button>
```

```
        <Button Grid.Column="1" Grid.Row="1">5</Button>
        <Button Grid.Column="2" Grid.Row="1">6</Button>
        <Button Grid.Column="0" Grid.Row="2">7</Button>
        <Button Grid.Column="1" Grid.Row="2">8</Button>
        <Button Grid.Column="2" Grid.Row="2">9</Button>
</Grid>
```

When you run this application, you'll see that the nine buttons are arranged in a 3×3 grid, as shown in Figure 5-21.

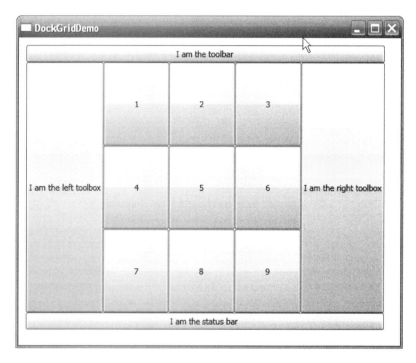

Figure 5-21. *Arranging controls on the grid*

In this example, each row and each column is automatically sized, so each is equally sized. You can override this by specifying desired column widths and row heights either by dragging on a column and row within the designer or by using the Collection Editor.

Figure 5-22 shows where the columns and widths have been edited in the designer.

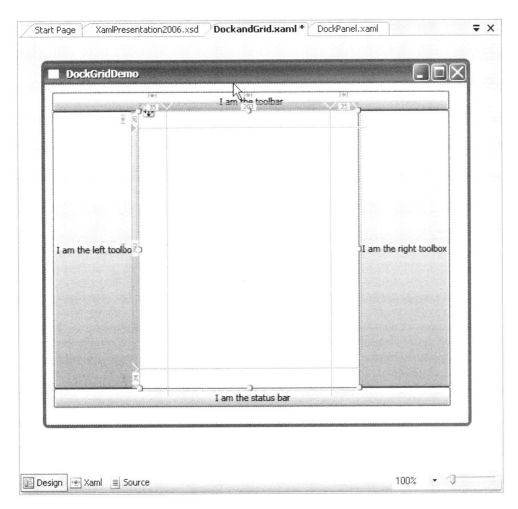

Figure 5-22. *Resizing columns and rows*

Building the UI with Columns and Rows

You can put a control into a grid cell as mentioned earlier—it's very straightforward. You simply place the control's declaration on the grid and set its Grid.Column and Grid.Row properties to the position you desire.

This works well if you are putting a single control in the cell, but when you are putting more than one control, you have to lay them out using margins, as mentioned earlier. This, of course, has the aforementioned drawbacks that occur when you resize the screen. However, a grid cell can also contain another container, and you can use another Grid or container control such as a StackPanel. This will then organize the controls for you.

Consider the following example where you place a StackPanel in the upper-left corner of the grid. You can use this to place multiple controls along the top of the client area.

```
<StackPanel Grid.Column="0"
            Grid.Row="0"
            Orientation="Horizontal">
 <Label>Your Name:</Label>
 <TextBox>Enter Name Here</TextBox>
 <Button>...</Button>
</StackPanel>
```

Now when you view this, you see a problem. You'd expect the StackPanel controls to be rendered across the top of the Grid control, but only the beginning of the Label control is visible. This is because the XAML dictates that the StackPanel should be within the grid at Column 0, Row 0. In this case, you don't want that; you want the StackPanel to be visible across the full width of the client area. To do this, you use the ColumnSpan property:

```
<StackPanel Grid.Column="0" Grid.Row="0"
        Grid.ColumnSpan="3" Orientation="Horizontal">
  <Label>Your Name:</Label>
  <TextBox>Enter Name Here</TextBox>
  <Button>...</Button>
</StackPanel>
```

This instructs the renderer to use three columns to render this information starting at Column 0, Row 0. This gives you the flexibility to specify which column you start rendering at and how many columns to span the rendering across. In a similar manner, you can specify the rows to span if you are using a vertical layout that you want to span across different rows.

Using the Canvas Control

Earlier you looked at the Grid control and how you can use it to place controls at free locations but with the drawback that the Margin property is used, which leads to problems when the application is resized. And as such, the Grid property is best used as a way of laying out controls and containers in a tabular format using rows, columns, and spanning.

Should you want to lay out controls in a fixed top and left manner like with Windows forms, you use a Canvas layout control.

Now this may seem nice, because it is following a method that gives you precise control over how your UI will appear, by dragging and dropping controls in the location you want and using the size you want. But you also have to consider the runtime behavior. Canvas controls will not provide automatic layout and positioning when the application is resized. Also, consider what happens when your application is internationalized where the text in your user interface resources can change drastically in size.

Using a Canvas is straightforward; you just place your child controls inside it and specify their top and left properties.

So, for example, consider the UI in Figure 5-23.

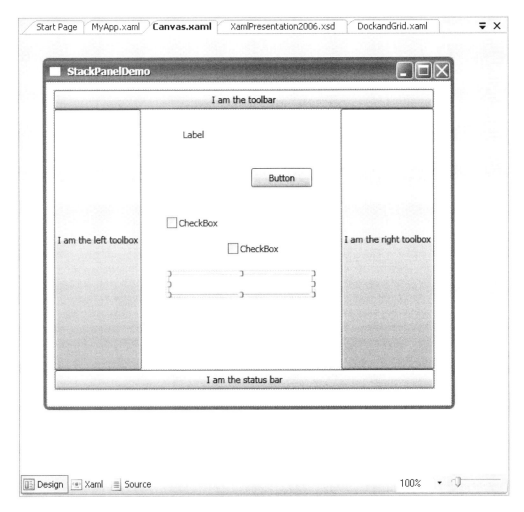

Figure 5-23. *Using the Canvas control for flexible layout*

You can see that this allows the Label, Button, CheckBox, and TextBox controls to be freely positioned on the screen. Examining the XAML in Listing 5-10 shows a straightforward structure, with the controls as children of the Canvas with their Canvas.Top and Canvas.Left properties set.

Listing 5-10. *XAML with Canvas.Top and Canvas.Left Properties*

```
<Canvas>
    <Label Canvas.Left="46.77"
           Canvas.Top="18.72"
           Name="label1">Label</Label>
    <Button Canvas.Left="135.41"
            Canvas.Top="71"
            Name="button5">Button</Button>
```

```
<CheckBox Canvas.Left="31.42"
          Canvas.Top="129.72"
          Name="checkBox1">CheckBox</CheckBox>
<CheckBox Canvas.Left="106.42"
          Canvas.Top="160.72"
          Name="checkBox2">CheckBox</CheckBox>
<TextBox Canvas.Left="33.41"
         Canvas.Top="197.72"
         Name="textBox1"
         Width="177"
         Height="25.28"></TextBox>
</Canvas>
```

If you run an application with a Canvas like this in it, you'll see some interesting behavior. In this case, the Canvas is put in the client area of the four-button DockPanel that was used earlier in this chapter. When you resize the window, you'll see something like Figure 5-24.

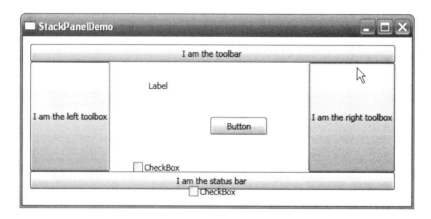

Figure 5-24. *Resizing an application using a Canvas control*

As you can see, the CheckBox not only appears on top of the bottom docked area (*status bar*), but it also appears in the margin of the application. This is because it is set with clear top and left properties dictating the screen position in which it is drawn. The fact that it is on a Canvas that is a child of the DockPanel is irrelevant.

When placing controls on a Canvas using the Cider designer, you place it relative to the top left of the Canvas. Should you want a child control to be present on the screen if the window is made narrower or shorter, you can also place it using the right and bottom properties. For this example, place one label on the top left of the screen, and place another one on the bottom right of the screen. When using the Cider designer, you'll see that the top and left properties are set for each. To change the Bottom Right label to appear always at the bottom right, you have to set the Canvas.Top and Canvas.Left properties to NaN and the Canvas.Bottom and Canvas.Right properties to something meaningful like 20.

Now your XAML will look like Listing 5-11.

Listing 5-11. *Using Right and Bottom Properties*

```
<Window x:Class="StackPanelDemo.Canvas2"
    xmlns="http://schemas.microsoft.com/winfx/2006/xaml/presentation"
    xmlns:x="http://schemas.microsoft.com/winfx/2006/xaml"
    Title="StackPanelDemo"
    Height="300" Width="300">    >
    <Grid>
      <Canvas MinHeight="50" MinWidth="50"
              VerticalAlignment="Stretch"
              HorizontalAlignment="Stretch"
              Grid.Column="0" Grid.ColumnSpan="1"
              Grid.Row="0" Grid.RowSpan="1"
              Margin="7,8,15,21"
              Width="NaN" Height="NaN"
              Name="canvas1">
      <Label Canvas.Left="12.37"
              Canvas.Top="8.72"
              Name="label1">Top Left</Label>
      <Label Canvas.Left="NaN"
              Canvas.Top="NaN"
              Name="label2"
              Canvas.Bottom="20"
              Canvas.Right="20">Bottom Right</Label>
      </Canvas>
    </Grid>
</Window>
```

When you run your application, the Bottom Right label will always be on the bottom right regardless of the window dimensions, as shown in Figures 5-25 and 5-26.

Figure 5-25. *The Canvas panel with labels of Top Left and Bottom Right before resizing*

Figure 5-26. *The same panel after resizing*

Thanks to the absolute positioning of the label element relative to the bottom right of the window, the Bottom Right label is always correctly positioned.

Using the TabPanel for Tabbed Layout

You can use a TabPanel control to specify an area of the screen to lay out tabbing. Although it isn't necessary to use a TabPanel when you want to put tabs on your page, it is useful to have, because it can act as a container for the TabControl. Thus, you need to manage layout for only one item (the TabPanel) instead of a group of them (the TabControl and all its children).

Using a TabPanel in XAML is straightforward; Listing 5-12 shows a simple example.

Listing 5-12. *XAML for TabPanel*

```
<TabPanel VerticalAlignment="Top"
        HorizontalAlignment="Stretch"
        Grid.Column="0" Grid.ColumnSpan="1"
        Grid.Row="0" Grid.RowSpan="1"
        Margin="0,29,0,0" Width="243"
        Height="195" Name="tabPanel1">
    <TabControl VerticalAlignment="Top"
                HorizontalAlignment="Stretch"
                Grid.Column="0"
                Grid.ColumnSpan="1"
                Grid.Row="0"
                Grid.RowSpan="1"
                Name="tabControl1">
        <TabItem Name="tabItem1" Header="Item1">Item 1</TabItem>
        <TabItem Name="tabItem2" Header="Item2">Item 2</TabItem>
        <TabItem Name="tabItem3" Header="Item3">Item 3</TabItem>
        <TabItem Name="tabItem4" Header="Item4">Item 4</TabItem>
    </TabControl>
</TabPanel>
```

This gives you an application that looks like Figure 5-27.

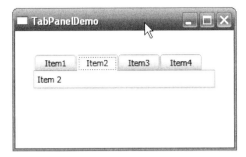

Figure 5-27. *Using the TabPanel*

Each tab when selected will render the child of the <TabItem> node that defines it. In the previous case, the tabs contain a simple string. However, you can place other layout controls such as a Grid or a StackPanel inside a tab and receive the appropriate UI when that tab is selected.

So, for example, if you amend the XAML markup for tabItem1 to this:

```
<TabItem Name="tabItem1" Header="Item1">
  <StackPanel>
    <Button>Button1</Button>
    <Button>Button2</Button>
    <Label>Label1</Label>
  </StackPanel>
</TabItem>
```

it will define that when the tab with the ID tabItem1 and the text Item1 is selected, the content defined by the StackPanel will be rendered. You can see this in Figure 5-28.

Figure 5-28. *Populating a tab in a TabPanel*

Using the WrapPanel Control

The WrapPanel control acts in a similar manner to the StackPanel in that it allows you to arrange controls either horizontally or vertically, but when the appropriate screen real estate isn't available, the controls will wrap into the available space. By default, the controls will arrange themselves left to right until the line is full, and then they will break and continue to the next line.

So, consider the XAML shown in Listing 5-13.

Listing 5-13. *Using the WrapPanel in XAML*

```
<Grid>
  <WrapPanel MinHeight="50" MinWidth="50"
      VerticalAlignment="Top"
      HorizontalAlignment="Left"
      Grid.Column="0"
      Grid.ColumnSpan="1"
      Grid.Row="0"
      Grid.RowSpan="1"
      Margin="12,16,0,0"
      Width="227"
      Height="69"
      Name="wrapPanel1">
    <Button>1</Button>
    <Button>2</Button>
    <Button>3</Button>
    <Button>4</Button>
    <Button>5</Button>
    <Button>6</Button>
    <Button>7</Button>
  </WrapPanel>
</Grid>
```

This will give a UI that looks like Figure 5-29.

Figure 5-29. *The WrapPanel wraps the buttons in a left-to-right fashion.*

Now if you change the width of the WrapPanel, you'll see that the controls automatically reorient themselves, as shown in Figure 5-30.

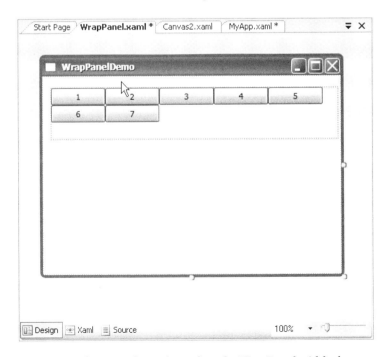

Figure 5-30. *The controls reorient when the WrapPanel width changes.*

Setting the Wrap Flow Direction

In the previous example, the controls are oriented from left to right. You can change this using the FlowDirection property, which you can set to be either LeftToRight or RightToLeft. Consider the XAML shown in Listing 5-14 where FlowDirection has been set to RightToLeft.

Listing 5-14. *Using Wrap Flow Direction*

```
<WrapPanel MinHeight="50"
           MinWidth="50"
           VerticalAlignment="Stretch"
           HorizontalAlignment="Stretch"
           Grid.Column="0" Grid.ColumnSpan="1"
           Grid.Row="0" Grid.RowSpan="1"
           Margin="12,16,4,49" Width="Auto"
           Height="Auto" Name="wrapPanel1"
           Orientation="Horizontal"
           FlowDirection="RightToLeft">
    <Button>1</Button>
    <Button>2</Button>
    <Button>3</Button>
    <Button>4</Button>
    <Button>5</Button>
    <Button>6</Button>
    <Button>7</Button>
</WrapPanel>
```

When rendered, this will appear like in Figure 5-31.

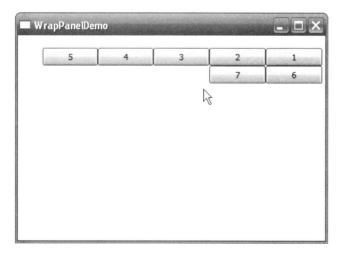

Figure 5-31. *RightToLeft control flow*

Setting the Orientation

In addition to setting the control flow direction, you can also set the orientation, using the Orientation property, which can be Horizontal or Vertical. The previous examples show a Horizontal flow where controls are arranged across the screen. If the Orientation property is set to Vertical, the controls will be arranged down the screen and wrapped across it.

Should FlowDirection be RightToLeft, the controls will appear vertically on the right side of the screen; otherwise, they will appear on the left. Listing 5-15 shows a vertical flow.

Listing 5-15. *Using FlowDirection for Vertical Flow*

```
<Grid>
  <WrapPanel MinHeight="50"
             MinWidth="50"
             VerticalAlignment="Stretch"
             HorizontalAlignment="Stretch"
             Grid.Column="0"
             Grid.ColumnSpan="1"
             Grid.Row="0"
             Grid.RowSpan="1"
             Margin="12,16,4,49"
             Width="Auto"
             Height="Auto"
             Name="wrapPanel1"
             Orientation="Vertical"
             FlowDirection="LeftToRight">
    <Button>1</Button>
    <Button>2</Button>
    <Button>3</Button>
    <Button>4</Button>
    <Button>5</Button>
    <Button>6</Button>
    <Button>7</Button>
  </WrapPanel>
</Grid>
```

This will give the vertical flow shown in Figure 5-32.

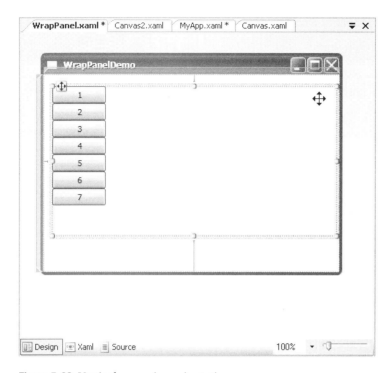

Figure 5-32. *Vertical wrapping orientation*

Summary

In this chapter, you looked at the various layout controls that are available to you as a WPF developer. Layout controls are essential to help you specify and implement the perfect UI. You took a tour of the various panels such as the StackPanel and the DockPanel and how you can use them with each other to lay out the controls for your UI effectively.

Now that you see how you can lay out your controls, you'll take a tour in the next chapter of the common controls in WPF, including learning how they work, how they hang together, and how you can use them in XAML user interfaces.

CHAPTER 6

Working with XAML Controls

Up to now you've explored the architecture of Extensible Application Markup Language (XAML) applications, the tools you can use the build them, a real-world example of an application, and details on how you can lay out the controls.

In this chapter, you'll get into the controls themselves, looking at each one in turn, how it works, and how you can use its events, methods, and properties. The Windows Presentation Foundation (WPF) application programming interface (API) for controls is enormous, so you won't look at every property method and event available; instead, you'll get a good grip on how to use each control so you can get up and running quickly. You'll also be equipped to go into the technical documentation and do more.

In addition, you'll look at data binding in XAML and how you specify the different types of bindings.

Your primary tool in this chapter will be Visual Studio 2005 with the Cider designer. It's a good idea to start using this to play with putting controls on XAML pages and manipulating them. If you want to get hands-on, follow along with the examples in this chapter. It should be a fun ride!

Using the Button Control

One of the simplest and most fundamental controls you'll use in any application is the Button control. This is a simple control that presents a three-dimensional (3D) push button that has a variety of presentation formats and that handles user interaction when the user clicks the button.

A Button control is a XAML ContentControl, meaning it can contain text, images, or even container controls such as panels.

The button has several states. The first, the default state, is the simple button, like this:

When the pointer hovers over a XAML button, it enters the PointerFocused state, which gives nice feedback to the user as they move around the screen, and it looks like this:

The keyboard is also a valid input device but doesn't indicate where the user is currently like a mouse does. Instead, it has *focus*, a visual indicator showing which control will get the keyboard input. You can click a button using the spacebar when it has the focus. It looks like this:

When a button is clicked, it will be "indented" into the screen, like this:

Getting Started with the Button Control

You can create a button by using the Visual Studio 2005 integrated development environment (IDE) to drag and drop it onto a XAML form or code it directly in XAML. The XAML Button declaration is straightforward and looks like this:

```
<Button Name="b1">Button</Button>
```

You add the Click event functionality to the button by adding a Click attribute and using it to specify the name of the event handler function you'll use in your C# code-behind file:

```
<Button Name="b1" Click="b1_Click">Button</Button>
```

You should then write an event handler as a void function in the code-behind file. This function should accept the sender as an object as its first argument and a RoutedEventArgs as its second, like this:

```
private void b1_Click(object sender, RoutedEventArgs e)
{
    // Write code to handle the event here
}
```

Using Rich Content in a Button

Buttons can contain rich content such as images. For example, if you want to specify the image for a button, you can do so with the XAML shown in Listing 6-1.

Listing 6-1. *Using Rich Content in a Button*

```
<Button HorizontalAlignment="Stretch"
        Margin="70,85,35,96"
        VerticalAlignment="Stretch"
        Height="Auto" Width="Auto"
        Grid.RowSpan="1" Grid.Column="0"
        Grid.Row="0" Grid.ColumnSpan="1">
```

```
<Image Source="fish.jpg"
       Height="77.259375"
       Width="147.926143024619" />
</Button>
```

Note that if you use an image within the Button control like this, you cannot also add text, because the <Button> element can hold only one child.

If you want to use something more complex within the button, you use a panel as this child. The panel can then contain multiple children. So, if you consider the XAML in Listing 6-2, it will give you a complex child on the button, which contains the picture and some text.

Listing 6-2. *Adding Pictures and Text*

```
<Button HorizontalAlignment="Stretch"
        Margin="57,37,48,111"
        VerticalAlignment="Stretch"
        Height="Auto" Width="Auto"
        Grid.RowSpan="1" Grid.Column="0"
        Grid.Row="0" Grid.ColumnSpan="1">
  <DockPanel Width="142.926143024619"
             Height="90.5360416666667">
    <Image DockPanel.Dock="Top"
           Source="fish.jpg"
           Height="73.259375"
           Width="96.9343493552169" />
    <TextBlock DockPanel.Dock="Bottom">
        Here is the caption!
    </TextBlock>
  </DockPanel>
</Button>
```

This will give you a button containing a panel that has an image and a text block forming the image caption. You can see this running in Figure 6-1.

Figure 6-1. *A Button control containing a complex child*

You can also change how a button is styled. The following properties allow you to change the appearance:

Background: Sets the background color of the button

Foreground: Sets the foreground (text) color of the button

FontSize: Sets the size of the text used in the button caption

FontWeight: Sets the weight of the font, from extra light to extra bold

FontFamily: Sets the family of the font to use, for example Verdana or Arial

Here's an example of a button with some of these properties set; you can see how it will look in Figure 6-2:

```
<Button Background="Beige"
        Foreground="Black"
        FontSize="12"
        FontWeight="ExtraBold"
        FontFamily="Verdana"
        VerticalAlignment="Top"
        HorizontalAlignment="Stretch"
        Height="73" Width="Auto">

        Changing presentation!
</Button>
```

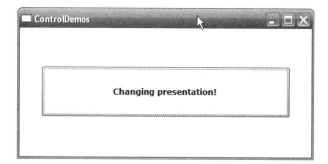

Figure 6-2. *Using a button with custom presentation properties*

As you can see, the XAML button is flexible, allowing you to use a child element to define its presentation. This child element can be a simple, single element such as text or an image or something more complex such as a panel that will contain multiple child elements. Additionally, you can use the styling properties of your button to dictate its appearance. Overall, when using XAML, this simple user interface (UI) element can take on some pretty complex functionality!

Using the CheckBox Control

A check box allows a user to give basic yes/no input by clicking it to change its state. Because the check box is a content control, similar to a button, it can contain a child element that can host a panel containing multiple controls, giving you the flexibility to have some complex presentation on your check box.

Despite the presentation flexibility, the interface of the CheckBox control is simple, giving either a checked state or an unchecked state, as shown here:

☑ Checked   ☐ Unchecked

Getting Started with the CheckBox Control

You can place the CheckBox control on your window using the Cider designer or declare it using the <CheckBox> tag in XAML. Here's an example of some XAML containing two CheckBox elements:

```
<CheckBox Name="checkBox1">Selection 1</CheckBox>
<CheckBox Name="checkBox2">Selection 2</CheckBox>
```

To handle the user input in an event handler, you need to use the Checked attribute on the XAML tag to specify the name of the event handler function. Here's an example of the XAML that defines the event handler:

```
<CheckBox Name="checkBox1" Checked="HandleCheck">Selection 1</CheckBox>
```

Your event handler function is then a void function in the code-behind file that takes two parameters: an object as the first and a RoutedEventArgs as the second. Here's an example:

```
private void HandleCheck(object sender, RoutedEventArgs e)
{
    checkBox1.Content = "Thanks for clicking on me";
}
```

Using Rich Content in a CheckBox Control

Because CheckBox is a content control, you can use a child element within it other than just simple text as in the previous examples. This content can be a single control or a panel containing multiple panels and controls. This gives you great flexibility in presenting your control.

Consider the example in Listing 6-3 that allows you to use image check boxes. It contains a StackPanel, which stacks three check boxes on top of each other. Each check box contains a horizontal StackPanel giving an image and a caption.

Listing 6-3. *Using Rich Content in CheckBox Controls*

```
<StackPanel>
  <CheckBox>
    <StackPanel Orientation="Horizontal">
```

```
        <Image Source="fishtn.jpg" ></Image>
        <TextBlock FontSize="24" Height="35"
                  Width="133.19">Tropical Fish</TextBlock>
    </StackPanel>
    </CheckBox>
    <CheckBox>
      <StackPanel Orientation="Horizontal">
        <Image Source="archtn.jpg" ></Image>
        <TextBlock FontSize="24" Height="35"
                  Width="133.19">Pretty Arch</TextBlock>
      </StackPanel>
    </CheckBox>
    <CheckBox>
      <StackPanel Orientation="Horizontal">
        <Image Source="lilytn.jpg" Height="192.5" Width="256"></Image>
        <TextBlock FontSize="24" Height="35"
                  Width="133.19">Water Lilies</TextBlock>
      </StackPanel>
    </CheckBox>
</StackPanel>
```

When you run the application containing these definitions, it will look like Figure 6-3.

Figure 6-3. *Picture CheckBox controls*

In a similar manner to the button, using XAML makes it much easier for you as a developer to implement your designer dreams, putting together complex designs for a simple control without resorting to a lot of programming, and as you saw in this example, you can override your basic check box with custom images and labels in an easy and purely declarative manner.

Using the ComboBox Control

The ComboBox control combines the functionality of a button and a list. It allows the user to click a button and, from that button, get a list of selectable items. It is a useful UI component because it hides the list, saving valuable screen real estate until the user activates it. It also encapsulates a text box that allows the user to enter information to be added to the list should the requirements desire this.

The standard Combo box appears like this:

And when the button is clicked, the list will drop down, appearing like this:

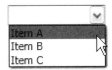

Getting Started with the ComboBox Control

You can define a ComboBox control using the <ComboBox> tag in XAML, and you can define its items as <ComboBoxItem> elements. Here's an example:

```
<ComboBox>
    <ComboBoxItem>Item A</ComboBoxItem>
    <ComboBoxItem>Item B</ComboBoxItem>
    <ComboBoxItem>Item C</ComboBoxItem>
</ComboBox>
```

The ComboBox control supports a number of events. You implement them by specifying the function using attributes on the XAML declaration and then writing a code-behind file that has the event handler.

DropDownOpened Event

The event that fires when the user clicks the button to render the list is DropDownOpened. You can then implement the event handler with a void function that accepts an object sender and an EventArgs argument.

First, here's the XAML:

```
<ComboBox DropDownOpened="cb1_DropDownOpened" Name="cb1" />
```

and now here's the event handler code:

```
void cb1_OnDropDownOpened(object sender, EventArgs e)
{
    // Event Handler Code
}
```

DropDownClosed Event

In a similar manner to the DropDownOpened event, you define the event handler to call when the DropDown is closed using the DropDownClosed attribute. This event handler is then implemented with a void function that accepts an object sender and an EventArgs argument.

First, here's the XAML:

```
<ComboBox DropDownClosed="cb1_DropDownClosed" Name="cb1" />
```

and now here's the event handler code:

```
void cb1_DropDownClosed(object sender, EventArgs e)
{
    // Event Handler Code
}
```

Handling Selection Changes

When the user selects an item on your list, you can capture this using the SelectionChanged event handler. You specify this using the SelectionChanged attribute on the <ComboBox> element like this:

```
<ComboBox SelectionChanged="cb1_SelectionChanged" Name="cb1" />
```

The event handler is implemented in the code-behind file using two parameters: a general object representing the sender and an EventArgs object that carries any event arguments:

```
void cb1_SelectionChanged(object sender, EventArgs e)
{
    // Event handler code here
}
```

Handling Mouse Moves

You can perform an action in response to the user moving the mouse over the items in your combo list. You specify this event on the <ComboBoxItem> element instead of the <ComboBox> element. You specify it with the MouseMove attribute like this:

```
<ComboBox>
    <ComboBoxItem MouseMove="cb1_MouseMove">Item A</ComboBoxItem>
```

```
    <ComboBoxItem MouseMove="cb1_MouseMove">Item B</ComboBoxItem>
    <ComboBoxItem MouseMove="cb1_MouseMove">Item C</ComboBoxItem>
</ComboBox>
```

You can map each ComboBoxItem to the same event handler as in the previous example. You can use the sender parameter in the event handler function to decide which item originated the event call if necessary. It also accepts a RoutedEventArgs parameter (routed because the item is a child of the combo box and the events are routed through the parent).

The event handler code will look like this in C#:

```csharp
void cb1_MouseMove(object sender, RoutedEventArgs e)
{
    // Event Handler Code here
    ComboBoxItem X = (ComboBoxItem)sender;
    MessageBox.Show(X.Content.ToString());

}
```

Using the Edit Area on the Combo Box

The combo box also implements a text editor, allowing the user to enter text that may or may not be added to the list of combo items (you'd have to write code to do that if that is what you want). You enable this functionality using the IsEditable property, which you can set to True or False. Should you want the list to remain open while you are editing, you can use the StaysOpenOnEdit property, which is also True or False. Thus, if you want a ComboBox control that is editable and stays open while you edit, you specify it like this:

```
<ComboBox StaysOpenOnEdit="True" IsEditable="True">
```

Using Rich Content in a Combo Box

You aren't limited to <ComboBoxItem> children in a ComboBox control and, in fact, can use any control as a child instead. So, for example, you can easily implement a graphical combo box by using a panel as the child element and then populating that panel.

So, for example, consider the XAML shown in Listing 6-4.

Listing 6-4. *Using Rich Content in Combo Boxes*

```
<ComboBox Height="Auto" Width="Auto"
    SelectionChanged="OnSelectionChanged"
    Grid.RowSpan="1" Grid.Row="0"
    Margin="16.5,12,13.5,12"
    VerticalAlignment="Stretch"
    HorizontalAlignment="Stretch"
    Grid.Column="0" Grid.ColumnSpan="1">
  <StackPanel Orientation="Horizontal">
    <Image Source="fishtn.jpg" ></Image>
    <TextBlock FontSize="24" Height="35"
               Width="133.19">
```

```
                Tropical Fish
    </TextBlock>
  </StackPanel>
  <StackPanel Orientation="Horizontal">
    <Image Source="archtn.jpg" ></Image>
    <TextBlock FontSize="24" Height="35"
              Width="133.19">
                Pretty Arch
    </TextBlock>
  </StackPanel>
  <StackPanel Orientation="Horizontal">
    <Image Source="lilytn.jpg"
          Height="192.5" Width="256"></Image>
    <TextBlock FontSize="24" Height="35"
              Width="133.19">
                Water Lilies
    </TextBlock>
  </StackPanel>
</ComboBox>
```

When this XAML is used in an executing application, you then get a nice picture combo
box, as shown in Figure 6-4.

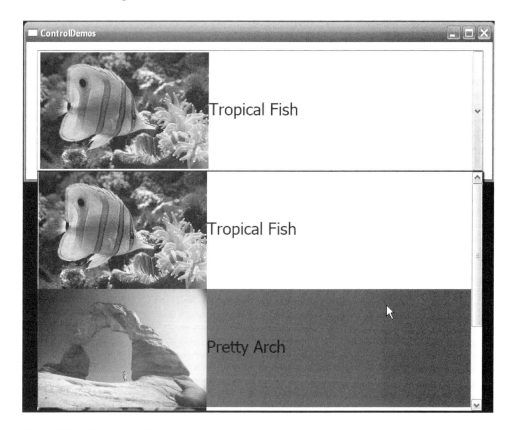

Figure 6-4. *An image combo box*

Using the Slider Control

The Slider control allows your users to specify a value that lies between a low range and a high range visually. It provides an easier-to-understand value than typing a number, and it also provides visual feedback on the value that has been entered relative to the desired range.

A Slider control can be either horizontal, like this:

or vertical, like this:

Getting Started with the Slider

You define a Slider control in your XAML with the <Slider> tag. A simple declaration for a Slider control will look like this:

```
<Slider Name="sl1" />
```

This defines a simple horizontal Slider control with a minimum value of 0, a maximum value of 10, and a current value of 0.

To change the range that the Slider control supports, you use the Minimum and Maximum properties. So, for example, to implement a Slider control that encompasses the values 0 through 100, with the starting value of 50, you would use this definition:

```
<Slider Name="sl1" Minimum="0" Maximum="100" Value="50" />
```

The Slider control has two components: the track and the thumb. The *thumb* is the piece you pick up and drag; the *track* is the line along which you drag it.

Using Tick Marks for Improved Feedback

You can provide better feedback for your users by implementing tick marks at regular intervals along the track. You do this with a number of properties:

IsSnapToTickEnabled: Takes the value True or False. This ensures that the thumb will snap to a tick mark; if, for example, you have ticks every 10 spaces from 0 through 100, you can select only the values 10, 20, 30, and so on.

TickPlacement: This determines where the ticks are located. This can be Top-Left, Bottom-Right, Both, or None.

TickFrequency: This determines how often a tick is placed on your slider. So, for example, if you want a tick for every five values, you use 5 in this property.

Here's an example of a slider with the values 0 through 100, a default of 50, and tick marks placed every 5 values in both locations (top left and bottom right):

```
<Slider Name="sl1"
        Minimum="0"
        Maximum="100"
        Value="50"
        IsSnapToTickEnabled="True"
        TickPlacement="Both"
        TickFrequency="5" />
```

Figure 6-5 shows how this looks in action. The thumb is rectangular because the tick marks are on both sides. If you set TickPlacement to either Top-Left or Bottom-Right, you'll get an upward- and downward-pointing thumb, respectively.

Figure 6-5. *Slider with tick bar*

Using a Selection Range in a Slider

Sometimes you may want to show the entire range of possible values that the slider can do, but at this moment you are limited to a smaller range. Say, for example, your entire range is 0 through 100, but currently you are allowed only to move within the range 60 through 90. You can implement this using a selection range.

You set up a selection range using three properties:

IsSelectionRangeEnabled: This can be True or False. If True, it turns on the selection range and reads it from the next two properties.

SelectionStart: Specifies the start value for the selection range.

SelectionEnd: Specifies the end value for the selection range.

Thus, you can update the earlier slider to support a selection range using XAML like this:

```
<Slider Name="sl1"
        Minimum="0"
        Maximum="100"
        Value="50"
        IsSnapToTickEnabled="True"
```

```
TickPlacement="BottomRight"
TickFrequency="5"
IsSelectionRangeEnabled="True"
SelectionStart="60"
SelectionEnd="90"/>
```

This will render a slider as shown in Figure 6-6.

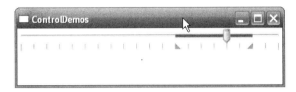

Figure 6-6. *A slider with a selection range*

Note that the slider will not enforce that the thumb remains in the selection range. You, as the developer, will have to do this.

Capturing Value Changes on the Slider

When the user changes the value of the slider by dragging the thumb, the ValueChanged event will get fired. You can capture this by setting the ValueChanged property of the slider and using it to specify the event handler function name. The event handler function can then be present in the code-behind file.

The following XAML will show this definition:

```
<Slider Name="sl1"
        Minimum="0"
        Maximum="100"
        Value="50"
        IsSnapToTickEnabled="True"
        TickPlacement="BottomRight"
        TickFrequency="5"
        IsSelectionRangeEnabled="True"
        SelectionStart="60"
        SelectionEnd="90"
        ValueChanged="sl1_ValueChanged"/>
```

The ValueChanged event handler can then be written in the code-behind file. Here is an example where the ValueChanged event handler ensures that the slider value must remain within the selection range, ensuring that the thumb cannot be dragged out of it:

```
private void sl1_ValueChanged(object sender, EventArgs e)
{
    if (sl1.Value < sl1.SelectionStart)
        sl1.Value = sl1.SelectionStart;

    if (sl1.Value > sl1.SelectionEnd)
        sl1.Value = sl1.SelectionEnd;
}
```

Using the Image Control

The Image control stores and renders images. It enables you to use the following image types: .bmp, .gif, .ico, .jpg, .png, and .tiff. If the image is a multiframe image such as an animated GIF, only the first frame in the animation is displayed. Multiframe images are not supported in WPF. When you use an image in WPF, the default is that the image area is sized according to the dimensions of the picture. You can override this by setting the width and height using properties.

Getting Started with the Image Control

You declare the Image control using the <Image> tag in XAML. The Source attribute specifies the location of the image to load into the control. It will look like this:

```
<Image Source="Fish.jpg" />
```

If you want the image to fit within a specified area, you can do so using the Width and Height properties. So, for example, the following XAML will fit an image into a 200×200 square, regardless of its original ratio:

```
<Image Source="Fish.jpg" Height="200" Width="200" />
```

If you want to keep the original aspect ratio of the image but limit it to 200 pixels high, you'll use this:

```
<Image Source="Fish.jpg" Height="200" />
```

Taking Care of Memory

A good practice for performance reasons is to use DecodePixelWidth or DecodePixelHeight alongside Width or Height and to set it to the same respective size. These cache the resized image instead of the source one, saving lots of application memory.

To use these, you use the <BitmapImage> tag, which is available in the XAML schema as a child of Image.Source. Thus, instead of declaring an image using this syntax:

```
<Image Source="Fish.jpg" Height="200">
```

you can get more fine-grained control using this syntax:

```
<Image Height="200">
  <Image.Source>
    <BitmapImage DecodePixelHeight="200" UriSource="Fish.jpg" />
  </Image.Source>
</Image>
```

Cropping an Image

You can crop an image by defining it in the Resources section, defining the cropped image in the Resources section with the dimensions of the crop, and then using this as the source for an image on the window. Your XAML will look like this:

```
<Grid>
  <Grid.Resources>
    <BitmapImage x:Key="Master"
                 UriSource="Fishtn.jpg" />
    <CroppedBitmap x:Key="Cropped"
                   SourceRect="20, 20, 100, 20"
                   Source="{StaticResource Master}" />
  </Grid.Resources>
  <Image Height="200" Source="{StaticResource Cropped}" />
</Grid>
```

When you run this, you'll see the cropping on the image like in Figure 6-7.

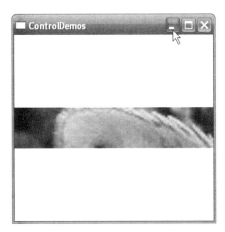

Figure 6-7. *Cropping an image*

Rotating an Image

You can rotate an image using the Rotation property of the BitmapImage image source. As with the "Taking Care of Memory" section earlier, you will use the <Image.Source> child of the <Image> tag for fine-grained control over the image source and then use this to specify the image using the <BitmapImage> tag. This has a Rotation property that allows you to rotate the image 90, 180, or 270 degrees. Here's an example:

```
<Image>
  <Image.Source>
    <BitmapImage UriSource="Fishtn.JPG" Rotation="Rotate90" />
  </Image.Source>
</Image>
```

When you run this in an application, you can see the rotated image like in Figure 6-8.

Figure 6-8. *Rotating an image*

Converting an Image

The <FormatConvertedBitmap> tag allows you to convert the image's color depth to produce dithered black-and-white images, grayscales, different color depths, and more. You use it by implementing it as a static resource, which converts an image in another static resource. The on-page image is then bound to the converted source. This may seem a little confusing, but investigating the code will clarify:

```
<Grid>
  <Grid.Resources>
    <BitmapImage x:Key="Master"
          UriSource="Fishtn.jpg" />
    <FormatConvertedBitmap x:Key="Converted"
          Source="{StaticResource Master}"
          DestinationFormat="BlackWhite" />
  </Grid.Resources>
  <Image Height="200" Source="{StaticResource Converted}" />
</Grid>
```

In this case, the grid resources contain a <BitMapImage> tag that contains the reference to the underlying image. The <FormatConvertedBitmap> tag then refers to the <BitmapImage> tag and has a DestinationFormat property that allows you to specify how the image can be converted. In this case, it converts to BlackWhite, which produces a dithered black-and-white image. You can use lots of formats here, including 2-bit to 32-bit grayscales, different RGB formats, and different CMYK formats.

You can see the output of this XAML in Figure 6-9.

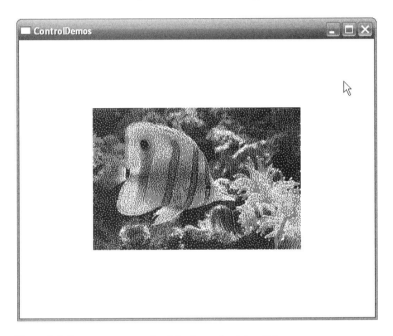

Figure 6-9. *Image converted to black-and-white dither*

Here's another example, where the image is converted to a 2-bit grayscale (in other words, four shades of gray):

```
<Grid>
  <Grid.Resources>
    <BitmapImage x:Key="Master"
        UriSource="Fishtn.jpg" />
    <FormatConvertedBitmap x:Key="Converted"
        Source="{StaticResource Master}"
        DestinationFormat="Gray2" />
  </Grid.Resources>
  <Image Height="200" Source="{StaticResource Converted}" />
</Grid>
```

Figure 6-10 shows the output of this.

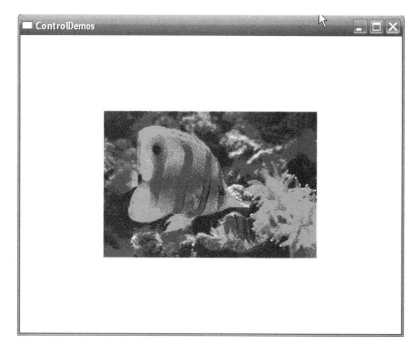

Figure 6-10. *Grayscale conversion*

Using the ListBox Control

The ListBox control presents a list of items from which the user can select one or more. It is a standard UI element in many applications and is generally used in a data-bound environment where the list is populated from a database source. You'll learn more about this later in this chapter in the "Performing Data Binding with XAML Controls" section.

A typical ListBox looks like Figure 6-11, with the selected item(s) being highlighted.

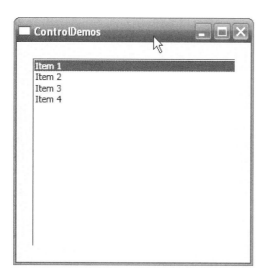

Figure 6-11. *A typical ListBox control*

Getting Started with the ListBox

You define a ListBox control in XAML with the <ListBox> tag. The children of this tag form the items in the list. Basic list items use the <ListItem> tag, but you can also use more complex list items such as images by using panels as the children and then putting images and text in these panels.

Listing 6-5 shows an example of a basic ListBox control, which renders a list like that shown previously in Figure 6-11.

Listing 6-5. *XAML for ListBox*

```
<ListBox BorderThickness="1"
         Margin="20,20,20,20"
         Width="290" Height="238"
         VerticalAlignment="Stretch"
         HorizontalAlignment="Stretch"
         Grid.Column="0" Grid.ColumnSpan="1"
         Grid.Row="0" Grid.RowSpan="1"
         SelectedIndex="0"
         Name="listBox1" BorderBrush="Blue">
  <ListBoxItem>Item 1</ListBoxItem>
  <ListBoxItem>Item 2</ListBoxItem>
  <ListBoxItem>Item 3</ListBoxItem>
  <ListBoxItem>Item 4</ListBoxItem>
</ListBox>
```

ListBox Selection Modes

The list box has three modes of selection, and these determine how many and which items may be selected by the user.

The default mode for a ListBox is *single* when only one item may be selected. When you want the user to be able to select multiple items, you can use the *multiple* mode. Finally, you can use the *extended* mode, which allows the user the most flexibility, so they can hold the Ctrl key to select multiple ranges of items.

To determine the selection mode, you use the SelectionMode property. Listing 6-6 shows an example of the same list as shown previously but multiple list items may be selected.

Listing 6-6. *Multiple Selection List Box*

```
<ListBox BorderThickness="1"
         Margin="20,20,20,20"
         Width="290" Height="238"
         VerticalAlignment="Stretch"
         HorizontalAlignment="Stretch"
         Grid.Column="0" Grid.ColumnSpan="1"
         Grid.Row="0" Grid.RowSpan="1"
         Name="listBox1" BorderBrush="Blue"
         SelectionMode="Multiple">
```

```
    <ListBoxItem>Item 1</ListBoxItem>
    <ListBoxItem>Item 2</ListBoxItem>
    <ListBoxItem>Item 3</ListBoxItem>
    <ListBoxItem>Item 4</ListBoxItem>
    <ListBoxItem>Item 5</ListBoxItem>
    <ListBoxItem>Item 6</ListBoxItem>
    <ListBoxItem>Item 7</ListBoxItem>
    <ListBoxItem>Item 8</ListBoxItem>
</ListBox>
```

Figure 6-12 shows how this appears at runtime when several items are selected. No ranges are allowed; if you want a range of items, you have to click each one individually.

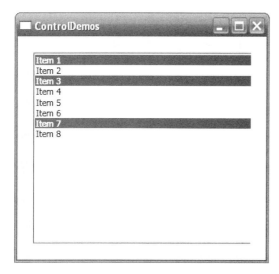

Figure 6-12. *Multiple-item selection list*

Configuring the list for extended selection is straightforward. You simply set the SelectionMode property to Extended. Listing 6-7 shows an example.

Listing 6-7. *ListBox with Extended Selection*

```
<ListBox BorderThickness="1"
        Margin="20,20,20,20"
        Width="290" Height="238"
        VerticalAlignment="Stretch"
        HorizontalAlignment="Stretch"
        Grid.Column="0" Grid.ColumnSpan="1"
        Grid.Row="0" Grid.RowSpan="1"
        Name="listBox1" BorderBrush="Blue"
        SelectionMode="Extended">
    <ListBoxItem>Item 1</ListBoxItem>
    <ListBoxItem>Item 2</ListBoxItem>
```

```
    <ListBoxItem>Item 3</ListBoxItem>
    <ListBoxItem>Item 4</ListBoxItem>
    <ListBoxItem>Item 5</ListBoxItem>
    <ListBoxItem>Item 6</ListBoxItem>
    <ListBoxItem>Item 7</ListBoxItem>
    <ListBoxItem>Item 8</ListBoxItem>
</ListBox>
```

Figure 6-13 shows how this will appear onscreen. You can select a range of items by click-ing the first item in the range and then holding Shift and clicking the last item in the desired range.

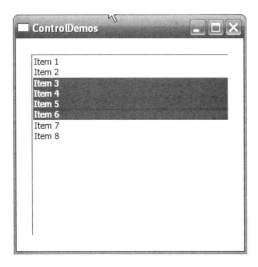

Figure 6-13. *Extended list allows for range selection*

Using Complex List Items

In addition to the ListItem control, a ListBox control can contain complex list items where any type of control can be a list item in XAML. So, for example, if you want a list of images, you can specify the list items to be panels, and these panels can contain an image and a text block. You can see an example of an image list in Listing 6-8.

Listing 6-8. *ListBox with Complex List Items*

```
<ListBox BorderThickness="1"
         Margin="20,20,20,20"
         VerticalAlignment="Stretch"
         HorizontalAlignment="Stretch"
         Grid.Column="0" Grid.ColumnSpan="1"
         Grid.Row="0" Grid.RowSpan="1"
         Name="listBox1" BorderBrush="Blue"
         SelectionMode="Extended">
  <StackPanel Orientation="Horizontal">
```

```
      <Image Source="fishtn.jpg" ></Image>
      <TextBlock FontSize="24" Height="35"
                 Width="133.19">Tropical Fish
      </TextBlock>
   </StackPanel>
   <StackPanel Orientation="Horizontal">
      <Image Source="archtn.jpg" ></Image>
      <TextBlock FontSize="24" Height="35"
                 Width="133.19">Pretty Arch
      </TextBlock>
   </StackPanel>
   <StackPanel Orientation="Horizontal">
      <Image Source="lilytn.jpg" Height="192.5" Width="256"></Image>
      <TextBlock FontSize="24" Height="35"
                 Width="133.19">Water Lilies
      </TextBlock>
    </StackPanel>
 </ListBox>
```

Figure 6-14 shows the image list this generates.

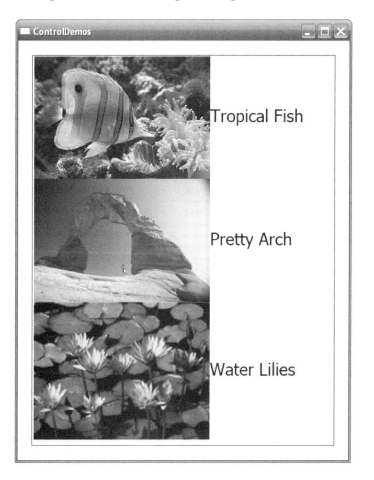

Figure 6-14. *List using complex list items*

Handling ListBox Events

The main event you'll handle is when a user selects an item on your list box. You specify this using the SelectionChanged attribute in XAML to name the event handler function. Listing 6-9 shows an example.

Listing 6-9. *Handling List Box Events*

```
<ListBox BorderThickness="1"
         Margin="20,20,20,20"
         VerticalAlignment="Stretch"
         HorizontalAlignment="Stretch"
         Grid.Column="0" Grid.ColumnSpan="1"
         Grid.Row="0" Grid.RowSpan="1"
         Name="listBox1" BorderBrush="Blue"
         SelectionMode="Single"
         SelectionChanged="listBox1_SelectionChanged">
   <ListBoxItem>Item 1</ListBoxItem>
   <ListBoxItem>Item 2</ListBoxItem>
   <ListBoxItem>Item 3</ListBoxItem>
   <ListBoxItem>Item 4</ListBoxItem>
   <ListBoxItem>Item 5</ListBoxItem>
   <ListBoxItem>Item 6</ListBoxItem>
   <ListBoxItem>Item 7</ListBoxItem>
   <ListBoxItem>Item 8</ListBoxItem>

 </ListBox>
```

You can then implement the event handler in your code-behind file. Because this ListBox supports single-selection mode, you will get only one item selection, which can be derived using the SelectedItem property like this:

```
public void listBox1_SelectionChanged
   (object sender, SelectionChangedEventArgs args)
{
  ListBoxItem myItem = (ListBoxItem) listBox1.SelectedItem;
  string strTest = myItem.Content;
}
```

Should you have a multiple or extended selection type, the SelectedItems property will contain a collection of the selected items. You can iterate through this collection to derive the user's selections. Here's an example that uses the Count property to get the number of items in the collection and then loops through them using their indices:

```
public void listBox1_SelectionChanged
   (object sender, SelectionChangedEventArgs args)
{
   int nCount = listBox1.SelectedItems.Count;
   string strTest = "";
   for(int lp=0; lp<nCount; lp++)
```

```
        {
            ListBoxItem myItem = (ListBoxItem) listBox1.SelectedItems[lp];
            string strTest = myItem.Content;
        }
}
```

Using the RadioButton Control

The RadioButton control, sometimes referred to as an *option button*, is similar to the Check-
Box control, except it constrains the selection within the range of controls to only one option.
So, if you want to present the user with a list of items and want to constrain them to only one
choice, you could use a list with the single selection type or a group of RadioButton controls.
An additional difference from the CheckBox control is that when a user clicks the radio button
when it is selected, the selection will not clear. The only way to clear a selection is to click
another RadioButton control.

Figure 6-15 shows an example of the RadioButton control in action.

Figure 6-15. *Using the RadioButton control*

Getting Started with the RadioButton

You use the <RadioButton> tag in XAML to specify the use of a RadioButton control. When you
use RadioButton controls together within a panel, they form an option group where only one
item may be selected.

Here's an example:

```
<StackPanel>
    <RadioButton Name="radioButton1">USA</RadioButton>
    <RadioButton Name="radioButton2">Japan</RadioButton>
    <RadioButton Name="radioButton3">Brazil</RadioButton>
    <RadioButton Name="radioButton4">Germany</RadioButton>
</StackPanel>
```

Specifying Option Groups

You can have multiple groups within the same panel by specifying the group name. Thus, you can have a single visible group of RadioButton controls and multiple selectable subgroups. This may sound confusing, so consider the following code:

```
<StackPanel Margin="30,30,30,30">
        <RadioButton GroupName="Jerseys">
          Blue Jerseys</RadioButton>
        <RadioButton GroupName="Jerseys">
          White Jerseys</RadioButton>
        <RadioButton GroupName="Shorts">
          Red Shorts</RadioButton>
        <RadioButton GroupName="Shorts">
          White Shorts</RadioButton>

</StackPanel>
```

This specifies two groups of options: one for Jersey colors and one for Shorts colors. The user can select one option from each range despite that all four RadioButton controls are in the same StackPanel.

You can see this in action in Figure 6-16.

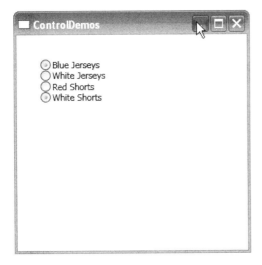

Figure 6-16. *Using GroupName to define multiple option ranges*

Using Complex RadioButton Types

With the RadioButton control, you aren't limited to simple text selections as in the previous sections. The RadioButton control is a content control, allowing you to specify either a single control or a panel (which can contain multiple controls) as its child. Here's an example of a RadioButton selection list that allows you to select from a number of images. The images are stored in a DockPanel, which contains a StackPanel for each image, and this StackPanel contains the image and the text block containing the label for that image.

Listing 6-10 shows an example.

Listing 6-10. *Complex RadioButtons in XAML*

```
<StackPanel>
  <RadioButton>
    <StackPanel Orientation="Horizontal">
      <Image Source="fishtn.jpg" ></Image>
      <TextBlock FontSize="24"
          Height="35" Width="133.19">
          Tropical Fish</TextBlock>
    </StackPanel>
  </RadioButton>
  <RadioButton>
    <StackPanel Orientation="Horizontal">
      <Image Source="archtn.jpg" ></Image>
      <TextBlock FontSize="24"
          Height="35" Width="133.19">
          Pretty Arch</TextBlock>
    </StackPanel>
  </RadioButton>
  <RadioButton>
    <StackPanel Orientation="Horizontal">
      <Image Source="lilytn.jpg"
          Height="192.5" Width="256"></Image>
      <TextBlock FontSize="24"
          Height="35" Width="133.19">
          Water Lilies</TextBlock>
    </StackPanel>
  </RadioButton>
</StackPanel>
```

Figure 6-17 shows this in action. You now have a RadioButton selection group where you can pick one image from the range.

Figure 6-17. *Selecting an image from a RadioButton list*

Handling RadioButton Events

When the user selects a RadioButton control, the Click event fires. Thus, you can use the Click attribute on the RadioButton control to specify the function to call as the event handler when this happens.

You can add an event handler for each object simply by specifying a function with a different name for each one, so if you have the following (within a container such as a StackPanel so they don't appear on top of each other):

```
<RadioButton Name="rb1" Click="rb1_Click">Item 1</RadioButton>
<RadioButton Name="rb2" Click="rb2_Click">Item 1</RadioButton>
<RadioButton Name="rb3" Click="rb3_Click">Item 1</RadioButton>
```

you would need three event handler functions, with each looking something like this:

```
void rb1_Click(object sender, RoutedEventArgs e)
{
    rb1.Content = "You Selected Me!";
}
```

Alternatively, you can map all three to the same event handler and use the "object sender" parameter to work with the source RadioButton control. So, the previous XAML would change to this:

```
<RadioButton Name="rb1" Click="rb_Click">Item 1</RadioButton>
<RadioButton Name="rb2" Click="rb_Click">Item 1</RadioButton>
<RadioButton Name="rb3" Click="rb_Click">Item 1</RadioButton>
```

This would require only one event handler function, like this:

```
void rb_Click(object sender, RoutedEventArgs e)
{
    System.Windows.Controls.RadioButton b =
        (sender as System.Windows.Controls.RadioButton);
    b.Content = "You Selected Me!";
}
```

Handling Events for Complex Types

As demonstrated earlier, the RadioButton control is a content control that can handle complex types such as an image list. Should you want to derive the details of the selection, such as the text in the text block that is part of the StackPanel that is a child of the RadioButton control, you can use "object sender" in the event handler too. So, for example, you can use this XAML to declare a group of RadioButton controls that are all mapped to the same event handler code, as shown in Listing 6-11.

Listing 6-11. *Handling Events with XAML Radio Buttons*

```
<StackPanel>
  <RadioButton Click="HandleSelection" Name="r1">
    <StackPanel Orientation="Horizontal">
      <Image Source="fishtn.jpg" ></Image>
      <TextBlock FontSize="24" Height="35"
          Width="133.19">Tropical Fish</TextBlock>
    </StackPanel>
  </RadioButton>
```

```
<RadioButton Click="HandleSelection" Name="r2">
   <StackPanel Orientation="Horizontal">
     <Image Source="archtn.jpg" ></Image>
     <TextBlock FontSize="24" Height="35"
        Width="133.19">Pretty Arch</TextBlock>
   </StackPanel>
 </RadioButton>
 <RadioButton Click="HandleSelection" Name="r3">
   <StackPanel Orientation="Horizontal">
     <Image Source="lilytn.jpg" Height="192.5"
        Width="256"></Image>
     <TextBlock FontSize="24" Height="35"
        Width="133.19">Water Lilies</TextBlock>
   </StackPanel>
 </RadioButton>
</StackPanel>
```

You can now write a single event handler, called HandleSelection, that casts the sender object to a RadioButton control and then looks at its content. It knows that the RadioButton control contains a StackPanel control and that the child at Index [1] is a text block. It can then derive the text in that text block.

Here's the code:

```
public void HandleSelection(Object sender, RoutedEventArgs e)
  {
    System.Windows.Controls.RadioButton b = (
      sender as System.Windows.Controls.RadioButton);
    StackPanel d = (StackPanel)b.Content;
    TextBlock t = (TextBlock)d.Children[1];
    string strTest = t.Text;
  }
```

Using the Menu Control

The Menu control allows you to create a set of organized elements that raise a Click event (much like a button) when the user selects them. The elements can be hierarchical in nature. In XAML, you use the <Menu> tag along with the <MenuItem> tag (which specifies individual items) and the <Separator> tag (which draws a line on the menu allowing you to gradually link items).

Figure 6-18 shows an example of a menu with multiple levels and separators.

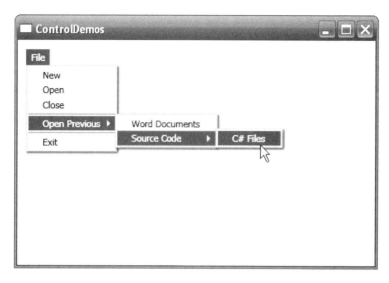

Figure 6-18. *An example menu*

Getting Started with the Menu Control

You declare your menu using the <Menu> item in XAML. This creates a new, empty menu that can have items added to it using the <MenuItem> tag. The textual description within a menu item is stored in its Header property. Additionally, <MenuItem> nodes are hierarchical, so a menu item can have one or more menu item children. To logically segregate your menu as shown in Figure 6-18, you use a <Separator> tag.

So, Listing 6-12 shows the XAML to build the menu structure you saw in Figure 6-18.

Listing 6-12. *Building a Menu Structure in XAML*

```
<Menu Width="30" Margin="10, 10, 5, 5"
      HorizontalAlignment="Left" Background="White">
  <MenuItem Header="_File">
    <MenuItem Header="_New" IsCheckable="true"/>
    <MenuItem Header="_Open" IsCheckable="true"/>
    <MenuItem Header="_Close" IsCheckable="true"/>
    <Separator/>
    <MenuItem Header="Open Previous">
      <MenuItem Header="Word Documents" />
      <MenuItem Header="Source Code" >
        <MenuItem Header="C# Files" />
```

```
            </MenuItem>
        </MenuItem>
        <Separator/>
        <MenuItem Header="E_xit">
        </MenuItem>
    </MenuItem>
</Menu>
```

If you look closely, you can see that the menu nesting comes from nesting the <MenuItem> nodes. Thus, the Word Documents and Source Code nodes are children of the Open Previous one, and C# Files is a child of Source Code. As a result, you get the nested behavior you can see in Figure 6-18.

Using Complex Menu Types

You aren't limited to the menu being a text menu. Because the MenuItem control is a container control, you can define different controls or panels as menu items. So, for example, Listing 6-13 shows a menu that gives three graphical elements as menu items.

Listing 6-13. *Building Complex Menu Types in XAML*

```
<Menu>
  <MenuItem Header="Graphical Menu">
    <StackPanel Orientation="Horizontal">
      <Image Source="Fishtn.jpg"></Image>
      <Label>Tropical Fish</Label>
    </StackPanel>
    <StackPanel Orientation="Horizontal">
      <Image Source="Archtn.jpg"></Image>
      <Label>Pretty Arch</Label>
    </StackPanel>
    <StackPanel Orientation="Horizontal">
      <Image Source="lilytn.jpg"></Image>
      <Label>Water lilies</Label>
    </StackPanel>
  </MenuItem>
</Menu>
```

You can see the results of running this in Figure 6-19.

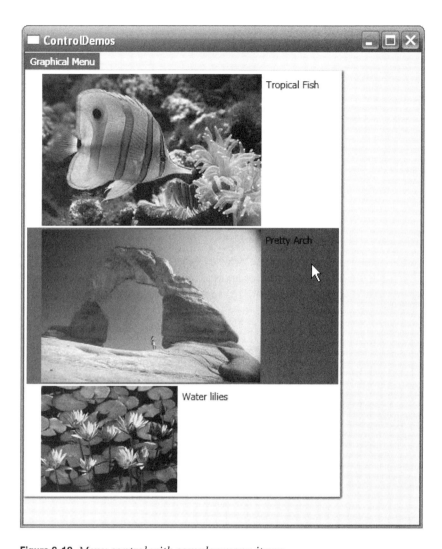

Figure 6-19. *Menu control with complex menu items*

Checkable Items

In some cases, you may require your menu items to be checkable, where the state of the menu item being selected is maintained and visually represented by a check mark. To achieve this and to implement a checkable menu item, you use the IsCheckable property. This can be True or False. The default is False, and if the property isn't specified, then it is considered not to be checkable. Additionally, you can set the initial state of the menu item to checked using the IsChecked property. Note that even if it is not checkable, if you set the IsChecked property to True, you'll get the check mark beside the menu.

Here's an example of a menu with checkable items:

```
<Menu>
  <MenuItem Header="CheckStates">
    <MenuItem Header="Is Checkable And Is Checked"
      IsCheckable="True" IsChecked="True"></MenuItem>
    <MenuItem Header="Is Checkable But Is Not Checked"
      IsCheckable="True" IsChecked="False"></MenuItem>
    <MenuItem Header="Is Not Checkable And Is Not Checked"
      IsCheckable="False" IsChecked="False"></MenuItem>
    <MenuItem Header="Is Not Checkable But I Set The IsChecked Property"
      IsCheckable="False" IsChecked="True"></MenuItem>
    </MenuItem>
</Menu>
```

Figure 6-20 shows how this menu will appear on the screen.

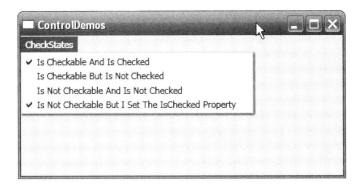

Figure 6-20. *Different check states on menu items*

Using Menu ToolTips

To give more information about a menu entry, you can add a tooltip to your menu by using the <MenuItem.ToolTip> tag. The tooltip will appear automatically and stay onscreen for about five seconds.

You can see the XAML for a simple tooltip in Listing 6-14.

Listing 6-14. *Building Menu Tooltips in XAML*

```
<Menu>
  <MenuItem Header="CheckStates">
    <MenuItem Header="Is Checkable And Is Checked"
      IsCheckable="True" IsChecked="True"></MenuItem>
    <MenuItem Header="Is Checkable But Is Not Checked"
      IsCheckable="True" IsChecked="False"></MenuItem>
    <MenuItem Header="Is Not Checkable And Is Not Checked"
      IsCheckable="False" IsChecked="False"></MenuItem>
```

```
    <MenuItem Header="Is Not Checkable But I Set The IsChecked Property"
      IsCheckable="False" IsChecked="True">
      <MenuItem.ToolTip>
      <ToolTip>You see how the menu item is
            checked even though it isn't checkable? :)
      </ToolTip>
  </MenuItem.ToolTip>
    </MenuItem>
    </MenuItem>
</Menu>
```

Now when you run the application and hover over the menu item, you can see the tooltip. Figure 6-21 shows it in action.

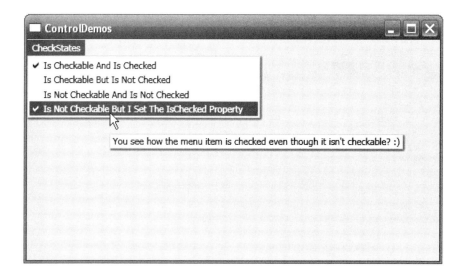

Figure 6-21. *Using a tooltip on a menu*

And, because flexibility is the name of the game in WPF and because the tooltip is a container, you can implement complex tooltip types by using other controls within the <MenuItem.ToolTip> tag. So, for example, you could put a StackPanel containing an image and a label as shown in Listing 6-15.

Listing 6-15. *Building a Complex Tooltip in XAML*

```
<Menu>
  <MenuItem Header="CheckStates">
    <MenuItem Header="Is Checkable And Is Checked"
      IsCheckable="True" IsChecked="True"></MenuItem>
    <MenuItem Header="Is Checkable But Is Not Checked"
      IsCheckable="True" IsChecked="False"></MenuItem>
    <MenuItem Header="Is Not Checkable And Is Not Checked"
      IsCheckable="False" IsChecked="False"></MenuItem>
```

```
    <MenuItem Header="Is Not Checkable But I Set The IsChecked Property"
      IsCheckable="False" IsChecked="True">
      <MenuItem.ToolTip>
     <ToolTip>
      <StackPanel Orientation="Horizontal">
        <Image Source="Fishtn.jpg"></Image>
        <Label>Here is my stackpanel picture tooltip, weird, huh?</Label>
      </StackPanel>
     </ToolTip>
  </MenuItem.ToolTip>
    </MenuItem>
    </MenuItem>
</Menu>
```

You can see the effect of this in Figure 6-22.

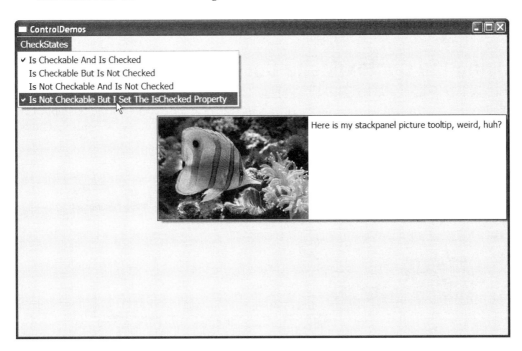

Figure 6-22. *Menu with graphical tooltip*

Handling Menu Events

The Menu item fires a Click event when it is selected, and you specify this using the Click
property. You can then handle the event in your code-behind file with a standard event handler function.

Here's an example:

```
<Menu>
  <MenuItem Header="CheckStates">
    <MenuItem Header="Is Checkable And Is Checked"
        IsCheckable="True" IsChecked="True"
        Name="mnuItem1" Click="mnuItem1_Click">
    </MenuItem>
  </MenuItem>
</Menu>
```

The event handler for this will then look like this:

```
private void mnuItem1_Click(object sender, EventArgs e)
{
  string strTest = "Hello";
}
```

Using the ContextMenu Control

The ContextMenu control is similar to the Menu control except that a context menu is initially hidden and can appear anywhere on the screen, instead of at the assigned, fixed position. The ContextMenu control is typically invoked when the user right-clicks a specific control; it pops up in response.

Figure 6-23 shows a ContextMenu control in action.

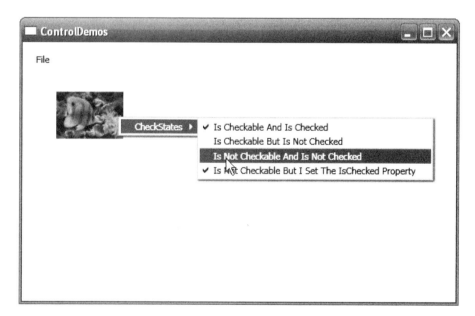

Figure 6-23. *A ContextMenu control*

Getting Started with the ContextMenu

You define a ContextMenu control with the <ContextMenu> tag in XAML. You also need to assign it to another control, and you do so with that control's ContextMenu property.

So, in Figure 6-23, you saw that the image has a context menu. When the user right-clicks it, the menu appears. This was implemented using the XAML shown in Listing 6-16. Note how the ContextMenu property of the image was used.

Listing 6-16. *Building a Context Menu Item in XAML*

```
<Image VerticalAlignment="Top"
       HorizontalAlignment="Left"
       Grid.Column="0" Grid.ColumnSpan="1"
       Grid.Row="0" Grid.RowSpan="1"
       Margin="41,59.4453125,0,0"
       Width="84" Height="56.109375"
       Name="image1"
       Source="Fishtn.jpg">
    <Image.ContextMenu>
      <ContextMenu>
        <MenuItem Header="CheckStates">
          <MenuItem Header="Is Checkable And Is Checked"
                    IsCheckable="True" IsChecked="True"
                    Name="mnuItem1" >
          </MenuItem>
          <MenuItem Header="Is Checkable But Is Not Checked"
                    IsCheckable="True" IsChecked="False">
          </MenuItem>
          <MenuItem Header="Is Not Checkable And Is Not Checked"
                    IsCheckable="False" IsChecked="False">
          </MenuItem>
          <MenuItem Header="Is Not Checkable
            But I Set The IsChecked Property"
                    IsCheckable="False" IsChecked="True">
          </MenuItem>
        </MenuItem>
      </ContextMenu>
    </Image.ContextMenu>
  </Image>
```

Handling a context menu for complex data types, checking and unchecking items, writing event handlers, and so on are all the same as for a traditional menu, so check out the "Using the Menu Control" section for details about this.

Using the ListView Control

The ListView control presents a list of items that can be reviewed in different ways. A classic example of the ListView control is Windows Explorer, where you have a number of options for viewing the contents of a directory. You can view icons, thumbnails, details, and several other options in this case. The ListView control has a huge amount of functionality and probably merits a book in its own right. The following sections will give you a brief overview of it so you can start using it straightaway.

Figure 6-24 shows an example of a ListView control using several columns of Extensible Markup Language (XML) data. Each data item is stored within a column, and you can rearrange and resize the columns. With a little work, the columns can also be sortable. Additionally, as you move across the ListView with the mouse, you get a highlight and immediate feedback that the list is active.

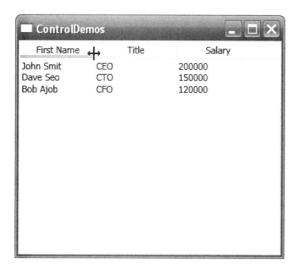

Figure 6-24. *A ListView control in action*

Getting Started with the ListView

The ListView control contains a number of ListItem controls when it is populated. Typically, you will not manually code these (although you could if you wanted) but instead dynamically create them at runtime using a data binding.

Listing 6-17 shows an example that binds to an XML data source.

Listing 6-17. *Binding a ListView to an XML Data Source*

```
<Window x:Class="ControlDemos.ListView_"
    xmlns="http://schemas.microsoft.com/winfx/2006/xaml/presentation"
    xmlns:x="http://schemas.microsoft.com/winfx/2006/xaml"
    Title="ControlDemos"
    Height="300" Width="300">
```

```
<Grid>
  <Grid.Resources>
    <XmlDataProvider x:Key="EmployeeSource"
         Source="employees.xml"/>
  </Grid.Resources>
  <ListView Name="lvwEmps"
            SelectionChanged="OnSelected"
            ItemsSource="{Binding Source={StaticResource EmployeeSource},
               XPath=/employees/employee}">
    <ListView.View>
    <GridView>
      <GridViewColumn Header="First Name"
           DisplayMemberBinding="{Binding XPath=Name}"
           Width="100"/>
      <GridViewColumn Header="Title"
           DisplayMemberBinding="{Binding XPath=Title}"
           Width="100"/>
      <GridViewColumn Header="Salary"
           DisplayMemberBinding="{Binding XPath=Salary}"
           Width="100"/>
    </GridView>
     </ListView.View>
  </ListView>
</Grid>
</Window>
```

I'll discuss data binding in the next section, so you'll see more details there. The ListView control is populated using the <ListView.View> nodes, where a <GridView> node is configured. Within the <GridView> node, you define a number of <GridViewColumn> nodes, which define both the columns (that is, headers and width, and so on) as well as the content (using DisplayMemberBinding). The ItemsSource property specifies the records to bind to in the data.

Thus, this XAML defines a ListView control that binds to the XML data source specified, with three columns, so that each ListViewItem control that gets created will have three columns, and they will map to the Name, Title, and Salary fields.

So, consider the following data:

```
<employees>
  <employee id="1">
    <Name>John Smit</Name>
    <Title>CEO</Title>
    <Salary>200000</Salary>
  </employee>
  <employee id="2">
    <Name>Dave Seo</Name>
    <Title>CTO</Title>
    <Salary>150000</Salary>
  </employee>
```

```
  <employee id="3">
    <Name>Bob Ajob</Name>
    <Title>CFO</Title>
    <Salary>120000</Salary>
  </employee>
</employees>
```

You'll see that the ListView control's ItemSource points to the /employees/employee XPath, which returns three records. Then, for each of these records, a column is defined on the ListView control using the <GridViewColumn> tags.

The result is the ListView you saw in Figure 6-23.

It's important to note that although you haven't explicitly created any ListViewItem controls here, there are now (in this case) three ListViewItem objects within the ListView. These can be interrogated in your code-behind file at runtime. You'll see some of this in the next section.

Handling ListView Events

When the user selects an item in the list or changes the list selection, the SelectionChanged event will fire. When you specify an event handler using the SelectionChanged property, you can then implement an event handler for it. This event handler takes two parameters: the sender as a generic object and a SelectionChangedEventArgs object you can use to query any arguments on the selection. Here's an example:

```
void OnSelected(object sender, SelectionChangedEventArgs e)
{
  int x = lvwEmps.Items.Count;
  int y = lvwEmps.SelectedItems.Count;
}
```

Performing Data Binding with XAML Controls

WPF provides a data binding methodology that is simple and consistent and allows you to "activate" your controls by binding them to data sources. You can bind to common language runtime (CLR) objects such as simple data types, properties of other controls, or object data sources, as well as to XML sources as you saw previously in the ListView example.

Ultimately, data binding is performing one of the processes that allows you to connect your UI presentation to your back-end business logic. If you consider the sample you ran through in Chapters 3 and 4, this was the logical flow you took. First, you built the application using a simple local cache of data to see how it would work and hang together. Next, you went through the process of binding it to "live" data on the server side, building a true *n*-tier application. The communication between the tiers was through WCF, but the perception of this came to the user through the use of data binding.

This demonstrates the typical use of data binding—placing middle- or upper-tier information into a format that the user can understand and interact with.

The concept of data binding is consistent regardless of the method you use. You have a binding source and a binding target. A property on the binding source object is bound to a dependency property on the binding target dependency object. You can see this pictorially in Figure 6-25.

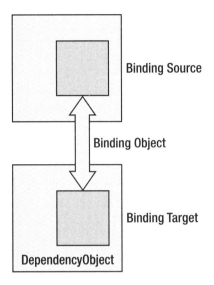

Figure 6-25. *Data binding architecture*

As you can see, data binding is, simply put, the creation of a bridge between two objects that are called the *source* and the *target*. The binding can have three direction settings:

OneWay: Where the binding goes from the source object to the dependency object

OneWayTosource: Where the binding goes from the dependency object to the source object

TwoWay: Where each binds to the other

In the next few sections, you'll go through some examples of how this works, starting with a simple control binding scenario.

Control Binding

The concept of control binding is simple. It allows you to declaratively define the bindings between two controls. It's useful when you want to have immediate feedback from your users' interaction.

Consider this example where you have a slider and a text block. As you drag the slider, the text block updates automatically to the value of the slider. Here's a portion of the XAML:

```
<Grid>
  <StackPanel>
    <Slider Name="sldValue" Minimum="0"
            Maximum="100"></Slider>
    <TextBlock
      Text="{Binding ElementName=sldValue, Path=Value}">
```

```
    </TextBlock>
  </StackPanel>
</Grid>
```

The interesting line is in bold. You can see here that the TextBlock assigns its Text property to this interesting string:

```
{Binding Elementname=sldValue, Path=Value}
```

This specifies that text is the dependency property, that TextBlock is the dependency object, that the slider (sldValue) is the source object, and that its Value property is the source property.

Now, when you run the application containing this XAML and move the slider, the text block will update showing the current value of the slider, as shown in Figure 6-26.

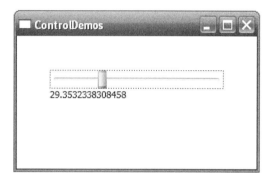

Figure 6-26. *Control binding example*

Using Conversions in Binding

You can write a class that implements the IValueConverter to handle the conversion of data from one type to another. Listing 6-18 shows an example that takes in a numeric value, and if it is greater than 50, it converts it to a red SolidColorBrush; otherwise, it converts it to a black SolidColorBrush.

Listing 6-18. *Using Conversions in Data Bindings*

```
using System;
using System.Collections.Generic;
using System.Text;
using System.Windows.Data;
using System.Windows.Media;

namespace ControlDemos
{
  class ColorConvert : IValueConverter
  {
```

```
  public object Convert(object value, Type targetType, object parameter,
                            System.Globalization.CultureInfo culture)
  {
    Color theColor = new Color();
    double theValue = (double)value;
    if (theValue > 50)
    {
      theColor = Colors.Red;
    }
    else
    {
      theColor = Colors.Black;
    }
    return new SolidColorBrush(theColor);
  }

  public object ConvertBack(object value, Type targetType, object parameter,
                            System.Globalization.CultureInfo culture)
  {
    return null;
  }

 }
}
```

Now you need to define this as a converter in your XAML code, which will look like the code in Listing 6-19.

Listing 6-19. *XAML for Binding Conversions App*

```
<Window x:Class="ControlDemos.SimpleBinding"
    xmlns="http://schemas.microsoft.com/winfx/2006/xaml/presentation"
    xmlns:x="http://schemas.microsoft.com/winfx/2006/xaml"
    xmlns:cnv="clr-namespace:ControlDemos"
    Title="ControlDemos" Height="300" Width="300">
  <Grid>
    <Grid.Resources>
      <cnv:ColorConvert x:Key="ColorConvert"></cnv:ColorConvert>
    </Grid.Resources>
    <StackPanel Margin="40,40,40,40">
      <Slider Name="sldValue" Minimum="0"
              Maximum="100">
      </Slider>
      <TextBlock
        Foreground="{Binding ElementName=sldValue,
         Path=Value,
         Converter={StaticResource ColorConvert}}">My Text
```

```
      </TextBlock>
    </StackPanel>
  </Grid>
</Window>
```

First, the converter support needs you to refer to the namespace in which the converter resides. So, if you look at the converter code, you'll see that it resides in the ControlDemos namespace. This namespace is defined in the XAML to use the cnv prefix like this:

```
xmlns:cnv="clr-namespace:ControlDemos"
```

Next, you specify the converter as a resource that is available to the page controls using the <Grid.Resources> section like this:

```
<Grid.Resources>
  <cnv:ColorConvert x:Key="ColorConvert"></cnv:ColorConvert>
</Grid.Resources>
```

Finally, on the Destination control, you specify the binding and configure the converter to use. In this case, you will be changing the foreground color of the control based on the value of the slider, so you bind to the Foreground property. Then, as part of the binding specification, you use Converter= to point at the static resource, defined in the Grid.Resources, which runs the color converter.

You can see that here:

```
<TextBlock
 Foreground="{Binding ElementName=sldValue,
  Path=Value,
  Converter={StaticResource ColorConvert}}">My Text
</TextBlock>
```

Now, when you run the application, you can move the slider to change the color of the text in the text block. You can see this in Figure 6-27.

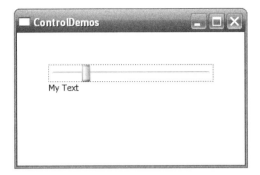 

Figure 6-27. *On the left, the slider is less than 50, so text is black. On the right, the slider is greater than 50, so the text is red.*

Performing XML Binding

A powerful feature of data binding in WPF is the facility to bind one or more controls on your page to an XML data source. This data can be external and referenced by your page, or it can be inline on the page as an XML data island. In the following sections, you'll look at how you can use each of these.

Using XML Data Islands

When using an XML *data island*, you define the XML inline on the XAML page using the <XMLDataProvider> tag. This is useful when you have small amounts of data and don't want to externalize it, making it easier to understand and develop your page as you are editing it.

Listing 6-20 shows an example of a page that contains an XML data island and a ListView control.

Listing 6-20. *Binding to XML Data Islands*

```
<Window x:Class="ControlDemos.xmldataisland"
    xmlns="http://schemas.microsoft.com/winfx/2006/xaml/presentation"
    xmlns:x="http://schemas.microsoft.com/winfx/2006/xaml"
    Title="ControlDemos" Height="300" Width="300">
  <Window.Resources>
    <XmlDataProvider x:Key="SoccerTeams">
      <x:XData>
        <Teams xmlns="">
          <Country Name="USA">
            <BestPlayer>Kasey Keller</BestPlayer>
          </Country>
          <Country Name="England">
```

```
            <BestPlayer>Joe Cole</BestPlayer>
          </Country>
          <Country Name="Japan">
            <BestPlayer>Nakata</BestPlayer>
          </Country>
        </Teams>
      </x:XData>
    </XmlDataProvider>


  </Window.Resources>
  <Grid>
    <ListView Name="lvwPlayers"
        ItemsSource="
         {Binding Source={StaticResource SoccerTeams},
         XPath=/Teams/Country}">
      <ListView.View>
        <GridView>
          <GridViewColumn Header="Country"
            DisplayMemberBinding="{Binding XPath=@Name}"
            Width="100"/>
          <GridViewColumn Header="Best Player"
            DisplayMemberBinding="{Binding XPath=BestPlayer}"
            Width="100"/>
        </GridView>
      </ListView.View>
    </ListView>
    </Grid>
</Window>
```

The XMLDataProvider tag is implemented in the Windows.Resources section. You need to give the island a name (using the key attribute). If you want to use an XML data island, you then specify the XML within an <x:Data> node so the parser bypasses the tags when validating the document. Your custom XML data (in this case, soccer teams) are not part of any of the XAML schemas and will cause an error if they are not wrapped in this node. The XMLDataProvider tag, containing the XML data, is then a static resource for your XAML page.

To bind to this data, you then specify your binding source using this static resource. When using a ListView, as in this example, you bind to this static resource using the ItemsSource attribute like this:

```
{Binding Source={StaticResource SoccerTeams}, XPath=/Teams/Country}
```

You then bind to items by specifying their XPath. So, when using a ListView, you can do it with the <GridViewColumn> tag. In this case, you use its DisplayMemberBinding attribute to generate the rows for that column.

You can see this in action in Figure 6-28.

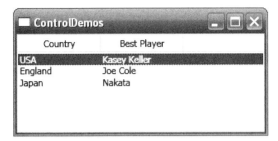

Figure 6-28. *ListView binding to an XML data island*

Using a Data Template

You can also specify a data template that defines how your items will appear when doing a data binding. This can be defined either as a static resource in the Resources section of your page or directly on the destination control. Listing 6-21 shows an example of binding a list box to an XML island where the data is formatted using a DataTemplate.

Listing 6-21. *Binding Using DataTemplates*

```
<Window x:Class="ControlDemos.xmldataisland"
    xmlns="http://schemas.microsoft.com/winfx/2006/xaml/presentation"
    xmlns:x="http://schemas.microsoft.com/winfx/2006/xaml"
    Title="ControlDemos" Height="300" Width="300">
  <Window.Resources>
    <XmlDataProvider x:Key="SoccerTeams" >
      <x:XData>
        <Teams xmlns="">
          <Country Name="USA">
            <BestPlayer>Kasey Keller</BestPlayer>
          </Country>
          <Country Name="England">
            <BestPlayer>Joe Cole</BestPlayer>
          </Country>
          <Country Name="Japan">
            <BestPlayer>Nakata</BestPlayer>
          </Country>
        </Teams>
      </x:XData>
    </XmlDataProvider>
  </Window.Resources>
```

```xaml
<Grid>
  <StackPanel>
    <TextBlock FontSize="14"
               FontWeight="Bold"
               Margin="10">Best Players
    </TextBlock>
    <ListBox>
      <ListBox.ItemsSource>
        <Binding
           Source="{StaticResource SoccerTeams}"
           XPath="/Teams/Country"/>
      </ListBox.ItemsSource>
      <ListBox.ItemTemplate>
        <DataTemplate>
          <StackPanel>
            <TextBlock FontSize="16"
                       FontWeight="Bold"
                       Foreground="Black">
              <TextBlock.Text>
                <Binding XPath="BestPlayer"/>
              </TextBlock.Text>
            </TextBlock>
            <TextBlock FontSize="10"
                       Foreground="Black">
              <TextBlock.Text>
                <Binding XPath="@Name"/>
              </TextBlock.Text>
            </TextBlock>
          </StackPanel>
        </DataTemplate>
      </ListBox.ItemTemplate>
    </ListBox>
  </StackPanel>
</Grid>
</Window>
```

You can see the data template in bold in the previous example. Typically, a list box allows only a single item to be a list item in it, so you use a DataTemplate to define a single Stack-Panel. This StackPanel contains a couple of TextBlock controls with their font size and colors being set. When you run the application, the DataTemplate gives you a nicely formatted list item with the players' names in a large font and their countries as a subtitle in a smaller font. You can see this in Figure 6-29.

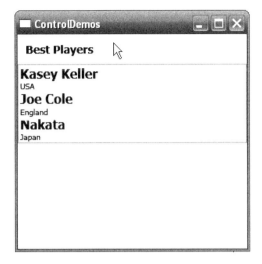

Figure 6-29. *Using a data template*

Using an External XML Data Source

The <XMLDataProvider> tag isn't limited to using an XML data island. You can also use it to specify an external XML file. You can provide this XML as a uniform resource locator (URL) to a hosted XML file or as a path to a file. Listing 6-22 shows an example of binding a ListView control to an external XML file that is hosted on a web server.

Listing 6-22. *Binding to an XML Data Source*

```
<Window x:Class="ControlDemos.ListView_"
  xmlns="http://schemas.microsoft.com/winfx/2006/xaml/presentation"
  xmlns:x="http://schemas.microsoft.com/winfx/2006/xaml"
  Title="ControlDemos" Height="300" Width="300">
  <Grid>
    <Grid.Resources>
      <XmlDataProvider x:Key="EmployeeSource"
        Source="http://localhost/employees.xml"/>
    </Grid.Resources>
    <ListView Name="lvwEmps"
        SelectionChanged="OnSelected"
        ItemsSource="
        {Binding Source={StaticResource EmployeeSource},
          XPath=/employees/employee}">
    <ListView.View>
     <GridView>
      <GridViewColumn Header="First Name"
        DisplayMemberBinding="{Binding XPath=Name}"
        Width="100"/>
```

```
        <GridViewColumn Header="Title"
            DisplayMemberBinding="{Binding XPath=Title}"
            Width="100"/>
        <GridViewColumn Header="Salary"
            DisplayMemberBinding="{Binding XPath=Salary}"
            Width="100"/>
      </GridView>
    </ListView.View>
  </ListView>
 </Grid>
</Window>
```

In this situation, your syntax is straightforward. You put the <XMLDataProvider> tag in the Resources section, give it a name (using x:Key), and then point it at a source, be it a URL like in this example or the path to a file. You then bind to it in the typical way.

This example uses the same data and bindings as an earlier one, and thus you can see the output from it in Figure 6-24.

Object Data Source Binding

The .NET 2.0 ObservableCollection allows you to create object data sources. You can then bind these object data sources to your XAML applications, giving you great flexibility, particularly in your middleware. So, for example, you can create a middle-tier service that retrieves data from a resource tier such as a database and then represents it as an ObservableCollection data object. Then, you can easily bind to this from your XAML. This prevents you from writing custom logic to iterate through each field and manually set your properties to the required data.

This is best demonstrated by example. Consider the example shown in Listing 6-23 of a simple e-mail address book, where you have an Entry class that stores a person's name and e-mail address.

Listing 6-23. *The Entry Class*

```
using System;
using System.Collections.Generic;
using System.Text;
using System.Collections.ObjectModel;

namespace ControlDemos
{
    public class Entry
    {
      public Entry (string Inname, string InemailAddress)
      {
       this.Name = Inname;
       this.EmailAddress = InemailAddress;
      }
```

```
    private string mEmailAddress;
    public string EmailAddress
    {
     get { return mEmailAddress; }
     set { mEmailAddress = value; }
    }

    private string mName;
    public string Name
    {
     get { return mName; }
     set { mName = value; }
    }

    public override string ToString ()
    {
     return this.Name + " : " + this.EmailAddress;
    }
   }
}
```

You can now implement an Entries class that builds an ObservableCollection of Entry items. A simple one that builds three entries can look like Listing 6-24.

Listing 6-24. *The ObservableCollection Entries Class*

```
using System;
using System.Collections.Generic;
using System.Text;
using System.Collections.ObjectModel;

namespace ControlDemos
{
    public class Entries:ObservableCollection<Entry>
    {
        public Entries()
        {
            base.Add(new Entry("Bill Gates",
              "billg@microsoft.com"));
            base.Add(new Entry("landon Donovan",
              "landycakes@hotmail.com"));
            base.Add(new Entry("Susan Ivanova",
              "angelofdeath@b5.com"));
        }

    }
}
```

Although this version uses several hard-coded name/e-mail address pairs, you could easily connect to a database, run a query, and then start adding the results from that query to the collection.

Now, to bind to this in your UI, you have to create a namespace reference to the classes, which as you can see from the listing are in the ControlDemos namespace.

The syntax for this is here:

```
xmlns:ent="clr-namespace:ControlDemos"
```

The ent text can be whatever you like—this is just the prefix you'll use when defining the classes in XAML. Here, I choose ent because they are the first three letters in *Entries*.

Next, in your Resources section, you will use an <ObjectDataProvider> tag to specify the data source. The declaration looks like this:

```
<ObjectDataProvider x:Key="Entries" ObjectType="{x:Type ent:Entries}"  />
```

You can see that this implements an <ObjectDataProvider> tag called Entries. This is given an object type using the ObjectType attribute—the object type is an Entries object specified in the code you saw earlier, which is referred to using the ent namespace. So, you use {x:Type ent:Entries} to tell XAML that you want to use a custom type called Entries that is defined in the ent XML namespace.

Once you have your <ObjectDataProvider> tag set up, then the binding is the same as for the <XMLDataProvider> tag. Listing 6-25 shows the full example of the XAML to bind a ListBox to the Entries object data source.

Listing 6-25. *XAML to Bind to the ObjectDataSource*

```
<Window x:Class="ControlDemos.ObjectDataBinding"
    xmlns="http://schemas.microsoft.com/winfx/2006/xaml/presentation"
    xmlns:x="http://schemas.microsoft.com/winfx/2006/xaml"
    xmlns:ent="clr-namespace:ControlDemos"
    Title="ControlDemos" Height="300" Width="300">
  <Window.Resources>
    <ObjectDataProvider x:Key="Entries"
      ObjectType="{x:Type ent:Entries}"  />

    <DataTemplate DataType="{x:Type ent:Entry}">
      <StackPanel Orientation="Vertical">
        <TextBlock Foreground="Red"
          Text="{Binding Name}"
          FontSize="14" />
        <TextBlock Foreground="Blue"
          Margin="8,8,8,8"
          Text="{Binding EmailAddress}"
          FontSize="12"/>
      </StackPanel>
    </DataTemplate>
  </Window.Resources>
```

```
<Grid>
  <ListBox
    ItemsSource="{Binding Source={StaticResource Entries}}" />
</Grid>
</Window>
```

As you can see, a DataTemplate is used, and its type is specified as an Entry, which is present in the namespace defined by ent, which of course is the ObservableCollection you built earlier.

Within the DataTemplate, a StackPanel is defined, which gives two TextBlock controls, one bound to Name and one bound to EmailAddress.

The result of this is visible in Figure 6-30.

Figure 6-30. *Binding a ListBox control to ObjectDataSource*

Summary

The XAML API is colossal with too many controls and subcontrols to go into detail on in one chapter. However, it is important to get a good grounding in each of the major controls so you know how to use them and can further explore their APIs. Each control in XAML can have hundreds of properties, events, and methods you can use, and it would take several books to document them all, so this chapter showed you how to use them in your graphical user interface (GUI) applications in a typical manner. You took a tour of all the major control types and built simple applications using them and using their major events. You also looked into the different types of data binding and how you can use them. You looked at how to bind properties of controls to each other so your user interfaces can dynamically update their state based on user interaction. You investigated XML data, with the XMLDataProvider implementing XML data islands as well as referencing external XML files, be they on the file system or at a distant URL.

Additionally, I outlined the powerful ObjectDataProvider. This is an enormously powerful tool for your toolbox, where you can build your own types using the ObservableCollection interface in .NET 2.0 and bind your XAML GUI to them. A great scenario for this is in building middleware; you can expose your data resources as custom types, collected into an ObservableCollection, and then define this as a data source to which your GUI elements can bind.

By now you should have the confidence and ability to determine the key differences between developing in XAML and traditional Windows forms. You have the tools and the knowledge to go out and build the next generation of forms-based UI applications. In the next chapter, you'll learn about some of the powerful new multimedia features of WPF that allow you to use graphics, video, and other media in your applications.

CHAPTER 7

■ ■ ■

Working with Graphics and Media

One of the core design tenets of the Windows Presentation Foundation (WPF) is to build applications that are visually stunning. Built on top of the highly performing DirectX application programming interface (API), which is typically used for games, WPF offers a full array of drawing capabilities that are designed to exploit the full capabilities of modern graphics cards. It gives a much richer experience than the existing Windows graphics APIs that were designed for the graphics capabilities of much older generations of graphics hardware.

This gives the designer a much freer palette to work from than ever before—the management of colors is much freer and straightforward, there is no restriction on objects on the screen, animation is possible, and much more. Additionally, the graphics architecture empowers the programmer because of its deep integration with the rest of the programming model. As you saw in the previous chapter, image management through the Image control is as straightforward as any other type of programming, and it uses the same methodologies and APIs.

In this chapter, you will go through some of the fundamental graphics capabilities of WPF, including 2D and 3D drawing; you'll also learn about multimedia such as video and audio and how you can put multimedia applications together.

Introducing the Graphics APIs

The WPF graphics APIs comprise a number of objects. These fall into the following main categories:

Brushes: You can use brushes to paint areas of the screen in solid colors, patterns, images, or drawings.

Shapes: You can use shapes to render 2D shapes such as squares or ellipses.

Transformations: You can apply these effects, such as rotation and scaling, to graphic elements.

Imaging: You can use imaging to render and manipulate bitmapped images of various formats, as well as support image processing effects such as color depth manipulation or blurring.

Animations: Animation and timing APIs can move or otherwise affect objects. I'll discuss animation in more detail in Chapter 8.

Using Brushes

The Brush class is an abstract class that provides the functionality for painting an area. Classes derived from it show how the area can be painted.

Using Fill with a Predefined Brush

The simplest use of a brush is when you use the Fill property of any shape that supports it and then use a predefined brush such as Black, Beige, or White. For example, you can create an ellipse that fills the viewport and colors itself black like this:

```
<Ellipse Fill="Black" />
```

You can see the result of this in Figure 7-1.

Figure 7-1. *Ellipse using the Fill property of a brush*

Using Fill with a Hex Brush to Get Transparency

You can specify a 24-bit color brush with 8-bit alpha levels using a hexadecimal string where the first two digits specify the alpha (transparency), with FF being completely opaque and 00 being completely transparent. The next six digits specify the red, green, and blue components.

So, to specify a semitransparent blue ellipse, you could use the following Extensible Application Markup Language (XAML):

```
<Ellipse Fill="#BB0000FF" />
```

When rendered on a page along with a TextBlock that appears behind it, you can see the results in Figure 7-2.

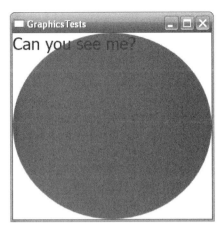

Figure 7-2. *Using a Fill property with a brush to get transparency*

Using the SolidColorBrush Object

To get finer-grained control on a fill, you can use the SolidColorBrush object to define fill attributes. This approach is useful because it also allows you to define transforms and relative transforms. You'll see some of that later in this chapter in the "Performing Transformations" section. The following is an example of using a SolidColorBrush object to fill an ellipse with semitransparent red:

```
<Ellipse>
  <Ellipse.Fill>
    <SolidColorBrush>
      <SolidColorBrush.Color>
        <Color A="200" R="255" G="0" B="0"></Color>
      </SolidColorBrush.Color>
    </SolidColorBrush>
  </Ellipse.Fill>
</Ellipse>
```

Figure 7-3 shows the result.

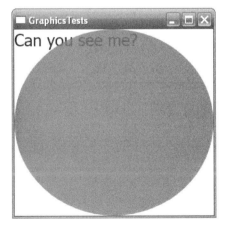

Figure 7-3. *Using the SolidColorBrush object to define the fill*

Using the LinearGradientBrush Class

This brush will allow you to fill an area with a linear gradient, where the color fades from value to value. Typically, a liner gradient will fade from one color to another, and with WPF you can specify a number of colors that the gradient will fade between. These are called *gradient stops.* So, if you define a linear gradient with four gradient stops called S1, S2, S3, and S4, WPF will automatically fade from S1 to S2, from S2 to S3, and from S3 to S4.

The following is an example of an ellipse with four gradient stops, where you fade from black to white through red and blue. Note that with gradient stops, if you use more than two, you also have to specify an Offset parameter, which specifies how far along the gradient the stop exists. This is a normalized value so that 0 is at the beginning, 1 is at the end, 0.5 is halfway along, and so on.

```
<Ellipse>
  <Ellipse.Fill>
    <LinearGradientBrush>
      <LinearGradientBrush.GradientStops>
        <GradientStop Color="Black" Offset="0"/>
        <GradientStop Color="Red" Offset="0.25" />
        <GradientStop Color="Blue" Offset="0.5" />
        <GradientStop Color="White" Offset="1" />
      </LinearGradientBrush.GradientStops>
    </LinearGradientBrush>
  </Ellipse.Fill>
</Ellipse>
```

You can see the results in Figure 7-4.

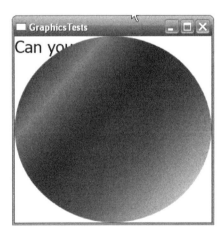

Figure 7-4. *Using a linear gradient fill with multiple gradient stops*

Using the RadialGradientBrush Class

The RadialGradientBrush object is a circular gradient that provides a bull's-eye effect when used. The coherent design of the WPF API gives an identical development experience to that used when defining a linear gradient. This XAML will define a radial gradient from black to white through red and blue in a similar manner to the linear gradient you saw earlier:

```
<Ellipse>
  <Ellipse.Fill>
    <RadialGradientBrush>
      <RadialGradientBrush.GradientStops>
        <GradientStop Color="Black" Offset="0"/>
        <GradientStop Color="Red" Offset="0.25" />
        <GradientStop Color="Blue" Offset="0.5" />
        <GradientStop Color="White" Offset="1" />
      </RadialGradientBrush.GradientStops>
    </RadialGradientBrush>
  </Ellipse.Fill>
</Ellipse>
```

You can see how this appears in Figure 7-5.

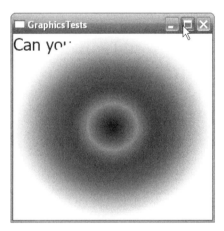

Figure 7-5. *A RadialGradientBrush object with multiple stops*

Using the Image Brush

You can also use an image as a brush. In this case, the shape to be filled is painted using a specified image. By default, the image will fill the area you are brushing it on, but you can also tile the image using the TileMode and Viewport properties.

The following is an example of painting an ellipse with a JPG image. The TileMode property specifies tiling, and the Viewport property is set to 0,0,0.25,0.25. This string may appear a little strange, but you can think of it as saying the tiling should start in the top-left corner (0,0) and the tiles should take up a quarter of the fill. This will give you a 4×4 tiling pattern. In a similar way, 0,0,0.1,0.1 will give you a 10×10 tiling pattern.

```
<Ellipse>
  <Ellipse.Fill>
    <ImageBrush ImageSource="Fishtn.jpg"
```

```
                TileMode="Tile"
                Viewport="0,0,0.25,0.25">
    </ImageBrush>
  </Ellipse.Fill>
</Ellipse>
```

Figure 7-6 shows the results.

Figure 7-6. *Using an image brush with tiling*

Using the SystemColors Class

One neat feature of WPF is that you can configure brushes to use system colors. For example, you can set a fill brush for a shape to use the same color as is used in the desktop background. Therefore, if you change the desktop background color, the fill color will update automatically without having to relaunch the application.

The following is an example of an ellipse being filled with a system color, in this case the desktop background color:

```
<Ellipse Fill="{DynamicResource
{x:Static SystemColors.DesktopBrushKey}}" >
</Ellipse>
```

Check out the System.Windows.SystemColors class in the Object Browser for more examples of the brushes you can use—some examples are MenuBrushKey, MenuBarBrushKey, WindowBrushKey, WindowTextBrushKey, and ActiveCaptionBrushKey.

You can see the previous XAML in action in Figure 7-7. As you can see, the ellipse is the same color as the desktop.

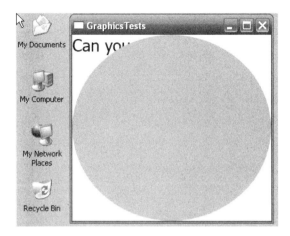

Figure 7-7. *Using DesktopColorBrush from the SystemColors class*

Using the VisualBrush Class

The visual brush allows you to paint an area with controls or other objects. So if you want to render a representation of a user interface on your screen for illustrative purposes, the visual brush will come in handy. The following is an example where the visual brush renders a simple user interface (UI) within an ellipse:

```
<Ellipse>
  <Ellipse.Fill>
    <VisualBrush>
      <VisualBrush.Visual>
        <StackPanel>
          <TextBlock>Here is a Textblock</TextBlock>
          <Button>Here is a Button</Button>
          <TextBox>Here is a Text Box</TextBox>
        </StackPanel>
      </VisualBrush.Visual>
    </VisualBrush>
  </Ellipse.Fill>
</Ellipse>
```

You can see the results in Figure 7-8.

Figure 7-8. *Painting with the visual brush*

Using Shapes

The WPF API supports a number of 2D shapes you can use in your user interfaces. You'll find them in the System.Windows.Shapes namespace.

Ellipse: Draws an ellipse or circle

Line: Draws a straight line between two defined points

Path: Draws a series of connected lines and curves

Polygon: Draws a straight-sided closed shape with a flexible number of lines

Polyline: Draws a series of connected straight lines

Rectangle: Draws a four-sided, straight-lined, closed shape that can be a rectangle or square

Using the Ellipse Class

You can use the Ellipse class to draw a circular or oval-shaped object. You use the Width and Height properties to define the shape of the ellipse. If they are the same, you will get a circle; if they are different, you will get an oval.

The following is an example of the XAML that will define a circle:

```
<Ellipse Height="100" Width="100" Fill="Black"></Ellipse>
```

This XAML will define a tall oval ellipse:

```
<Ellipse Height="200" Width="100" Fill="Black"></Ellipse>
```

This XAML will define a wide oval ellipse:

```
<Ellipse Height="100" Width="200" Fill="Black"></Ellipse>
```

You can see these in action in Figure 7-9.

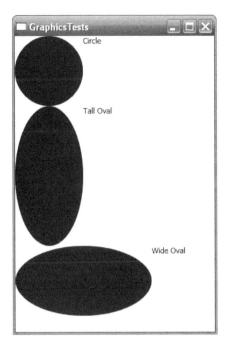

Figure 7-9. *Different ellipses*

In addition to filling the ellipse, as you saw earlier, you can also specify the *stroke* of the ellipse. This is the line that defines the border of the ellipse; the color is defined by the Stroke attribute, and the weight is defined by the StrokeThickness attribute. For example, you would define a yellow ellipse with a thick black outline like this:

```
<Ellipse Fill="Yellow" Stroke="Black" StrokeThickness="6"></Ellipse>
```

You can see this in Figure 7-10.

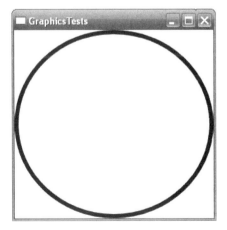

Figure 7-10. *Using the stroke with an ellipse*

Using the Line Class

You use the Line class to (surprise, surprise) draw line segments on the screen. You set its starting point using X1 and Y1 coordinates and its endpoint using X2 and Y2 coordinates. As with the ellipse in the previous example, you can also use the Stroke and StrokeThickness properties to define the line's color and weight.

For example, to draw a series of lines, you can use the XAML shown in Listing 7-1. This is the solution to a popular children's puzzle where you have to draw a specific shape without going over the same line twice.

Listing 7-1. *Drawing a Puzzle in XAML*

```
<Grid>
    <Line X1="200" Y1="200"
        X2="300" Y2="200"
        Stroke="Black" StrokeThickness="3"></Line>
    <Line X1="300" Y1="200"
        X2="300" Y2="100"
        Stroke="Black" StrokeThickness="3"></Line>
    <Line X1="300" Y1="100"
        X2="250" Y2="50"
        Stroke="Black" StrokeThickness="3"></Line>
    <Line X1="250" Y1="50"
        X2="200" Y2="100"
        Stroke="Black" StrokeThickness="3"></Line>
    <Line X1="200" Y1="100"
        X2="300" Y2="100"
        Stroke="Black" StrokeThickness="3"></Line>
    <Line X1="300" Y1="100"
        X2="200" Y2="200"
        Stroke="Black" StrokeThickness="3"></Line>
    <Line X1="200" Y1="200"
        X2="200" Y2="100"
        Stroke="Black" StrokeThickness="3"></Line>
    <Line X1="200" Y1="100"
        X2="300" Y2="200"
        Stroke="Black" StrokeThickness="3"></Line>
</Grid>
```

Figure 7-11 shows how the lines will appear when rendered.

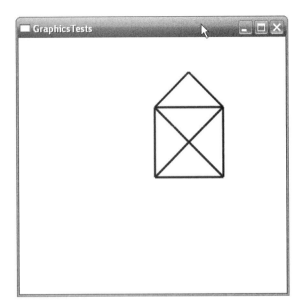

Figure 7-11. *The line segment in action*

Using the Path Class

You use the Path class to draw a connected series of lines and curves. A typical use of a Path class is to store user-initiated input like that from a pen or from dragging the mouse over a page area. For example, in Chapter 1, specifically in Figure 1-9, an attribution was drawn on an image using the mouse to highlight and "write" text in Microsoft Codenamed Max. This is ultimately stored as a path.

The Path class is flexible, and you can use it to draw shapes that are closed or open, lines, and curves. You define paths using geometries, including the flexible PathGeometry as well as fixed ones such as Ellipse, Line, and Rectangle. In the following sections, you'll look at some examples of where you can use the Path class with these geometries.

Getting Started with the Path Class

When defining a path, you specify, using the <Path.Data> tag, the geometry you'd like to use. For example, if you are using the PathGeometry type, your XAML would look like this:

```
<Path>
  <Path.Data>
    <PathGeometry>
    ...
    </PathGeometry>
  </Path.Data>
</Path>
```

Depending on the geometry type, you then use a different set of tags to define the specific geometry settings. So, in the case of the <PathGeometry> tag, you can specify the collection of path geometry figures to use, or in the case of the <LineGeometry> tag, you can specify the line to use.

So, when using a Path geometry, the next tag to specify is the collection of figures you want to use. You can also specify a transform, but that isn't detailed here; check the MSDN documentation or the "Performing Transformations" section later in this chapter for details.

You specify the figures like this:

```
<Path>
  <Path.Data>
    <PathGeometry>
      <PathFigure>
        ...
      </PathFigure>
    </PathGeometry>
  </Path.Data>
</Path>
```

The path figures can then be any of the segment types, including ArcSegment, BezierSegment, LineSegment, PolyLineSegment, and more. Here's the code that draws a couple of ArcSegments:

```
<Path Stroke="Black" StrokeThickness="1">
  <Path.Data>
    <PathGeometry>
      <PathFigure>
        <ArcSegment Size="100,50" RotationAngle="45"
            IsLargeArc="True"
            SweepDirection="Counterclockwise"
            Point="200,100" />
        <ArcSegment Size="100,50" RotationAngle="60"
            IsLargeArc="True"
            SweepDirection="Counterclockwise"
            Point="200,200" />

      </PathFigure>
    </PathGeometry>
  </Path.Data>
</Path>
```

You can see the result of this code in Figure 7-12.

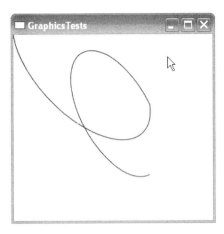

Figure 7-12. *Using the Path class to draw two ArcSegments*

Using Bezier Curves

The previous section demonstrated the ArcSegment type, but you can easily adapt it to show a Bezier curve. A Bezier curve is based on a start point, an endpoint, and two control points.

When using a Bezier curve in WPF, you define the start point using the parent PathFigure of the BezierSegment. You configure the control points using the Point1 and Point2 attributes, and you configure the endpoint using Point3.

The following is an example of a Bezier curve with the start point being in the top-left corner (0,0) and the endpoint being toward the bottom right (400,400). Two control points are configured at 100,0 and 0,100.

```
<Path Stroke="Black" StrokeThickness="1">
  <Path.Data>
    <PathGeometry>
      <PathGeometry.Figures>
        <PathFigure StartPoint="0,0">
          <BezierSegment Point1="100,0"
                         Point2="0,100"
                         Point3="400,400"/>
        </PathFigure>
      </PathGeometry.Figures>
    </PathGeometry>
  </Path.Data>
</Path>
```

You can see this curve in Figure 7-13.

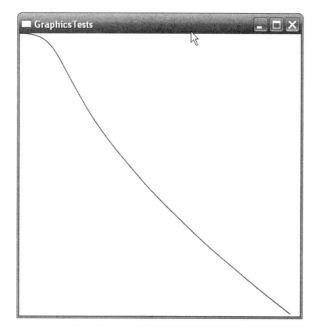

Figure 7-13. *Drawing a Bezier curve*

Using PolylineSegments

When using a PathGeometry, you can also specify polyline segments. With these, you specify points, and WPF draws lines between the points for you. Earlier when you used line segments to draw the children's puzzle, you specified the beginning point and then the endpoint of the first line. The endpoint of the first line was then the beginning point of the second line, but you had to specify that again, along with the endpoint of the second line, and so on. If you were using a polyline segment, then you'd just specify the points, and WPF would do the rest.

Listing 7-2 shows the same example, implemented using the polyline. In a similar manner to the Bezier curve, the start point is defined in the parent PathFigure.

Listing 7-2. *Drawing the Puzzle with PolyLine*

```
<Path Stroke="Black" StrokeThickness="1">
  <Path.Data>
    <PathGeometry>
      <PathGeometry.Figures>
        <PathFigure StartPoint="200,200">
          <PolyLineSegment>
            <PolyLineSegment.Points>
              <Point X="300" Y="200" />
              <Point X="300" Y="100" />
              <Point X="250" Y="50" />
              <Point X="200" Y="100" />
              <Point X="300" Y="100" />
```

```
            <Point X="200" Y="200" />
            <Point X="200" Y="100" />
            <Point X="300" Y="200" />

          </PolyLineSegment.Points>
        </PolyLineSegment>
      </PathFigure>
    </PathGeometry.Figures>
  </PathGeometry>
  </Path.Data>
</Path>
```

You can see the result of this in Figure 7-14.

Figure 7-14. *Using a polyline to draw the puzzle picture*

Using PolyBezierSegments

In a similar manner to the polyline segment type you saw earlier, you can also specify multiple Bezier curves by using a collection of points. Each curve requires three points: two control points and an endpoint. The end of the previous Bezier curve determines the starting point. So, take the XAML shown in Listing 7-3, for example.

Listing 7-3. *PolyBezierSegments*

```
<Path Stroke="Black" StrokeThickness="1">
  <Path.Data>
    <PathGeometry>
      <PathGeometry.Figures>
        <PathFigure StartPoint="200,200">
          <PolyBezierSegment>
```

```
        <PolyBezierSegment.Points>
          <Point X="100" Y="200" />
          <Point X="300" Y="100" />
          <Point X="300" Y="200" />
          <Point X="400" Y="400" />
          <Point X="400" Y="100" />
          <Point X="100" Y="100" />
        </PolyBezierSegment.Points>
      </PolyBezierSegment>
    </PathFigure>
   </PathGeometry.Figures>
  </PathGeometry>
 </Path.Data>
</Path>
```

This will form two Beziers. The first is from 200,200 (the StartPoint) to 300,200 using the control points at 100,200 and 300,100 (the first two points in the points collection). The second Bezier curve will start at 300,200 and go to 100,100. It will use 400,400 and 400,100 as its control points.

You can see the results in Figure 7-15.

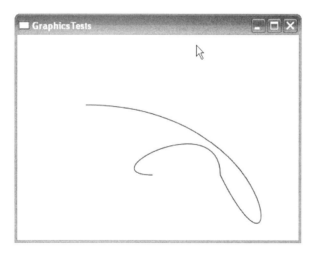

Figure 7-15. *Using PolyBezierSegments to draw multiple curves*

Using Geometry Groups

In the previous examples, you were able to do some stacking of different types such as lines and curves using PolyLineSegment and PolyBezierSegment. When it comes to mixing different types, you can use the <GeometryGroup> tag to specify different geometries and then configure each one of these separately. For example, Listing 7-4 shows the XAML to create a geometry group containing three ellipses, a rectangle, and a path containing a PolyBezierSegment.

Listing 7-4. *Using a Geometry Group*

```
<Path Stroke="Black" StrokeThickness="1">
  <Path.Data>
    <GeometryGroup>
      <EllipseGeometry Center="100,100"
        RadiusX="50" RadiusY="50" />
      <EllipseGeometry Center="200,100"
        RadiusX="50" RadiusY="50" />
      <EllipseGeometry Center="100,200"
        RadiusX="50" RadiusY="50" />
      <RectangleGeometry Rect="100,200,100,100" />
      <PathGeometry>
        <PathGeometry.Figures>
          <PathFigure StartPoint="200,200">
            <PolyBezierSegment>
              <PolyBezierSegment.Points>
                <Point X="100" Y="200" />
                <Point X="300" Y="100" />
                <Point X="300" Y="200" />
                <Point X="400" Y="400" />
                <Point X="400" Y="100" />
                <Point X="100" Y="100" />
              </PolyBezierSegment.Points>
            </PolyBezierSegment>
          </PathFigure>
        </PathGeometry.Figures>
      </PathGeometry>
    </GeometryGroup>
  </Path.Data>
</Path>
```

Figure 7-16 shows the Picasso-like results.

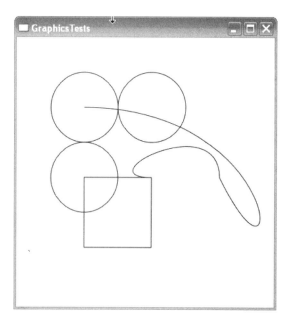

Figure 7-16. *Using a geometry group to combine paths*

Using Path to Close a Shape

When you define a shape using a path, you can specify for WPF to automatically close the shape. So if you use two line segments in a polyline, WPF will automatically close the shape into a triangle. Three line segments will close it into a polygon, possibly a rectangle or a square (depending on the coordinates of the three lines). You do this using the IsClosed attribute on the PathFigure attribute.

The following is an example:

```
<Path Stroke="Black" StrokeThickness="1">
  <Path.Data>
    <PathGeometry>
      <PathGeometry.Figures>
        <PathFigure StartPoint="10,100" IsClosed="True">
          <PolyLineSegment>
            <PolyLineSegment.Points>
              <Point X="200" Y="100" />
              <Point X="200" Y="200" />
            </PolyLineSegment.Points>
          </PolyLineSegment>
        </PathFigure>
      </PathGeometry.Figures>
    </PathGeometry>
  </Path.Data>
</Path>
```

This draws a polyline segment with two lines. One goes from 10,100 to 200,100. The other goes from 200,100 to 200,200. However, because IsClosed is set to True, you will get a triangle where WPF draws a third line from 200,200 to 10,100.

You can see this in Figure 7-17.

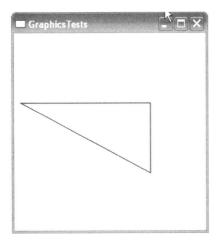

Figure 7-17. *WPF can automatically close a path into a shape.*

Using the Polygon Class

A polygon is a shape with a number of straight sides. It can be a square, a rectangle, a dodecahedron, or an irregular shape as long as its sides are straight.

In XAML, you can define the edges of the polygon by specifying a series of X,Y coordinates. Like with a polyline, WPF will draw the lines that connect these points and close the shape after the final point. The following is an example:

```
<Polygon Fill="Black">
  <Polygon.Points>
    <Point X="100" Y="100" />
    <Point X="100" Y="110" />
    <Point X="130" Y="125" />
    <Point X="200" Y="120" />
  </Polygon.Points>
</Polygon>
```

Figure 7-18 shows this polygon in action.

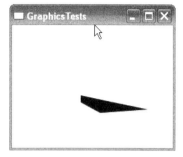

Figure 7-18. *Drawing a polygon with the Polygon class*

Performing Transformations

All shapes support transformation using the LayoutTransformation attribute. This specifies a single transformation or a group of transformations collected in a <TransformGroup> node. The available transforms are as follows:

MatrixTransform: In image processing, all transformations occur using matrix mathematics. This gives you low-level access, providing your own matrix with which to transform an element. Using it is beyond the scope of this book, so check out the MSDN articles and documentation for details.

RotateTransform: This rotates the image a number of degrees in the x-y plane.

ScaleTransform: This scales an object in the x-y plane.

SkewTransform: This skews an object along the x- or y-axis.

TranslateTransform: This translates (moves) the object a specified amount along the x- or y-axis.

So, if you want to rotate the previous polygon by 90 degrees, you would use the following XAML:

```
<Polygon Fill="Black">
  <Polygon.LayoutTransform>
    <RotateTransform Angle="90"></RotateTransform>
  </Polygon.LayoutTransform>
  <Polygon.Points>
    <Point X="100" Y="100" />
    <Point X="100" Y="110" />
    <Point X="130" Y="125" />
    <Point X="200" Y="120" />
  </Polygon.Points>
</Polygon>
```

To do a compound transform where you rotate it, as well as skew it, 20 degrees on the x-axis, you would use XAML like this:

```
<Polygon Fill="Black">
  <Polygon.LayoutTransform>
    <TransformGroup>
        <RotateTransform Angle="90"></RotateTransform>
        <SkewTransform AngleX="5"></SkewTransform>
    </TransformGroup>
  </Polygon.LayoutTransform>
  <Polygon.Points>
    <Point X="100" Y="100" />
    <Point X="100" Y="110" />
    <Point X="130" Y="125" />
    <Point X="200" Y="120" />
  </Polygon.Points>
</Polygon>
```

Using the Imaging APIs

WPF imaging provides a major upgrade over how imaging was handled in previous versions of the development APIs. The majority of the APIs are in the System.Windows.Media.Imaging namespace, though some also reside in System.Windows.Media; the basic Image control, which as you saw in the previous chapter, is a member of System.Windows.Controls.

The WPF imaging API provides built-in support (via codecs) for each of the following image formats: Bitmap (.BMP), Joint Photographic Experts Group (.JPG or .JPEG), Tagged Image File Format (.TIF or .TIFF), Graphics Interchange Format (.GIF), the Windows Media Photo format (.WDP), Portable Network Graphics (.PNG), and Icon (.ICO). In addition, the Windows Imaging Component (WIC) for WPF provides an extensible architecture that makes it possible to create new image codecs so that other image formats can be supported as well.

In the following sections, you'll look at some of the major classes that are used by the imaging API and how you can use them in your applications to beef up your graphical UI.

Using the BitmapSource Class

The BitmapSource class provides a way of representing a single constant set of pixels at a known size and resolution. It is present in the System.Windows.Media.Imaging namespace, which requires you to reference the PresentationCore.dll file in your project. It's an abstract class from which many of the imaging classes you'll use derive.

Using the BitmapImage class

The BitmapImage class derives from the BitmapSource and is designed to be used easily within XAML. Using a BitmapImage is straightforward. The following is an example:

```
<Image>
  <Image.Source>
    <BitmapImage UriSource="FishTn.JPG" />
  </Image.Source>
</Image>
```

As you can see, the UriSource attribute specifies the image you want to use. You can use other properties to manipulate the image in various ways. For example, if you want to rotate the image, you can do so using the Rotation property, which allows you to specify how the image is rotated in 90-degree increments.

```
<Image>
  <Image.Source>
    <BitmapImage UriSource="FishTn.JPG" Rotation="Rotate270" />
  </Image.Source>
</Image>
```

Converting Images with FormatConvertedBitmap

Additionally, you can convert the color depth of the image to a different format. You do this using a derived class from BitmapImage called FormatConvertedBitmap. You specify the image using its Source property and the new color depth using the DestinationFormat property.

The following is an example:

```
<Image>
  <Image.Source>
    <FormatConvertedBitmap Source="FishTn.jpg"
        DestinationFormat="Gray16" />
  </Image.Source>
</Image>
```

The available DestinationFormats include the following:

- Indexed1, Indexed2, Indexed4, and Indexed8, which provide palette-based bitmaps with fixed palettes of 2, 4, 16, and 256 colors, respectively

- BlackWhite, which dithers the image into two colors

- Gray2, Gray4, Gray8, Gray16, and Gray32, which provide 4, 16, and 256 16-bit and 32-bit grayscale images

- Bgr555, which specifies a 15-bit per pixel color format

- Bgr565, which also specifies a 16-bit per pixel color format with 6 green bits

- Rgb128Float, which specifies 128 bits per pixel

For a full specification of the available color depths, check out the members of the System.Windows.Media.PixelFormats class.

Cropping Images

You can crop an image using the Clip property of an image. Within the Clip property, you can then specify a geometry, and WPF will crop the image according to that geometry.

So, if you use an image and set its clip to a closed path, you will crop the image with the contents of the shape defined by that path. Listing 7-5 shows an example of an image and a PathGeometry that defines a clipping triangle.

Listing 7-5. *Clipping Triangle*

```
<Grid>
  <StackPanel>
  <Image Source="FishTn.jpg" Height="256.84375" Width="392">
    <Image.Clip>
      <PathGeometry>
        <PathGeometry.Figures>
          <PathFigure StartPoint="10,100" IsClosed="True">
            <PolyLineSegment>
              <PolyLineSegment.Points>
                <Point X="200" Y="100" />
                <Point X="200" Y="200" />
              </PolyLineSegment.Points>
            </PolyLineSegment>
          </PathFigure>
        </PathGeometry.Figures>
      </PathGeometry>
    </Image.Clip>
  </Image>
  </StackPanel>
</Grid>
```

Figure 7-19 shows the results of this. The full image is at the top of the StackPanel, and the cropped pixels appear at the bottom.

Figure 7-19. *Cropping an image using a path*

Stretching Images

The image classes provide a Stretch property that defines how you stretch an image to fit its container. You can use several types of stretch mode:

None: Image isn't stretched, as shown in Figure 7-20. If it is smaller than its container, it gets padded with whitespace; if it is larger than the container, it gets cropped.

```
<Image Stretch="None" Height="300" Width="200" Source="smile.jpg"/>
```

Figure 7-20. *No stretching on the image*

Fill: The image is stretched to fit the Height and Width properties independently. As such, the image may be distorted when it fills the frame.

```
<Image Stretch="Fill" Height="300" Width="200" Source="smile.jpg"/>
```

In this case, the image appears stretched vertically, as shown in Figure 7-21. Because the source image is small, you also see distortion in the stretching of the image.

Figure 7-21. *Stretching an image with the Fill method*

Uniform: The image is scaled so it fits neatly within the output area while preserving its aspect ratio, as shown in Figure 7-22. In the case where the aspect ratio of the container and the image are different, the area will be padded with whitespace. So, in this example, the image has a square aspect ratio and the container is a tall rectangle, so you see whitespace padding above and below the image.

```
<Image Stretch="Uniform" Height="300" Width="200" Source="smile.jpg"/>
```

Figure 7-22. *Image with uniform stretching*

UniformToFill: The image is stretched to fit the container area while preserving its aspect ratio. If the resulting image is too big for the container, it will be cropped. In this example, the image is a square, and the container is a tall rectangle. As such, the image is scaled to fit the larger axis of the rectangle, causing the horizontal axis of the image to be too large for the container; thus, it is cropped. You can see the results in Figure 7-23.

```
<Image Stretch="UniformToFill" Height="300" Width="200" Source="smile.jpg"/>
```

Figure 7-23. *Stretching an image with UniformToFill*

Using Images As Brushes

You can also use images as brushes when painting an area using an ImageBrush. You can see many examples of this in Chapter 7, but here's another one, where a button can be painted using an image:

```
<Button Height="100" Width="100">
  <Button.Background>
    <ImageBrush ImageSource="smile.jpg" />
  </Button.Background>
</Button>
```

This renders a button on the screen using smile.jpg as its image.

Using Multimedia

The core of multimedia in WPF comes with the MediaElement class, which is present in the System.Windows.Controls namespace. In a similar manner to the Image element, you specify the media file (audio or video) to play using the Source property.

Using the MediaElement Class

The following is an example:

```
<MediaElement Source="c:\\clock.avi" />
```

This automatically loads and runs the media file. You can provide controls to how the media file is executing using methods of MediaElement class. You can use the Play, Pause, and Stop methods to control this playback. The following is an example:

```
<StackPanel>
  <MediaElement LoadedBehavior="Manual"
      Name="mdElement"
      Source="c:\\clock.avi" />
  <StackPanel Orientation="Horizontal">
    <Button Name="bPlay" Click="bPlay_Click">Play</Button>
    <Button Name="bPause" Click="bPause_Click">Pause</Button>
    <Button Name="bStop" Click="bStop_Click">Stop</Button>
  </StackPanel>
</StackPanel>
```

The code-behind file to handle play, pause, and stop is as follows:

```
private void bPlay_Click(Object sender, EventArgs e)
{
  mdElement.Play();
}
private void bPause_Click(Object sender, EventArgs e)
{
  mdElement.Pause();
}
```

```
private void bStop_Click(Object sender, EventArgs e)
{
  mdElement.Stop();
}
```

If you are using Visual Studio 2005 and the Cider XAML designer, you will see the video load and play, but when you run the application, you will not see it. This is, presumably, because Visual Studio is holding the file open. To execute this application and see the video, you need to compile it, close Visual Studio .NET, and the run the file directly from the directory to which you compiled it. Also, the source isn't compiled and deployed with the application, so make sure the Source attribute points to an absolute directory or uniform resource indicator (URI). In the previous example, you can see it pointing to clock.avi on the C: drive.

Figure 7-24 shows the application in action.

Figure 7-24. *Using the MediaElement control*

Using Transforms with Media

You can transform your multimedia elements using the transform classes. You define them using the LayoutTransform attribute of the MediaElement control to specify a transform type or a group of transform types. So, for example, to invert the media, you can specify a RotateTransform property to rotate it 180 degrees like this:

```
<MediaElement LoadedBehavior="Manual"
    Name="mdElement"
    Source="c:\\clock.avi">
  <MediaElement.LayoutTransform>
    <TransformGroup>
      <RotateTransform Angle="180" />
    </TransformGroup>
  </MediaElement.LayoutTransform>
</MediaElement>
```

You can use a <TransformGroup> tag to collect multiple transforms, so to transform a MediaElement class using a rotation and a skew, you'd have XAML like this:

```
<MediaElement LoadedBehavior="Manual"
    Name="mdElement"
    Source="c:\\clock.avi">
  <MediaElement.LayoutTransform>
    <TransformGroup>
      <RotateTransform Angle="180" />
      <SkewTransform AngleX="20" />
    </TransformGroup>
  </MediaElement.LayoutTransform>
</MediaElement>
```

You can see the resulting video in Figure 7-25.

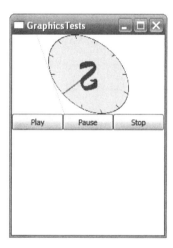

Figure 7-25. *Transforming a media element*

Summary

The graphics and multimedia elements in WPF present an enormous, flexible, and high-performing API. In this chapter, you took a whistle-stop tour of some of these elements. First, you looked at brushes and how you can use them to define and fill shapes using different types of effects and transforms, including achieving transparency and filling shapes with images. Next, you looked at the primitive shapes and paths and learned how points and lines can be connected; you also learned how to draw curves and Bezier curves. You looked into polygons and how to create them; you also learned about the WPF imaging API and how you can manipulate bitmapped images: scaling, sizing, and using them as fills. Finally, you looked at the MediaElement control and how you can use it to program multimedia interfaces. You've barely scratched the surface in this chapter, but it should give you a head start in building your WPF interfaces. The rest is up to you!

CHAPTER 8

■■■

Working with Animation

In addition to the user interface components, the graphical elements, and the multimedia features you can use to jazz up your user interfaces, the Windows Presentation Foundation (WPF) also offers animation, which can bring your application to life. In fact, the word *animation* means bringing something to life, and in WPF (as with all other animations) you create the illusion by cycling through a series of images, with each slightly different from the last. The brain interprets this as a single changing scene. For example, if you want to use a moving spotlight to highlight your scene (like in Microsoft Codenamed Max, discussed in Chapters 1 and 3), you would have a circle or ellipse highlighting the scene, which would then move around the scene little by little.

Having animation in your user interface provides an effective visual cue to direct your users' attention to where you want them to look. For example, in the bicycle browser application in Chapters 3 and 4, you could have the bicycle and its associated metadata "fly in" when the user selects one from the product list.

Animation works by using *timers*. In the previous example, the program would create a timer when the user selects a product from the list. Then, at regular intervals, it would check how much time has elapsed on the timer. At discrete steps it would then change the location of the panel containing the data, perhaps changing its y-axis coordinate to move it in off the top of the screen. The framework behind the scenes manages all this—you don't have to poll the timer yourself.

WPF and Extensible Application Markup Language (XAML) offer a native animation system that takes care of all the behind-the-scenes work of managing timing and redrawing.

Getting Started with Animation

The important point to remember with WPF is that when you animate objects, you do so by changing their individual properties as a result of a timer. For example, if you want to animate an object, making it fade in or out of the screen, you do so using its Opacity property. Listing 8-1 shows an example.

Listing 8-1. *Simple Animation Example*

```
<Window x:Class="AnimTest.Window1"
    xmlns="http://schemas.microsoft.com/winfx/2006/xaml/presentation"
    xmlns:x="http://schemas.microsoft.com/winfx/2006/xaml"
    Title="AnimTest" Height="300" Width="300" >
    <Grid>
        <Rectangle Name="Rect"
```

```
            Height="200" Width="200">
        <Rectangle.Fill>Red</Rectangle.Fill>
        <Rectangle.Triggers>
          <EventTrigger
                RoutedEvent="Rectangle.Loaded">
            <EventTrigger.Actions>
              <BeginStoryboard>
                <Storyboard>
                  <DoubleAnimation
                    Storyboard.TargetName="Rect"
                    Storyboard.TargetProperty="Width"
                    From="200" To="0"
                    Duration="0:0:10"
                    AutoReverse="True"
                    RepeatBehavior="Forever">
                  </DoubleAnimation>
                </Storyboard>
              </BeginStoryboard>
            </EventTrigger.Actions>
          </EventTrigger>
        </Rectangle.Triggers>
      </Rectangle>
    </Grid>
</Window>
```

This draws a simple red rectangle on the screen and animates its Width property. This causes the width of the rectangle to reduce from 200 to 0 over a ten-second period. The AutoReverse=True setting then reverses the animation so that over the next ten seconds, the rectangle will increase from 0 to 200 and then reverse again constantly (because of the RepeatBehavior=Forever setting). You will look into many of these settings in more detail as you progress through this chapter.

You can see this animation in action in Figure 8-1, where it has just begun. In Figure 8-2, you are five seconds into the application running, and the rectangle has reduced to half its original width.

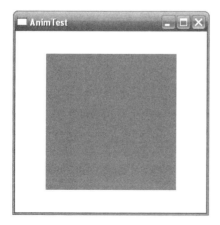

Figure 8-1. *Beginning the animation—the rectangle at full width*

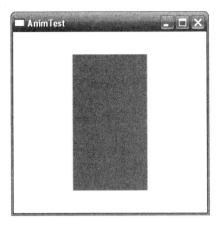

Figure 8-2. *Continuing the animation—the rectangle width reduced to half its original width*

Understanding the Animation Types

You can use a number of animation types. Animation works by setting various properties at timely intervals according to a rule for that property. In the case of the previous example, the Width property is animated, and because Width is a Double value, the DoubleAnimation type is used. In a similar manner, the ColorAnimation and PointAnimation types animate colors and point coordinates. These types of animations use the From, To, and By properties to specify the start value, end value, and increment value, respectively.

Listing 8-2 shows an example of an animation that changes the color of a rectangle using the ColorAnimation type. In this case, you fill the rectangle with a named SolidColorBrush and then animate its Color property. You cannot animate the Fill property of a rectangle because it is a brush, not a color. ColorAnimation can animate only a color. It's a little confusing at first, but you'll soon pick it up. This example also shows that animation types can be "stacked" in a storyboard. You can see that the ColorAnimation type that cycles the color and the DoubleAnimation type that cycles the width can happen in parallel. In this example, as the width changes from 200 to 0, the color changes from black to white.

Listing 8-2. *Animating Color and Dimension*

```
<Window x:Class="AnimTest.Window1"
    xmlns="http://schemas.microsoft.com/winfx/2006/xaml/presentation"
    xmlns:x="http://schemas.microsoft.com/winfx/2006/xaml"
    Title="AnimTest" Height="300" Width="300" >
    <Grid>
      <Rectangle Name="Rect" Height="200" Width="200">
        <Rectangle.Fill>
          <SolidColorBrush x:Name="FillBrush"
                Color="Black"></SolidColorBrush>
        </Rectangle.Fill>
        <Rectangle.Triggers>
```

```
            <EventTrigger RoutedEvent="Rectangle.Loaded">
              <EventTrigger.Actions>
                <BeginStoryboard>
                  <Storyboard>
                    <ColorAnimation
                      Storyboard.TargetName="FillBrush"
                      Storyboard.TargetProperty="(SolidColorBrush.Color)"
                      From="Black" To="White" Duration="0:0:10"
                      AutoReverse="True" RepeatBehavior="Forever">
                    </ColorAnimation>
                    <DoubleAnimation
                      Storyboard.TargetName="Rect"
                      Storyboard.TargetProperty="Width"
                      From="200" To="0" Duration="0:0:10"
                      AutoReverse="True" RepeatBehavior="Forever">
                    </DoubleAnimation>
                  </Storyboard>
                </BeginStoryboard>
              </EventTrigger.Actions>
            </EventTrigger>
          </Rectangle.Triggers>
        </Rectangle>
    </Grid>
</Window>
```

You can see this animation in Figures 8-3 and 8-4, with the rectangle fading from black to white through gray as its width decreases.

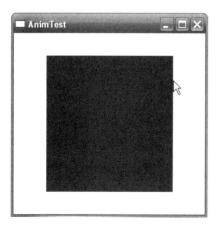

Figure 8-3. *Changing the color of the rectangle with ColorAnimation*

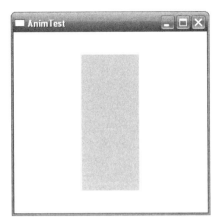

Figure 8-4. *The color fading to gray defined by ColorAnimation*

Another animation type you can use is PointAnimation, which animates a point property between two target values using linear interpolation. For example, if your starting point is at (X1,Y1) and your end point is at (X2,Y2), the PointAnimation type will create the transition between these two points over the specified time.

Listing 8-3 shows an example that moves a circle (created using EllipseGeometry) from 0,0 to 200,200 over ten seconds.

Listing 8-3. *Using a Path to Animate the Position of an Object*

```
<Path Fill="Black">
  <Path.Data>
    <EllipseGeometry x:Name="MyCircle" Center="0,0"
            RadiusX="50" RadiusY="50">
    </EllipseGeometry>
  </Path.Data>
  <Path.Triggers>
    <EventTrigger RoutedEvent="Path.Loaded">
      <EventTrigger.Actions>
        <BeginStoryboard>
          <Storyboard>
            <PointAnimation
                Storyboard.TargetName="MyCircle"
                Storyboard.TargetProperty="Center"
                Duration="0:0:10" From="0,0" To="200,200">
            </PointAnimation>
          </Storyboard>
        </BeginStoryboard>
      </EventTrigger.Actions>
    </EventTrigger>
  </Path.Triggers>
</Path>
```

Figure 8-5 shows the circle "in flight" as it migrates from the top-left corner toward the center of the window.

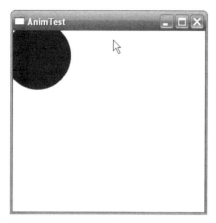

Figure 8-5. *Moving a shape using PointAnimation*

Using Keyframe-Based Animation

To exercise finer-grained control over your animations, you can use keyframe-based animation types, which allow you to specify any number of target values and to control how the interpolation occurs. You can control some types, such as StringAnimation, only by using keyframe animations.

Using Keyframes with a Color Animation

You can use three types of keyframes with a color animation that uses keyframes:

LinearColorKeyFrame: This animates the color value of the previous keyframe to its own using linear interpolation. This calculates the intermediate shades between the color values and over time changes the color values until the desired one is reached at the desired time.

DiscreteColorKeyFrame: This animates from the color value of the previous keyframe to its own using discrete interpolation. This does not calculate the intermediate shades. At the desired time, the color will be changed in a single "jump" from the old to the new.

SplineColorKeyFrame: This animates from the color value of the previous keyframe to its own using splines. This is similar to LinearColorKeyFrame interpolation but is more flexible, where the color interpolates linearly; however, you can adjust the times of interpolation using splines to give an effect of acceleration or deceleration. You can do this using the KeySpline property, which defines the control points for a quadratic curve.

In this case, the curve always begins at 0 and ends at 1, and the control points are defined as two points between these values. For example, if you want to define a KeySpline that slowly accelerates to a midway point between the colors and then rapidly accelerates after that, you could use a value like 0.5,0 0.9,0 as the KeySpline value.

Consider Listing 8-4, which uses all three types of keyframes, building on the earlier example of moving a circle.

Listing 8-4. *Using Keyframes for More Sophisticated Animation*

```
<Path>
  <Path.Fill>
    <SolidColorBrush x:Name="MyAnimatedFill" Color="Black" />
  </Path.Fill>
  <Path.Data>
    <EllipseGeometry x:Name="MyCircle" Center="0,0"
        RadiusX="50" RadiusY="50">
    </EllipseGeometry>
  </Path.Data>
  <Path.Triggers>
    <EventTrigger RoutedEvent="Path.Loaded">
      <EventTrigger.Actions>
        <BeginStoryboard>
          <Storyboard>
            <PointAnimation
                Storyboard.TargetName="MyCircle"
                Storyboard.TargetProperty="Center"
                Duration="0:0:10" From="0,0" To="200,200">
            </PointAnimation>
            <ColorAnimationUsingKeyFrames
                Storyboard.TargetProperty="(SolidColorBrush.Color)"
                Storyboard.TargetName="MyAnimatedFill"
                Duration="0:0:10"
                FillBehavior="HoldEnd"
                RepeatBehavior="Forever">
              <LinearColorKeyFrame
                  Value="Red" KeyTime="0:0:2" />
              <DiscreteColorKeyFrame
                  Value="Yellow" KeyTime="0:0:3" />
              <SplineColorKeyFrame
                  Value="Black" KeyTime="0:0:10"
                  KeySpline="0.5,0.0 0.9,0.0" />
            </ColorAnimationUsingKeyFrames>
          </Storyboard>
        </BeginStoryboard>
      </EventTrigger.Actions>

    </EventTrigger>
  </Path.Triggers>
</Path>
```

You can see that this example uses each type of color keyframe.

The first one is the LinearColorKeyFrame type that animates the color from black to red over the first two seconds of the animation. By specifying that its KeyTime is 0:0:2, you are saying that this key should be reached after two seconds of the animation.

Next, a DiscreteColorKeyFrame changes the color from red to yellow in one jump at the three-second mark.

Finally, a SplineColorKeyFrame trips, starting at the three-second mark and ending at the ten-second mark, that migrates from yellow to black. The KeySpline defines how the acceleration takes place with control points at halfway (.5,0) and near the end (.9,0), giving a smooth transition in the first half, a slightly faster transition afterward, and then a rapid transition right at the end. When running the application, you can see this in action. See Figures 8-6 through 8-8.

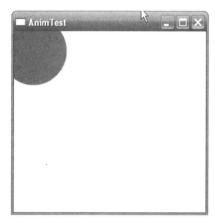

Figure 8-6. *Toward the start of the animation, the circle is red.*

Figure 8-7. *The DiscreteColorKeyFrame Animation changes it to yellow.*

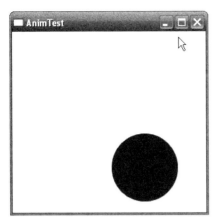

Figure 8-8. *The KeySpline animation changes it back to black at the end.*

Using Keyframes in a Double Animation

Earlier you looked at using a Double animation to specify the width of a rectangle, cycling that width from 0 to a value and back again. The interpolation did not use keyframes and thus was linear. You can change the behavior of this to get a finer-grained animation using keyframes. The types of keyframes available are as follows:

LinearDoubleKeyFrame: This acts as a linear interpolation method, moving the Double value from the old to the new through a series of values, determined by the timeline.

DiscreteDoubleKeyFrame: This acts as a single discrete "jump" from the old value to the new one at the specified key time.

SplineDoubleKeyFrame: This acts as a quadratic Bezier curve linking the old value to the new one with control points specified using the KeySpline property. It is analogous to a parallel projection of a Bezier curve onto a one-dimensional line, determining how the interpolation of the value between the two time points is calculated. If you can imagine a curve, you are moving an item along that curve. Now imagine a shadow underneath that curve—this is a parallel projection. Although the item moving along the curve moves at a constant rate, its shadow will look to accelerate and decelerate, depending on the way the curve is set up. Thus, using this method, you can create a "curved" increment, where the value can accelerate or decelerate from the old value to the new one.

Listing 8-5 moves a square from the top to the bottom of the screen using a LinearDoubleKeyFrame, with the bottom value defined at the five-second point in the timeline and the top value at the ten-second point. The animation then repeats forever, giving the effect of the square "bouncing" at the bottom of the screen.

Listing 8-5. *Using Linear Keyframes for a Bounce Effect*

```
<Canvas>
  <Rectangle Name="MyRect"
    Canvas.Top="0"
    Canvas.Left ="100"
    Height="100"
    Width="100"
    Fill="Black">
  <Rectangle.Triggers>
    <EventTrigger RoutedEvent="Rectangle.Loaded">
      <EventTrigger.Actions>
        <BeginStoryboard>
          <Storyboard RepeatBehavior="Forever">
            <DoubleAnimationUsingKeyFrames
                Storyboard.TargetName="MyRect"
                Storyboard.TargetProperty="(Canvas.Top)">
                <LinearDoubleKeyFrame Value="200"
                    KeyTime="0:0:5">
                </LinearDoubleKeyFrame>
                <LinearDoubleKeyFrame Value="0"
                    KeyTime="0:0:10">
                </LinearDoubleKeyFrame>
              </DoubleAnimationUsingKeyFrames>
            </Storyboard>
          </BeginStoryboard>
        </EventTrigger.Actions>
      </EventTrigger>
    </Rectangle.Triggers>
  </Rectangle>
</Canvas>
```

When using a DiscreteDoubleKeyFrame, the difference is obvious. In this case, the square doesn't flow smoothly to the bottom of the screen and back up; it will instead "jump" between the two. Listing 8-6 shows the XAML code.

Listing 8-6. *Using DiscreteDoubleKeyFrame for a "Jump" Effect*

```
<Canvas>
  <Rectangle Name="MyRect"
    Canvas.Top="0"
    Canvas.Left ="100"
    Height="100"
    Width="100"
    Fill="Black">
```

```
<Rectangle.Triggers>
  <EventTrigger RoutedEvent="Rectangle.Loaded">
    <EventTrigger.Actions>
      <BeginStoryboard>
        <Storyboard RepeatBehavior="Forever">
          <DoubleAnimationUsingKeyFrames
              Storyboard.TargetName="MyRect"
              Storyboard.TargetProperty="(Canvas.Top)">
            <DiscreteDoubleKeyFrame Value="200"
                KeyTime="0:0:5">
            </DiscreteDoubleKeyFrame>
            <DiscreteDoubleKeyFrame Value="0"
                KeyTime="0:0:10">
            </DiscreteDoubleKeyFrame>
          </DoubleAnimationUsingKeyFrames>
        </Storyboard>
      </BeginStoryboard>
    </EventTrigger.Actions>
  </EventTrigger>
</Rectangle.Triggers>
</Rectangle>
</Canvas>
```

The SplineDoubleKeyFrame allows you to use splines to make the animation accelerate and decelerate according to the quadratic Bezier curve control point settings. This causes the animation of the square to accelerate and decelerate as it moves along its path. Listing 8-7 shows an example.

Listing 8-7. *Using SplineDoubleKeyFrame to Accelerate and Decelerate Animation*

```
<Canvas>
  <Rectangle Name="MyRect"
    Canvas.Top="0"
    Canvas.Left ="100"
    Height="100"
    Width="100"
    Fill="Black">
  <Rectangle.Triggers>
    <EventTrigger RoutedEvent="Rectangle.Loaded">
      <EventTrigger.Actions>
        <BeginStoryboard>
          <Storyboard RepeatBehavior="Forever">
            <DoubleAnimationUsingKeyFrames
                Storyboard.TargetName="MyRect"
                Storyboard.TargetProperty="(Canvas.Top)">
```

```
                <SplineDoubleKeyFrame Value="200" KeyTime="0:0:5"
                        KeySpline="0.1,0 0.9,0">
                </SplineDoubleKeyFrame>
                <SplineDoubleKeyFrame Value="0" KeyTime="0:0:10"
                        KeySpline="0.05,0 0.1,0">
                </SplineDoubleKeyFrame>
                </DoubleAnimationUsingKeyFrames>
            </Storyboard>
          </BeginStoryboard>
        </EventTrigger.Actions>
      </EventTrigger>
    </Rectangle.Triggers>
    </Rectangle>
</Canvas>
```

Using Key Points in a Point Animation

The Point animation allowed for an animation from a point defined at X1,Y1 to X2,Y2. When using keyframes, you can exercise finer control over how the animation moves the value between these two points. You can use the following keyframe animation types:

LinearPointKeyFrame: This provides a linear interpolation between the points over the specified time frame. When used in a point animation, this moves both the X and Y values in a smooth linear manner.

DiscretePointKeyFrame: This provides a single "jump" from X1,Y1 to X2,Y2 at the specified key time.

SplinePointKeyFrame: This provides an interpolation from X1,Y1 to X2,Y2 along a projected Bezier quadratic curve, with the control points defined in the KeySpline property.

Listing 8-8 uses LinearPointKeyFrame to move a circle through a triangular path, starting in the top-left corner, moving to the bottom right, and then moving left and back up to the top-left corner.

Listing 8-8. *Using Linear Key Points*

```
<Canvas>
  <Path Fill="Black">
    <Path.Data>
      <EllipseGeometry x:Name="MyCircle" Center="0,0"
        RadiusX="20" RadiusY="20">
      </EllipseGeometry>
    </Path.Data>
    <Path.Triggers>
      <EventTrigger RoutedEvent="Rectangle.Loaded">
        <EventTrigger.Actions>
          <BeginStoryboard>
            <Storyboard RepeatBehavior="Forever">
```

```
            <PointAnimationUsingKeyFrames
               Storyboard.TargetName="MyCircle"
               Storyboard.TargetProperty="Center"
               Duration="0:0:12">
              <LinearPointKeyFrame
                 KeyTime="0:0:4" Value="200,200" />
              <LinearPointKeyFrame
                 KeyTime="0:0:8" Value-"0,200" />
              <LinearPointKeyFrame
                 KeyTime="0:0:12" Value="0,0" />
            </PointAnimationUsingKeyFrames>
          </Storyboard>
        </BeginStoryboard>
      </EventTrigger.Actions>
    </EventTrigger>
  </Path.Triggers>
  </Path>
</Canvas>
```

Listing 8-9 performs the same function but uses a DiscretePointKeyFrame that jumps the circle between the three points of the triangle.

Listing 8-9. *Using Discrete Key Points*

```
<Canvas>
  <Path Fill="Black">
    <Path.Data>
      <EllipseGeometry x:Name="MyCircle" Center="0,0"
         RadiusX="20" RadiusY="20">
      </EllipseGeometry>
    </Path.Data>
    <Path.Triggers>
      <EventTrigger RoutedEvent="Rectangle.Loaded">
        <EventTrigger.Actions>
          <BeginStoryboard>
            <Storyboard RepeatBehavior="Forever">
              <PointAnimationUsingKeyFrames
                 Storyboard.TargetName="MyCircle"
                 Storyboard.TargetProperty="Center"
                 Duration="0:0:12">
                <DiscretePointKeyFrame
                   KeyTime="0:0:4" Value="200,200" />
                <DiscretePointKeyFrame
                   KeyTime="0:0:8" Value="0,200" />
                <DiscretePointKeyFrame
                   KeyTime="0:0:12" Value="0,0" />
              </PointAnimationUsingKeyFrames>
            </Storyboard>
```

```
            </BeginStoryboard>
          </EventTrigger.Actions>
        </EventTrigger>
      </Path.Triggers>
    </Path>
</Canvas>
```

Finally, Listing 8-10 uses SplinePointKeyFrame to accelerate and decelerate the circle along a quadratic Bezier projection as it moves between the coordinates.

Listing 8-10. *Using Spline Key Points*

```
<Canvas>
  <Path Fill="Black">
    <Path.Data>
      <EllipseGeometry x:Name="MyCircle" Center="0,0"
          RadiusX="20" RadiusY="20">
      </EllipseGeometry>
    </Path.Data>
    <Path.Triggers>
      <EventTrigger RoutedEvent="Rectangle.Loaded">
        <EventTrigger.Actions>
          <BeginStoryboard>
            <Storyboard RepeatBehavior="Forever">
              <PointAnimationUsingKeyFrames
                  Storyboard.TargetName="MyCircle"
                  Storyboard.TargetProperty="Center"
                  Duration="0:0:12">
                <SplinePointKeyFrame
                    KeyTime="0:0:4" Value="200,200" KeySpline="0.1,0 0.9,0" />
                <SplinePointKeyFrame
                    KeyTime="0:0:8" Value="0,200" KeySpline="0.1,0 0.9,0" />
                <SplinePointKeyFrame
                    KeyTime="0:0:12" Value="0,0" KeySpline="0.1,0 0.9,0" />
              </PointAnimationUsingKeyFrames>
            </Storyboard>
          </BeginStoryboard>
        </EventTrigger.Actions>
      </EventTrigger>
    </Path.Triggers>
  </Path>
</Canvas>
```

String Animations Using Keyframes

An additional animation type is available only using keyframes, and that is the StringAnimation type. This animation type supports only those discrete keys that change the string from one value to another. Listing 8-11 shows an example.

Listing 8-11. *Using Discrete Strings for Animation*

```
<Grid>
  <StackPanel HorizontalAlignment="Center"
    VerticalAlignment="Center">
    <ContentControl Content="" FontSize="24" Name="Cont">
      <ContentControl.Triggers>
        <EventTrigger RoutedEvent="Window.Loaded" >
          <EventTrigger.Actions>
            <BeginStoryboard>
              <Storyboard>
                <StringAnimationUsingKeyFrames
                    RepeatBehavior="Forever"
                    Storyboard.TargetName="Cont"
                    Storyboard.TargetProperty="Content"
                    Duration="0:0:10">
                  <DiscreteStringKeyFrame
                      KeyTime="0:0:1"
                      Value="Let's Go" />
                  <DiscreteStringKeyFrame
                      KeyTime="0:0:3"
                      Value="MAR" />
                  <DiscreteStringKeyFrame
                      KeyTime="0:0:4"
                      Value="MAR IN" />
                  <DiscreteStringKeyFrame
                      KeyTime="0:0:5"
                      Value="MAR IN ERS" />
                  <DiscreteStringKeyFrame
                      KeyTime="0:0:8"
                      Value="Let's GO!" />
                </StringAnimationUsingKeyFrames>
              </Storyboard>
            </BeginStoryboard>
          </EventTrigger.Actions>
        </EventTrigger>
      </ContentControl.Triggers>
    </ContentControl>
  </StackPanel>
</Grid>
```

This causes the string in the content control to change at the assigned key times. It is discrete, so no interpolation takes place between the strings. For example, at one second, the string becomes "Let's Go," and at three seconds it becomes "MAR," and so on.

Animations Using Storyboards and TimeLine Classes

A TimeLine is a class that defines a segment of time. It contains the duration, the number of times it repeats, and how fast time should progress on it. In the examples in this chapter, you've been using the Storyboard timeline, which can target objects and properties to animate. It does this through the TargetName and TargetProperty properties, which you can use to specify the object on which the animation should occur as well as the property on that object to animate. For example, when moving an ellipse, you set TargetName to the name of the ellipse and TargetProperty to its Center property.

You start a storyboard by associating it with an EventTrigger object, which describes what actions to take place when the specified event fires. One of the available actions is the <BeginStoryBoard> tag, which, as its name suggests, will start the storyboard.

You'll see how this works in Listing 8-12.

Listing 8-12. *Animation with Triggers*

```
<Window x:Class="AnimTest.Window1"
    xmlns="http://schemas.microsoft.com/winfx/2006/xaml/presentation"
    xmlns:x="http://schemas.microsoft.com/winfx/2006/xaml"
    Title="AnimTest" Height="300" Width="300" >
    <Grid>
      <Rectangle Name="Rect"
          Height="200" Width="200">
        <Rectangle.Fill>Red</Rectangle.Fill>
        <Rectangle.Triggers>
          <EventTrigger
              RoutedEvent="Rectangle.Loaded">
            <EventTrigger.Actions>
              <BeginStoryboard>
                <Storyboard>
                  <DoubleAnimation
                    Storyboard.TargetName="Rect"
                    Storyboard.TargetProperty="Width"
                    From="200" To="0"
                    Duration="0:0:10"
                    AutoReverse="True"
                    RepeatBehavior="Forever">
                  </DoubleAnimation>
                </Storyboard>
              </BeginStoryboard>
            </EventTrigger.Actions>
          </EventTrigger>
        </Rectangle.Triggers>
      </Rectangle>
    </Grid>
</Window>
```

In this case, the rectangle is defined and named Rect like this:

```
<Rectangle Name="Rect"
    Height="200" Width="200">
```

Then, this has its triggers defined, and an event trigger is set up to fire when the rectangle gets loaded:

```
<Rectangle.Triggers>
  <EventTrigger
        RoutedEvent="Rectangle.Loaded">
```

Next, you specify you want to begin a new storyboard and define its storyboard as one containing a <DoubleAnimation>:

```
<EventTrigger.Actions>
                <BeginStoryboard>
                  <Storyboard>
                    <DoubleAnimation
                    ...
                    </DoubleAnimation>
                  </Storyboard>
                </BeginStoryboard>
              </EventTrigger.Actions>
```

Within the storyboard, you can then stack animations to achieve a compound animation effect. Additionally, you can specify keyframe animations, which contain multiple keyframe specifications (as you can see in the many examples earlier in this chapter), and these can also be stacked on top of each other to provide complex animations.

Because the storyboard is associated with an event, you can then apply animations to a number of different events. For example, with WPF you can animate the behavior of a button, specifying different behaviors for hovering, clicking, moving the mouse over, and enabling or disabling the button, amongst others. It makes for a flexible application programming interface (API) that gives you the powerful and fine-grained control you need to make your applications richer than ever before.

You can also exercise control over a storyboard using these storyboard commands:

PauseStoryboard: This pauses the storyboard activity.

ResumeStoryboard: Once you have paused a storyboard, you can make it resume using this command.

SetStoryboardSpeedRatio: This changes the speed at which the storyboard operates.

SkipStoryboardToFill: You can specify a fill action for a storyboard (using the FillBehavior property), which performs once the specified duration has elapsed. You can use this command to skip to that action regardless of the current time.

StopStoryboard: This stops the storyboard activity.

RemoveStoryboard: This removes the storyboard from the currently running application.

Working with Animation and Timelines with Interactive Designer

When using Microsoft Expression Interactive Designer, you can define timelines visually using drag and drop. This allows you to define complex animations quickly and easily because the tool generates the XAML for you.

Let's walk through a simple example. First, launch Expression Interactive Designer, and edit the default XAML scene. You can see this in Figure 8-9.

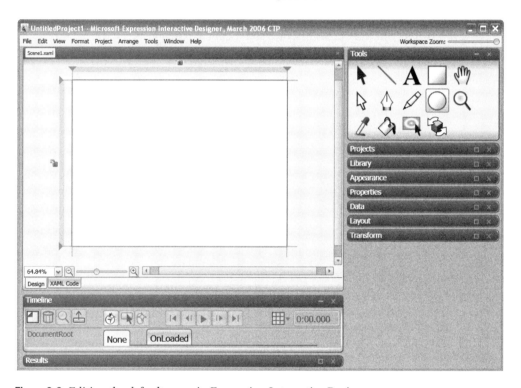

Figure 8-9. *Editing the default scene in Expression Interactive Designer*

At the bottom of the screen, you can see the Timeline window; it contains the default OnLoaded timeline. This is easy to use. For example, place an ellipse on the screen in the top-left corner, and fill it with a solid color, like in Figure 8-10.

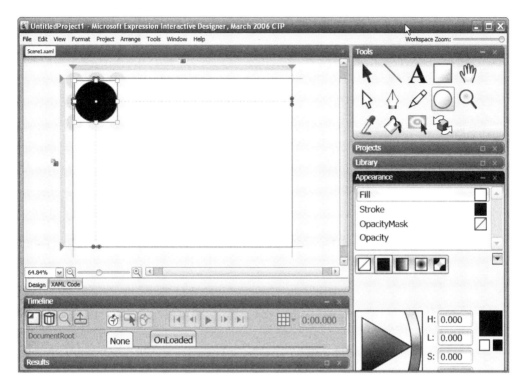

Figure 8-10. *Placing a control on the screen to define the start of the timeline*

Now, select the OnLoaded timeline tab. You'll see the timeline like in Figure 8-11.

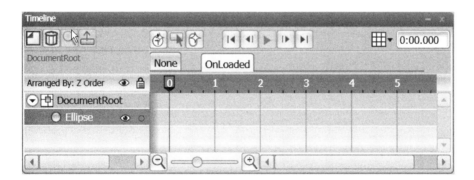

Figure 8-11. *The OnLoaded timeline*

On this timeline, you can see the document root and the ellipse you just placed. You can drag the thumb at the top of the timeline. For example, if you drag the thumb to the 2 setting (signifying two seconds into the timeline), the screen will update to show the status of the scene at that moment in time. Right now, nothing will be different. But if you drag the ellipse to a different location on the screen while the thumb is at the 2 mark, this will create an animation that moves the ellipse from its current spot to the new one over two seconds. Take a look at Figure 8-12 for an example.

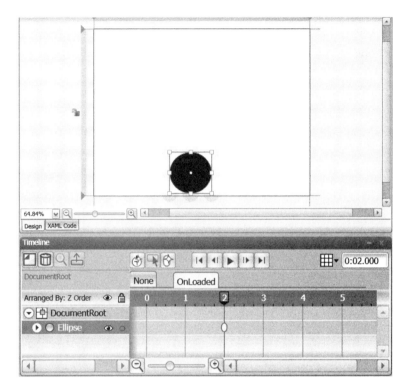

Figure 8-12. *Setting the animation visually*

Now when you view the scene, your circle will move from the original position to the new one over a two-second period.

You can also use keyframes with this type of animation to get better control over the animation. For example, in this case you can place a keyframe at the two-second mark to make this a *stop* in the animation path and then move the circle to another part of the screen at the four-second mark to change its direction. To place the keyframe, you click the Record Keyframe button at the desired point in the timeline. Figure 8-13 shows a keyframe being recorded at the two-second point.

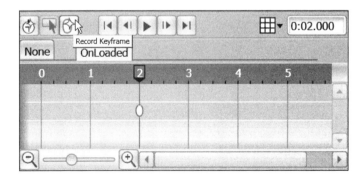

Figure 8-13. *Recording a new keyframe*

You'll see a small oval on the timeline indicating the keyframe. Next, you can move to another point on the timeline (say the four-second point) and move the circle elsewhere on the screen. You've now defined a keyframe-based animation moving the circle in a triangular path. With F5, you can now execute the scene and see your animation in action.

If you explore the XAML that is produced by Expression Interactive Designer, you can see the storyboard in action using DoubleAnimationUsingKeyFrames to implement the motion.

You can see this XAML in Listing 8-13.

Listing 8-13. *XAML from Expression Interactive Designer*

```
<Grid
  xmlns="http://schemas.microsoft.com
          /winfx/2006/xaml/presentation"
  xmlns:x="http://schemas.microsoft.com
          /winfx/2006/xaml"
  xmlns:mc="http://schemas.openxmlformats.org
          /markup-compatibility/2006"
  xmlns:d="http://schemas.microsoft.com
          /expression/interactivedesigner/2006"
  mc:Ignorable="d"
  Background="#FFFFFFFF"
  x:Name="DocumentRoot"
  x:Class="UntitledProject1.Scene1"
  Width="640" Height="480">

  <Grid.Resources>
    <Storyboard x:Key="OnLoaded">

      <DoubleAnimationUsingKeyFrames
          BeginTime="00:00:00"
          Storyboard.TargetProperty=
            "(UIElement.RenderTransform).
             (TransformGroup.Children)[5].
             (TranslateTransform.X)"
          Storyboard.TargetName="Ellipse">
        <SplineDoubleKeyFrame
          d:KeyEase="Linear;Linear;0.5;0.5;0.5;0.5"
          KeySpline="0.5,0.5,0.5,0.5"
          Value="0" KeyTime="00:00:00"/>
        <SplineDoubleKeyFrame
          d:KeyEase="Linear;Linear;0.5;0.5;0.5;0.5"
          KeySpline="0.5,0.5,0.5,0.5"
          Value="240" KeyTime="00:00:02"/>
        <SplineDoubleKeyFrame
          d:KeyEase="Linear;Linear;0.5;0.5;0.5;0.5"
          KeySpline="0.5,0.5,0.5,0.5"
          Value="500" KeyTime="00:00:04"/>
```

```xml
        </DoubleAnimationUsingKeyFrames>
        <DoubleAnimationUsingKeyFrames
            BeginTime="00:00:00"
            Storyboard.TargetProperty=
             "(UIElement.RenderTransform).
              (TransformGroup.Children)[5].
              (TranslateTransform.Y)"
            Storyboard.TargetName="Ellipse">
          <SplineDoubleKeyFrame
              d:KeyEase="Linear;Linear;0.5;0.5;0.5;0.5"
              KeySpline="0.5,0.5,0.5,0.5"
              Value="0" KeyTime="00:00:00"/>
          <SplineDoubleKeyFrame
              d:KeyEase="Linear;Linear;0.5;0.5;0.5;0.5"
              KeySpline="0.5,0.5,0.5,0.5"
              Value="371" KeyTime="00:00:02"/>
          <SplineDoubleKeyFrame
              d:KeyEase="Linear;Linear;0.5;0.5;0.5;0.5"
              KeySpline="0.5,0.5,0.5,0.5"
              Value="14" KeyTime="00:00:04"/>
        </DoubleAnimationUsingKeyFrames>
      </Storyboard>
    </Grid.Resources>

    <Grid.Triggers>
      <EventTrigger RoutedEvent="FrameworkElement.Loaded">
        <BeginStoryboard
            x:Name="OnLoaded_BeginStoryboard"
            Storyboard="{DynamicResource OnLoaded}"/>
      </EventTrigger>
    </Grid.Triggers>

    <Grid.ColumnDefinitions>
      <ColumnDefinition/>
    </Grid.ColumnDefinitions>
    <Grid.RowDefinitions>
      <RowDefinition/>
    </Grid.RowDefinitions>
    <Ellipse
          Stroke="#FF000000" Fill="#FFFFFFFF"
          HorizontalAlignment="Left"
          VerticalAlignment="Top"
          Margin="12,14,0,0" Width="102"
          Height="95" x:Name="Ellipse"
          RenderTransformOrigin="0.5,0.5">
      <Ellipse.RenderTransform>
        <TransformGroup>
```

```
            <TranslateTransform X="0" Y="0"/>
            <ScaleTransform ScaleX="1" ScaleY="1"/>
            <SkewTransform AngleX="0" AngleY="0"/>
            <RotateTransform Angle="0"/>
            <TranslateTransform X="0" Y="0"/>
            <TranslateTransform X="0" Y="0"/>
          </TransformGroup>
        </Ellipse.RenderTransform>
      </Ellipse>
</Grid>
```

One of the really nice features of using Expression Interactive Designer for animations is not only does the tool work out the correct keyframes for you but it also comes up with the correct transformations should you amend the scene in any way. Consider the scenario in Figure 8-14, where instead of a circle, an image appears in the top-left corner of the scene.

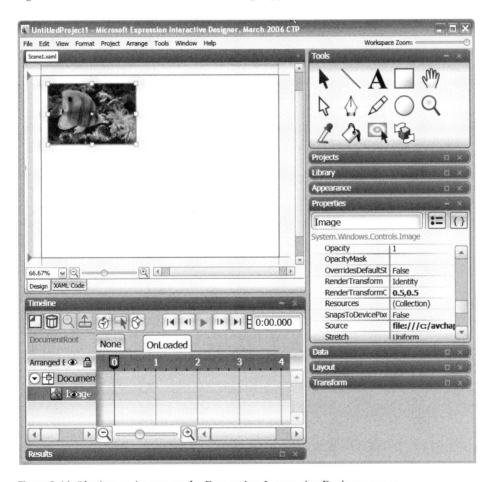

Figure 8-14. *Placing an image on the Expression Interactive Designer scene*

If you now advance the timeline to the two-second mark and then move the image to a new location, you will see similar behavior to earlier—with the image moving along that line in the time specified when you run the scene. However, this time you can also rotate the image using the Rotate Transformation tool. You get this tool when you rest your cursor on the corner of an image in the designer. You can see it in Figure 8-15.

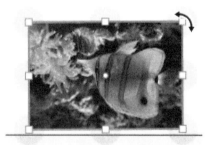

Figure 8-15. *Using the Rotate Transformation tool*

Now, you should have specified that the image is in the top left at the beginning of the timeline and somewhere else (in my case it is at the bottom right) after two seconds. Not only that, but it is inverted at the two-second point. WPF will then calculate the *tween* frames that take you from the start position to the end one, including what is needed to rotate the image. If you slide the cursor along the timeline, you can preview this behavior. Check out Figures 8-16 through 8-18 to see the image progress along its path, automatically rotating as it goes. Remember, you can use the designer to preview this; you do not need to run the application, which allows you to tweak and debug the animation in your applications without running them.

Note the position of the timeline and see how the animation is generating the correct rotation for the image at the correct time between Figures 8-16 through 8-18.

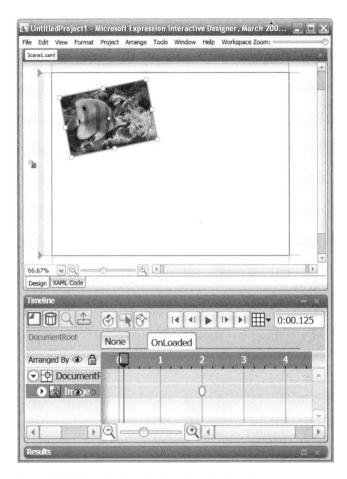

Figure 8-16. *Shortly after the timeline begins, the image starts to rotate.*

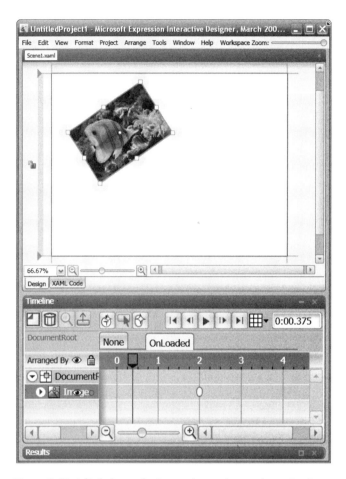

Figure 8-17. *A little later, the image is moving and continuing to rotate.*

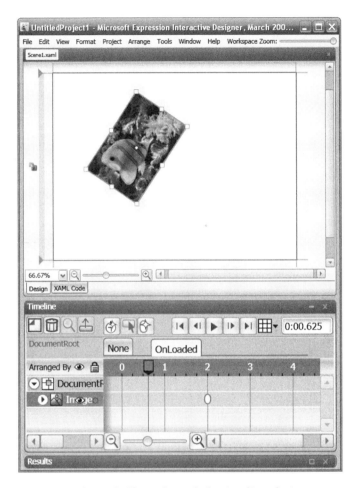

Figure 8-18. *Almost halfway through the timeline, the image approaches the halfway point and half its specified rotation.*

Assigning Animations to Events in Interactive Designer

Obviously, you want animations to occur at any time in your application, not just when the application first runs as in the previous examples. With Expression Interactive Designer, you can create a trigger that runs an application upon an event. For example, say that when you click a button, you want a specific animation to run. You can do this using a custom timeline.

As an example, place a button on a new scene using Expression Interactive Designer. Make it nice and big. On the Timeline palette, find the New Timeline control, and use it to create a new timeline called ButtonBounce. You can see this in Figure 8-19. Note the new tab for the new timeline.

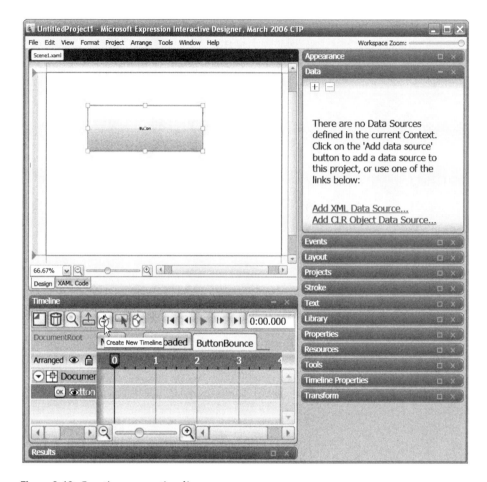

Figure 8-19. *Creating a new timeline*

Now use this timeline to create a simple animation by moving the button around the screen (and rotating it if you like) by selecting a new point on the timeline (say the two-second mark) and then moving the button when it is selected to generate a keyframe animation. Repeat this a number of times to make the button move around the screen.

Once you're done, open the Timeline Properties palette. You can see it on the right side of the screen in Figure 8-19. If you don't have it, you can find it on the View menu at the top of the screen. You can use this to assign a new trigger to run the ButtonBounce timeline when the user clicks the button. See Figure 8-20.

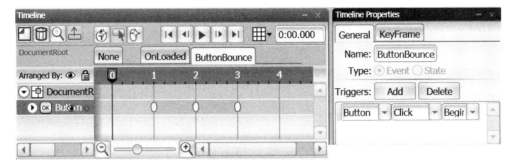

Figure 8-20. *Assigning a timeline to an event*

And that's all you need to do. Now when the user clicks the button, the animation will begin. In this example, the animation causes the button to bounce around the screen, rotating and changing shape as it goes. See Figures 8-21 and 8-22 for details.

Figure 8-21. *The basic application*

Figure 8-22. *The button is flying around the screen, rotating and reshaping after it is clicked.*

Summary

This chapter introduced you to the basic principles of animation using WPF. You looked at the animation types that are supported in XAML, using such examples as DoubleAnimation to change property dimensions or PointAnimation to change coordinates. You also explored the concepts behind splines and how you can use them to make varying linear animations, accelerating and decelerating the object along its path. You explored the concept of a timeline and how this is used for fine-tuning an animation, and you learned about keyframes, which can be seen as milestones along the animation path. Finally, you started playing with Expression Interactive Designer and seeing how easily it can put animation XAML together visually, with it doing all the grunt work of calculating keyframes along the timeline and the requisite animation types within the keyframe. You used this to create a simple animation that runs when you run the scene and another that runs in response to a user event, such as clicking a button.

Now that you've done a whistle-stop tour of the Avalon API, you'll notice that you've covered only two-dimensional (2D) graphics. WPF also has a pretty cool API for writing applications in 3D too—and in the next chapter you'll look into how you can use it to add an extra dimension to your applications! You will be equipped with what you need to know to distribute your latest and greatest application securely and easily.

CHAPTER 9

■■■

Working with 3D Graphics in WPF

As requirements for the user experience get more and more sophisticated and the demand increases for users to be more productive, the need for three-dimensional (3D) graphics for data representation (amongst other things) is fast becoming a priority. Luckily, the Windows Presentation Foundation (WPF) offers a full set of application programming interfaces (APIs) that allow you to develop 3D graphical applications in Extensible Application Markup Language (XAML) as well as in procedural C# code.

At the heart of 3D graphics in WPF is the ViewPort3D class. This provides a two-dimensional (2D) window into a 3D scene—it is a surface on which the 3D scene is projected. You use it just like any other element in WPF, and as such, you place it on a scene using XAML.

The problem with using XAML for 3D scenes is that to describe a 3D object, you require a lot of data points. These data points form what is called a *mesh* that describes the polygons used to make up the shape. Consider the simple scene in Figure 9-1.

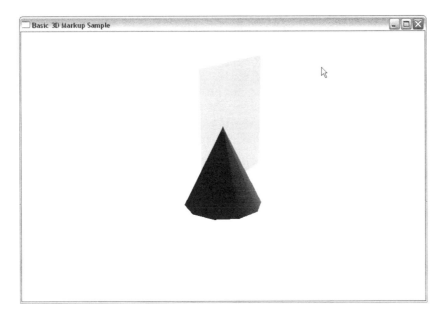

Figure 9-1. *A simple 3D scene*

The mesh used to describe these shapes is still pretty complex, with only a small snippet of it in Listing 9-1.

Listing 9-1. *Defining Complex Shapes*

```
<!-- Define a cone. -->
  <GeometryModel3D>
    <GeometryModel3D.Geometry>
      <MeshGeometry3D
            Positions="0.293893 -0.5 0.404509
              ... 30 lines cropped for brevity
              "
            Normals="0.7236065,0.4472139,0.5257313
            ... 30 lines cropped for brevity  "
            TriangleIndices="0 1 2 3 4 5 6 7 8 9 10 11
                    12 13 14 15 16 17 18 19 20 21 22 23
                    24 25 26 27 28 29 30 31 32 33 34 35
                    36 37 38 39 40 41 42 43 44 45 46 47
                    48 49 50 51 52 53 54 55 56 57 58 59 " />
    </GeometryModel3D.Geometry>
  <GeometryModel3D.Material>
  <DiffuseMaterial>
    <DiffuseMaterial.Brush>
      <SolidColorBrush Color="Red" Opacity="1.0"/>
    </DiffuseMaterial.Brush>
  </DiffuseMaterial>
</GeometryModel3D.Material>
</GeometryModel3D>
```

If you consider a more complex object, you end up with literally megabytes (or more) of numbers like these for positions, normals, indices, and so on. Figure 9-2 shows what is still a relatively simple model—and this requires 2MB worth of definitions.

As a result, the best methodology for programming in 3D with WPF is to use a 3D designer package to create models and meshes and then import them into WPF when you want to create lifelike experiences or games or when you want to use procedural code to model more basic 3D shapes when building applications such as graphing or charting apps.

Figure 9-2. *A 3D model mesh in WPF*

Understanding the Basics of 3D Programming

The representation of 3D objects projected onto a 2D surface is a huge area in its own right and has spawned many books and university courses dedicated to it. As such, this chapter only touches on 3D programming and scene representation. It is intended as a primer to get you up and running with the technology!

Introducing Points

In Figure 9-2, you saw the model of a turtle that was represented as a number of meshes, with each mesh being the representation of a surface. You create this by representing the surface as a series of points and lines, with the points (in 3D space) defining the high and low parts of the surface and the lines that connect them establishing how to get from one point to the next.

For example, you could represent a pyramid using four sets of three points. Each set of points defines a triangle on a plane, and these planes intersect each other in 3D space to form the pyramid. The reason why you wouldn't use one set of five points is that when you do that, the five points aren't on the same plane, so you cannot define the plane itself. Although this may not seem to be important now, it will be later when you consider lighting and shading—basically, you need to inform the API of the "direction" of the plane of the object so that light falls on its inside and outside correctly. You do this using the *normal* of the plane, which you will learn about in the "Introducing Normals" section.

When it comes to defining objects, the simplest plane object is a triangle, and as such it makes sense to define all complex objects in terms of many triangles.

Introducing Vertices

When using WPF to *draw* a triangle, you add the points, and then you draw the lines between the points by adding them as indices of the triangle. It's a little bit like defining a path. For example, if you have points X, Y, and Z, you first add these points to the mesh, and then you define the lines between them by adding them as indices. However, this has a slight quirk. WPF defines a triangle as having an "up" side that it shades and a "down" side that it doesn't shade. The "up" side is determined as being the one in which the lines defining the vertices are added in a counterclockwise direction.

This is known as the *right-hand rule*. Consider your right hand. Place it in a "thumbs-up" position. Your fingers are now curling clockwise (when viewing from tip to base). Thus, to define a triangle that is facing "up," you would add points X, Y, and Z, as shown in Figure 9-3.

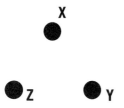

Figure 9-3. *Adding the points of a triangle*

Now, if you want to draw a triangle so the plane of the triangle that is on the page faces "up" and is thus drawn, you would add the vertices according to the right-hand rule; thus, you would add X first, then Z, and then Y. Of course, the normal of the triangle (which defines how light works when hitting the triangle) and the position of the camera are also important. In this case, the position of the camera is assumed to be your eyes as you are reading the page. Should the camera be behind the page, then by adding the vertices in the XZY order, you would be defining the "back" plane of the triangle as facing the camera, and thus it wouldn't be drawn, as shown in Figure 9-4.

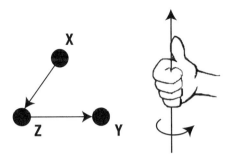

Figure 9-4. *Adding the vertices to the points so that the plane of the triangle is "up"*

Introducing Normals

Next you have to define the normals of the triangle. A *normal* is a vector that is perpendicular to the surface of the triangle. You can calculate it by getting the cross-product of the two vectors. Details on how to calculate a cross-product are beyond the scope of this book, but what is important is understanding the direction of the normal. You want the normal to also appear pointing toward the "up" direction of the triangle so the light will fall on the surface of the triangle to be drawn. You use a similar right-hand technique to what you used earlier to determine the normal. The best way to calculate one is to use two vertices of the triangle. For triangle XYZ that you defined earlier, the normal resulting from YX × YZ is in the "upward" direction. You can understand this by placing your right hand at point Y, then pointing your index finger at X (giving YX), and pointing your middle finger at Z (giving YZ). Now, according to the right-hand rule, your thumb gives the direction of the cross-product; thus, the normal is facing the "up" side of the triangle, as shown in Figure 9-5.

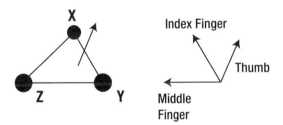

Figure 9-5. *Calculating the normal of the triangle*

In a similar manner, you can establish the normal pointing "down" the triangle by calculating the YZ × YX cross-product.

If you consider a pyramid in 3D space with a single light source, you would likely see only two faces of the pyramid, and these would be lit differently because they are not facing the light source in the same direction. The one that is closer to the vector of the light source would appear brighter than the other. This is what normals are used for—and by knowing the normal of a surface, WPF can calculate the appropriate lighting for that surface.

Enough Theory, Let's See the Code

OK, enough of the theory and the vector mathematics. This is a WPF book, and as such you probably want to see some C# code to achieve these effects. For your first task, you will put all this theory into practice by writing lots of code that will achieve the monumental task of drawing a red triangle. It might seem like overkill, but it is the principle that matters! By understanding the principles of how to program in 3D space in WPF, you'll soon be on your way to building more complex objects; however, you'll go one step at a time.

Create a new WinFX Windows project with Visual Studio 2005, and edit the basicWindow1. xaml file that is created by the wizard to include the contents shown in Listing 9-2. It's best to avoid editing the <Window> node and instead just put the <Grid> and its children into your application.

Listing 9-2. *Defining a 3D Viewport*

```
<Window x:Class="Chapter9Ex1.Window1"
    xmlns="http://schemas.microsoft.com/winfx/2006/xaml/presentation"
    xmlns:x="http://schemas.microsoft.com/winfx/2006/xaml"
    Title="Chapter9Ex1" Height="300" Width="300"
    >
    <Grid>
      <Viewport3D Name="vpt">
        <Viewport3D.Camera>
          <PerspectiveCamera
           FarPlaneDistance="100"
           LookDirection="-10,-10,-10"
           UpDirection="0,1,0"
           NearPlaneDistance="1"
           Position="10,10,10"
           FieldOfView="45" />
        </Viewport3D.Camera>
        <ModelVisual3D>
          <ModelVisual3D.Content>
            <DirectionalLight
             Color="White"
             Direction="-1,-1,-1" />
          </ModelVisual3D.Content>
        </ModelVisual3D>
      </Viewport3D>
    </Grid>
</Window>
```

This defines the 3D viewport and its camera and lighting information. You'll learn more about the camera and lighting in the "Setting Up the Camera" section, but suffice it to say for now that unless the camera is pointing at the object, you will not see it. In addition, the way the object appears depends on the light used. The code will create an object around the origin point 0,0,0, and the camera in this case is at point 10,10,10 looking through the origin toward the point at –10,–10,–10, so you will see the object. You've also defined the light as pointing in the same direction as the camera, and it is white light. The triangle is defined as red, so it will be rendered as red. If the light is defined as a different color, then the additive mixing of colors will occur. For example, if the light is defined as blue, the triangle will be rendered as black because in optics, an object is red because it reflects the red wavelengths of light. If it is under a white light, you see red. If it is under a blue light, with no red element, nothing is reflected, and thus it appears black.

Now, in your Window constructor, you can start writing the code to define the triangle.

You'll need three points to define the points of the triangle. You define them using the Point3D class, like this:

```
Point3D point0 = new Point3D(0, 0, 0);
Point3D point1 = new Point3D(2, -4, 0);
Point3D point2 = new Point3D(0, 0, 5);
```

If you think in terms of absolute Cartesian coordinates, you now have a point at the origin 0,0,0; another one at 2 on the X axis and at –4 on the Y axis (2,–4,0); and another one at 0 on X, at 0 on Y, and at 5 on Z. The human mind tends to think of X as being left and right on the paper, Y as being "up and down," and Z as being "in and out." As such, the triangle would be invisible to you because you would be looking at it edge on. However, remember that the camera is not at this position; it is at 10,10,10, and it is looking toward –10,–10,–10, so it is diagonally positioned above and to the right of the origin, looking through the origin toward its 3D opposite. Thus, later when you render the triangle, you will see it.

Next you want to add the points to the mesh. You first create the mesh as a MeshGeometry3D object like this:

```
MeshGeometry3D triangleMesh = new MeshGeometry3D();
```

Then you add the points to it:

```
triangleMesh.Positions.Add(point0);
triangleMesh.Positions.Add(point1);
triangleMesh.Positions.Add(point2);
```

So far, so good. Now, you need to start adding the indices to the triangle so the path defining the triangle becomes part of the mesh and the triangle becomes a shape instead of a collection of points. You'll use the right-hand rule to define the "up" direction of the triangle:

```
triangleMesh.TriangleIndices.Add(0);
triangleMesh.TriangleIndices.Add(2);
triangleMesh.TriangleIndices.Add(1);
```

Notice something unusual here? Other than the order being 0-2-1 as discussed earlier, you are also just adding references to the positions, rather than the points themselves. As such, it is important to add the points in the right order. Earlier you added point0, point1, point2 to the positions within the mesh in that order; thus, index 0 contains point0, index 1 contains point1, and so on. Had these been added out of order, then the indices would not be smart enough to figure out the correct values. Thus, the moral of the story is to be careful about the order in which you add your points!

You can calculate a normal if you want, or you can just define one manually. In this example, you will define one manually as running along the Y axis like this:

```
Vector3D normal = new Vector3D(0, 1, 0);
```

Then, you add the normal vector to the Normals collection for the mesh:

```
triangleMesh.Normals.Add(normal);
```

To build the model of the triangle, you need the mesh (which you have now finished defining) and the material that defines how the mesh will be painted. You want a red triangle so you'll build a simple red Material object like this:

```
Material material = new DiffuseMaterial(
            new SolidColorBrush(Colors.Red));
```

You can do lots more complex things with materials, but you will stick with a simple SolidColorBrush for now.

You are now ready to create the model of your triangle that WPF can understand and render. You do this by creating a GeometryModel3D using the mesh and the material and then using this to fill the content of a ModelVisual3D object like this:

```
GeometryModel3D triangleModel = new GeometryModel3D(
            triangleMesh, material);
ModelVisual3D model = new ModelVisual3D();
model.Content = triangleModel;
```

Finally, you add the model to the ViewPort3D object for rendering to occur:

```
this.vpt.Children.Add(model);
```

Listing 9-3 shows the complete code.

Listing 9-3. *Defining a Triangle*

```
using System.Windows.Media.Media3D;
public Window1()
{
  InitializeComponent();
  MeshGeometry3D triangleMesh = new MeshGeometry3D();
  Point3D point0 = new Point3D(0, 0, 0);
  Point3D point1 = new Point3D(2, -4, 0);
  Point3D point2 = new Point3D(0, 0, 5);
  triangleMesh.Positions.Add(point0);
  triangleMesh.Positions.Add(point1);
  triangleMesh.Positions.Add(point2);
  triangleMesh.TriangleIndices.Add(0);
  triangleMesh.TriangleIndices.Add(2);
```

```
triangleMesh.TriangleIndices.Add(1);
Vector3D normal = new Vector3D(0, 1, 0);
triangleMesh.Normals.Add(normal);
Material material = new DiffuseMaterial(
    new SolidColorBrush(Colors.Red));
GeometryModel3D triangleModel = new GeometryModel3D(
    triangleMesh, material);
ModelVisual3D model = new ModelVisual3D();
model.Content = triangleModel;
this.vpt.Children.Add(model);
}
```

When you run this application, you'll see the results shown in Figure 9-6.

Figure 9-6. *Your red triangle*

Examining the ViewPort3D Object

You use a ViewPort3D object to create the 3D scene. This control displays 3D content and provides properties for controlling that content such as clipping, height, width, and response to mouse events. The object contains a number of property classes that are used to dictate this behavior; you will look at some of those classes in the following sections.

Setting Up the Camera

Earlier you set up the XAML code for the ViewPort3D object, which included the definition of the camera that would provide the user's viewpoint on the scene. The camera specifies which part of the 3D scene is viewable. The PerspectiveCamera type is the most realistic of these; it's like a real camera, where the viewing surface is a single point, and it describes a viewing "pyramid," with the far plane of viewing being the base of the pyramid and the camera being the apex of the pyramid viewing everything between it and the distant plane using a method called *perspective foreshortening*. Another type of camera is the OrthographicCamera type, which performs a parallel projection of the 3D objects onto the 2D surface. In real-world terms, a perspective camera works similarly to a photographic camera, and an orthographic projection works similarly to you looking out a window at an object.

To set up a PerspectiveCamera, first you need to specify where the camera is—you do this using the Position property to specify where it is in 3D coordinate space. For example, if the camera is to be at position 1 on the X axis and 0 on Y and Z, you would specify its position as {1,0,0}.

Then, you need to specify the distance to the far plane of viewing (that is, how far the camera can see). This is an absolute distance from the camera, not a coordinate in space. For example, if your camera is looking along the X axis and is positioned at point 1 on this axis (that is, {1,0,0}) and the far plane distance is 100, then the far plane of viewing will be intersecting the X axis at {−99,0,0}.

Next, you need to specify the direction in which the camera is looking. If you consider the camera to be at a single point in 3D space, the direction it is looking in is a vector originating at that point. You specify the direction by specifying to which point the camera should look. So, if you look at the following XAML, you will see that the camera is at {10,10,10} and is looking at {−10,−10,−10} with the far plane distance being 100 units away. So if any other objects were in the scene behind the triangle, you would see them, unless they were farther than 100 units away.

Here's the XAML:

```
<Viewport3D.Camera>
  <PerspectiveCamera
  FarPlaneDistance="100"
  LookDirection="-10,-10,-10"
  Position="10,10,10" />
</Viewport3D.Camera>
```

You can use a plethora of other properties on a perspective camera that may be useful, such as the field of view, which allows you to specify (in degrees) the width of the field of view available into which to project. For example, if you see the camera as the tip of a pyramid, with the base being the far plane, you specify the width of the pyramid using the field of view. A narrow field of view will give you a tall, thin pyramid, and a wide field of view will give you a short, fat one.

You can also specify and use the camera in code. Thus, you can manipulate your camera to move it around the scene and make things more interesting. Here's an example of how you would create the same camera using C#:

```
PerspectiveCamera pCam = new PerspectiveCamera();
pCam.FarPlaneDistance = 100;
pCam.Position = new Point3D(10, 10, 10);
pCam.LookDirection = new Vector3D(-10, -10, -10);
vpt.Camera = pCam;
this.vpt.Children.Add(model);
```

Thus, you can manipulate the camera using code also. Here is an example of a small routine that changes the X position of the camera, which could be used on a mouse click or other event handler:

```
PerspectiveCamera pCam = (PerspectiveCamera) vpt.Camera;
Point3D pPos = pCam.Position;
pPos.X = pPos.X + 2;
pCam.Position = pPos;
```

This code creates a PerspectiveCamera from the Camera property of the viewport using a cast to the PerspectiveCamera class type. Then, it creates a Point3D using the camera's position, amends this Point3D by adding 2 to its X value, and resets the position of the camera to the resultant point. You can see the result of calling this routine in Figures 9-7 and 9-8.

Figure 9-7. *The triangle before you move it*

Figure 9-8. *The triangle after you move it*

These figures show a surprising result—you would have expected the figure to move to the right, but it moved to the left and slightly upward; its shape is also slightly distorted. So, what happened?

You didn't move the shape; you moved the *camera*. Don't forget that the shape is a triangle with one of its corners at {0,0,0}. You were previously at {10,10,10} looking at {–10,–10,–10}, so you were looking straight through the origin. As such, the corner that is at the origin would appear in the center of the viewport. This is, indeed, the case in Figure 9-7 where the "top" of the triangle is in the center of the screen. By Figure 9-8, the camera has moved to {16,10,10} and is still looking at {–10,–10,–10}, so it is no longer looking through the origin. By then, the camera has moved to the right on the X axis, causing the triangle to move to the left on the X axis, and it has been distorted because it is now projecting toward a different camera position! Remember that the triangle object itself has not moved—just the camera. You will look at moving the object in the "Using Transforms" section.

Setting Up the Lights

You can have one or more lights on a scene, and the lights don't necessarily have to be in the same position as the camera. It helps to picture yourself in a dark room. You are standing in one corner of the room, and a pyramid is in the center of the room. Without any lights, you cannot see it. Assume the pyramid is red, and you place a white light to your left. What will you see? One of the faces of the pyramid will be quite red, and the others will have different, darker shades of red. What happens if the light changes color? The pyramid will also appear to be a different color because it is reflecting light of a different wavelength.

WPF supports several lighting types:

- *AmbientLight* provides a nondirectional ambient lighting that illuminates all objects uniformly regardless of their location or orientation.

- *DirectionalLight* provides light heading in a specific direction along a defined vector. It has no specified location.

- *PointLight* acts like a real-world light—imagine a floating lightbulb in a specific location that casts light in all directions. Objects will be illuminated based on their position and distance from the light. You can set properties on a PointLight that dictates how the light will fade away with distance as well as how this fading will behave (linear, quadratic, or constant fade).

- *SpotLight* is similar to the PointLight except that it has an inherent direction, so instead of casting light in all directions, it casts it along a specific vector in a "cone" shape, and you can define the cone shape using the InnerConeAngle and OuterConeAngle properties.

All lights are Model3D objects, so you specify them in XAML as a child of the <ModelVisual3D> node. Here's the example from earlier:

```
<ModelVisual3D>
    <ModelVisual3D.Content>
        <DirectionalLight
                Color="White"
                Direction="-1,-1,-1" />
    </ModelVisual3D.Content>
</ModelVisual3D>
```

In this case, a directional light is used, running along the vector defined by {–1,–1,–1}, and is colored white.

You can programmatically add a light to your scene, too. This allows you to pull a reference for the light from your viewport and amend it. For example, to add a white light on vector {–1,–1,–1} as before, you could use the following C#:

```
ModelVisual3D light = new ModelVisual3D();

light.Content = new DirectionalLight(
      Colors.White, new Vector3D(-1, -1, -1));

this.vpt.Children.Add(model);
this.vpt.Children.Add(light);
```

If you keep track of the children that are lights, you can then amend them easily. In this case, I know that the child at index 1 is my light, so a simple routine that changes the color of the light would look like Listing 9-4.

Listing 9-4. *Changing Light Colors*

```
public void btnChange_Click(Object sender, RoutedEventArgs e)
{
  ModelVisual3D light = (ModelVisual3D) this.vpt.Children[1];
  DirectionalLight dl = (DirectionalLight) light.Content;
  if (dl.Color == Colors.White)
    dl.Color = Colors.Green;
  else
    dl.Color = Colors.White;
  light.Content = dl;
  this.vpt.Children.RemoveAt(1);
  this.vpt.Children.Add(light);
}
```

This pulls the lights from the collection of children on the viewport and casts it to a DirectionalLight. It checks the current color and, if it is green, sets it to white, and vice versa. Then, it removes the existing light and replaces it with the new one. You can see the results in Figures 9-9 and 9-10. If you don't know the index of the light or if you have a large and complex scene, it is easy to just loop through the collection of children of your ViewPort3D and check like this to establish whether the object is a light:

```
if (vpt.Children[index].Content is DirectionalLight == true)
```

The same can be said for all content types of a ModelVisual3D. This is a useful technique for iterating through a scene and making changes based on the content type of a particular model within the scene.

Figure 9-9. *The red triangle with a white light*

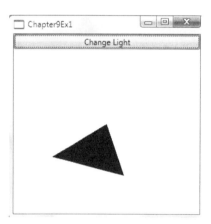

Figure 9-10. *The red triangle with a green light*

You can see that the two objects are considerably different, with the second appearing to be a dark red and almost black in color because of the mixing of the red and green colors.

Using Materials

As you saw in the previous section, a light is a type of model, and a scene consists of one or more models. When you want to render objects in 3D space, you define the object using a mesh as you saw earlier and using a material to determine how it should be lit. These combine to form a Geometry3DModel, which can then be used as the content for a ModelVisual3D and thus added to the viewport.

Earlier you saw how to set up the triangle mesh by defining points and indices. You then associated a normal with them to complete the mesh. To get an object that can be rendered in 3D space, you then added a material. The simplest form of material is a DiffuseMaterial type, which can take a single flat color like this:

```
Material material = new DiffuseMaterial(
    new SolidColorBrush(Colors.Red));
```

Then, you use this in the constructor for the Geometry3DModel along with the triangle mesh like this:

```
GeometryModel3D triangleModel = new GeometryModel3D(
    triangleMesh, material);
```

The DiffuseMaterial is the simplest material type, supporting a single flat color defined with a SolidColorBrush or a TiledColorBrush. Image brushes are not supported. The model does not reflect any light other than the overall color of the surface. As such, the object isn't considered shiny.

The SpecularMaterial brush allows the brush to be applied as if the surface of the model were hard and/or shiny so it would reflect a highlight. This highlight is based on the SpecularPower that you associate with the material. The lower the number, the more reflective the material is.

You can add a SpecularMaterial to the existing material by using a MaterialGroup. This allows you to combine different materials on the same surface.

Thus, for example, you can use code like this to make your triangle red but have a white specular material that is reflective:

```
Material material = new DiffuseMaterial(
  new SolidColorBrush(Colors.Red));
Material material2 = new SpecularMaterial(
  new SolidColorBrush(Colors.White),
  1);
MaterialGroup mg = new MaterialGroup();
mg.Children.Add(material);
mg.Children.Add(material2);

GeometryModel3D triangleModel = new GeometryModel3D(
  triangleMesh, mg);
```

You can see the results of this in Figure 9-11.

Figure 9-11. *Triangle with SpecularMaterial surface*

Finally, the EmissiveMaterial type allows you to specify that the texture will be applied as though the model were emitting light that is the color of the brush. It doesn't make the model a brush, but it does allow it to handle effects such as shadowing differently. For example, if the triangle is red and an EmissiveMaterial that is purple in color is applied to it, then the appearance would be that the triangle will be shaded in lilac (assuming you are also using the white specular material mentioned previously). For example, consider the code in Listing 9-5.

Listing 9-5. *Using Emissive Materials*

```
Material material = new DiffuseMaterial(
  new SolidColorBrush(Colors.Red));
Material material2 = new SpecularMaterial(
  new SolidColorBrush(Colors.White),
  1);
Material material3 = new EmissiveMaterial(
  new SolidColorBrush(Colors.Purple));

MaterialGroup mg = new MaterialGroup();
mg.Children.Add(material);
mg.Children.Add(material2);
mg.Children.Add(material3);

GeometryModel3D triangleModel = new GeometryModel3D(
  triangleMesh, mg);
```

This will result in the lilac triangle shown in Figure 9-12.

Figure 9-12. *Using an emissive light*

Seeing a More Complex Example in Action

Now that you've played with a single triangle, you can start looking at a more complex example where you will draw a 3D surface that will appear like a rubber sheet whose troughs and peaks can be determined by some known values. This type of sheet makes a useful business graphic when the values are derived from a database—forming a three-dimensional bar chart–like view of your data—but for now you will just use random values, and you can fill in the rest later.

To get started, create a new WPF Windows application, and create a new ViewPort3D in the XAML for Window1, like this:

```
<Window x:Class="Chapter9Ex2.Window1"
    xmlns="http://schemas.microsoft.com/winfx/2006/xaml/presentation"
    xmlns:x="http://schemas.microsoft.com/winfx/2006/xaml"
    Title="Chapter9Ex2" Height="300" Width="300"
    >
    <Grid>
      <Viewport3D Name="vpt" />
    </Grid>
</Window>
```

This is straightforward and just sets up a ViewPort3D called vpt.

Now, on the Constructor for Window1, add this code:

```
public Window1()
{
  Point3D[,] myPoints = new Point3D[10, 10];
  InitializeComponent();
```

```
    InitializeSurface(myPoints);
    DrawTriangles(myPoints);
    DrawLight();
    DrawCamera();
}
```

This creates a 10×10 array of points that will be used to represent the surface. These points will have the X and Y coordinates of their index within the array and a random Z coordinate. For example, myPoints[0,0] will be {0,0,something}, and so on. You set this up in the InitializeSurface function, as shown in Listing 9-6.

Listing 9-6. *Building a Mesh of Triangles*

```
private void InitializeSurface(Point3D[,] myPoints)
{
    int x = 0;
    int y = 0;
    double z = 0.0;
    Random r = new Random();
    for (x = 0; x < 10; x++)
    {
        for (y = 0; y < 10; y++)
        {
            z = (Convert.ToDouble(r.Next(20))-10)/10;
            myPoints[x, y] =
                new Point3D(Convert.ToDouble(x),
                            Convert.ToDouble(y),
                            z);
        }
    }
}
```

This just goes through a nested loop on X and Y and creates a value for Z, which is a value from −1 to +1, by getting a whole number from −10 to +10 and then dividing that by 10.

Now that you have your surface, you want to draw the triangles indicated by that surface. Remember, the points are stored in a 2D 10×10 grid. To draw triangles of this grid, you will iterate through the grid and for each point draw two triangles with that point at its apex. The first triangle will be with the other two points to the right and above it on the matrix. The second triangle will be with the points to the right and below right from it on the matrix.

Listing 9-7 shows the code to achieve this.

Listing 9-7. *Drawing the Mesh of Triangles*

```
private void DrawTriangles(Point3D[,] myPoints)
{
  int x - 0;
  int y = 0;

  for (x = 0; x <= 8; x++)
  {
    for (y = 0; y <= 8; y++)
    {
      Point3D p1 = myPoints[x, y];
      Point3D p2 = myPoints[x + 1, y];
      Point3D p3 = myPoints[x, y + 1];
      DrawSingleTriangle(p1, p2, p3);
    }
    for (y = 1; y <= 9; y++)
    {
      Point3D p1 = myPoints[x, y];
      Point3D p2 = myPoints[x + 1, y - 1];
      Point3D p3 = myPoints[x + 1, y];
      DrawSingleTriangle(p1, p2, p3);
    }
  }
}
```

Two loops make sure the bounds checking is correct. The first loop draws the triangle using the points to the right and above the current point. The second loop uses the points to the right and below right.

This function then calls DrawSingleTriangle, which as you might have guessed draws the model of the triangle and adds it to the viewport. You can see it in Listing 9-8.

Listing 9-8. *Drawing the Triangles and Calculating Their Normals*

```
private void DrawSingleTriangle(Point3D p1, Point3D p2, Point3D p3)
{
  MeshGeometry3D triangleMesh = new MeshGeometry3D();
  triangleMesh.Positions.Add(p1);
  triangleMesh.Positions.Add(p2);
  triangleMesh.Positions.Add(p3);
  triangleMesh.TriangleIndices.Add(0);
  triangleMesh.TriangleIndices.Add(1);
  triangleMesh.TriangleIndices.Add(2);
```

```
    Vector3D normal = CalculateNormal(p1, p2, p3);
    triangleMesh.Normals.Add(normal);
    Material material = new DiffuseMaterial(
      new SolidColorBrush(Colors.Green));
    Material material2 = new SpecularMaterial(
      new SolidColorBrush(Colors.White),
      80);
    MaterialGroup mg = new MaterialGroup();
    mg.Children.Add(material);
    mg.Children.Add(material2);
    GeometryModel3D triangleModel = new GeometryModel3D(
      triangleMesh, mg);
    ModelVisual3D model = new ModelVisual3D();
    model.Content = triangleModel;
    this.vpt.Children.Add(model);
}
private Vector3D CalculateNormal(Point3D p1, Point3D p2, Point3D p3)
{
    Vector3D v0 = new Vector3D(
      p2.X - p1.X, p2.Y - p1.Y, p2.Z - p1.Z);
    Vector3D v1 = new Vector3D(
      p3.X - p2.X, p3.Y - p2.Y, p3.Z - p2.Z);
    return Vector3D.CrossProduct(v0, v1);
}
```

All that remains now is to draw the light and the camera, as shown in Listing 9-9, and you'll see your sheet in glorious 3D!

Listing 9-9. *Adding Lights and Camera*

```
private void DrawLight()
{
    ModelVisual3D light = new ModelVisual3D();
    light.Content = new DirectionalLight(
      Colors.White, new Vector3D(-1, -1, -1));
    this.vpt.Children.Add(light);
}
private void DrawCamera()
{
    PerspectiveCamera pCam = new PerspectiveCamera();
    pCam.FarPlaneDistance = 100;
    pCam.Position = new Point3D(20, 20, 15);
    pCam.LookDirection = new Vector3D(-20, -20, -20);
    pCam.UpDirection = new Vector3D(0, 0, 1);
    vpt.Camera = pCam;
}
```

Now, when you execute the application, you will see your surface with all the different lighting shades like in Figure 9-13.

Figure 9-13. *Running your surface*

Now, all this has a catch; this may seem to be the natural way of developing the scene—generating triangles and building the scene from that—but when you look at these lines in the DrawSingleTriangle method, you will notice that each triangle is being added as a separate model to the scene:

```
GeometryModel3D triangleModel = new GeometryModel3D(
    triangleMesh, mg);
ModelVisual3D model = new ModelVisual3D();
model.Content = triangleModel;
this.vpt.Children.Add(model);
```

This is a valid way of doing it and is the way you will likely do it when you first start building 3D applications in WPF. The problem with this is that you will then have to manage each triangle separately if you are doing any changes to the scene, which will involve lots of extra code, as well as have a performance impact. You may prefer to group all the triangles for a single object into a single model and make that model the child of the scene.

In this case, to do that, you would use a Model3DGroup to collect all the triangles into a single group. In DrawTriangles, you would have code like this:

```
Model3DGroup model = new Model3DGroup();
GeometryModel3D tri;
```

Then your calls to DrawSingleTriangle would no longer be void calls but would return a GeometryModel3D like this:

```
tri = DrawSingleTriangle(p1, p2, p3);
```

Listing 9-10 shows the complete code for DrawTriangles and DrawSingleTriangle.

Listing 9-10. *Handling the Triangles in 3D Space*

```
private void DrawTriangles(Point3D[,] myPoints)
{
  int x = 0;
  int y = 0;
  Model3DGroup model = new Model3DGroup();
  GeometryModel3D tri;
  for (x = 0; x <= 8; x++)
  {
    for (y = 0; y <= 8; y++)
    {
      Point3D p1 = myPoints[x, y];
      Point3D p2 = myPoints[x + 1, y];
      Point3D p3 = myPoints[x, y + 1];

      tri = DrawSingleTriangle(p1, p2, p3);

      model.Children.Add(tri);
    }
    for (y = 1; y <= 9; y++)
    {
      Point3D p1 = myPoints[x, y];
      Point3D p2 = myPoints[x + 1, y - 1];
      Point3D p3 = myPoints[x + 1, y];
      DrawSingleTriangle(p1, p2, p3);
      tri = DrawSingleTriangle(p1, p2, p3);
      model.Children.Add(tri);
    }
  }
  ModelVisual3D mainmodel = new ModelVisual3D();
  mainmodel.Content = model;
  this.vpt.Children.Add(mainmodel);

}

private GeometryModel3D
      DrawSingleTriangle(Point3D p1, Point3D p2, Point3D p3)
{
  MeshGeometry3D triangleMesh = new MeshGeometry3D();
  triangleMesh.Positions.Add(p1);
```

```
triangleMesh.Positions.Add(p2);
triangleMesh.Positions.Add(p3);
triangleMesh.TriangleIndices.Add(0);
triangleMesh.TriangleIndices.Add(1);
triangleMesh.TriangleIndices.Add(2);
Vector3D normal = CalculateNormal(p1, p2, p3);
triangleMesh.Normals.Add(normal);
Material material = new DiffuseMaterial(
  new SolidColorBrush(Colors.Green));
Material material2 = new SpecularMaterial(
  new SolidColorBrush(Colors.White),
  80);
MaterialGroup mg = new MaterialGroup();
mg.Children.Add(material);
mg.Children.Add(material2);
GeometryModel3D triangleModel = new GeometryModel3D(
  triangleMesh, mg);

return triangleModel;

}
```

In the next section, "Using Transforms," you'll see why this technique is useful—now you can pull the entire model representing the landscape from Figure 9-13 and apply a transform to it in one swoop.

Using Transforms

Another artifact of 3D programming is the *transform*, which uses some pretty heavy matrix mathematics (which I won't go into here) to allow you to move, rotate, resize, and change the form of your models. Because a model is stored as a set of 3D coordinates and the paths that link them, you can use these mathematics to perform such actions.

Luckily, as a developer, you don't need to brush up on the heavy-duty math and understand how features such as identity matrices work; instead, WPF handles this for you using the Transform property of any model.

One confusing part of WPF, particularly to newcomers, is how transforms work—they change the coordinates of the object in its model space but not in absolute space. In other words, they do not change the absolute coordinates of the primitives but instead where it is rendered. So if you have a triangle with an apex at {1,0,0} and you translate it to {2,0,0}, the coordinate of the apex is still stored in the model as {1,0,0} so that if you apply the transform *again*, it will be at {2,0,0} and not {3,0,0} as you might expect. Thus, when you want to compound transforms, you use a transform group. Now, this may appear to be inefficient, where you would have to, for example, apply the transform ten times if you are making ten moves, but it isn't. In this case, the transform group calculates a transformation matrix of a compound of the ten moves and applies that matrix to the model only once.

You can use a number of transforms in WPF, the first of which is the transform that is used to move your model around the 3D space. This is called a *translation* transform.

Using Translations

Translations are handled in WPF using the TranslateTransform3D class. This moves all the points in your model in the direction of an offset specified by a vector. Under the hood, your points are stored using the mathematical construct called a *matrix*, and a translation involves multiplying this matrix by another, which represents a vector in which the translation occurs. In WPF, you just use the TranslateTransform3D class and construct it with the parameters that determine the vector direction in X, Y, and Z coordinates using the OffsetX, OffsetY, and OffsetZ parameters.

Here's an example:

```
private void TranslateModel()
{
  ModelVisual3D model = (ModelVisual3D) this.vpt.Children[0];
  Transform3D myTranslation = new TranslateTransform3D(0.1,0.0,0.0);
  tGroup.Children.Add(myTranslation);
  model.Transform = tGroup;
}
```

This function will move the model by 0.1 units on the X axis, but for a continuous movement, you have to add it to a transformation group, which in this case is called tGroup and is defined elsewhere in the program (in fact, in this case it is a member variable of the host window). Then, you assign the transformation group to the .Transform property of the model, and the transformation occurs. Had you repeatedly applied myTranslation to the model, the model would move only along the X axis once.

Using Scaling

You transform the scale of a model using the ScaleTransform3D. Remember, this doesn't change the *size* of your model, just the scaling to use when rendering it. You scale the model by specifying the amount to scale on the X, Y, and Z axes, using a normalized value. In other words, 1.0 means keep the scale the same, 0.9 is 10 percent smaller, 1.1 is 10 percent bigger, and so on.

Here's an example:

```
ModelVisual3D model = (ModelVisual3D)this.vpt.Children[0];
Transform3D myScaling = new ScaleTransform3D(1.01, 1.01, 1.01);
tGroup.Children.Add(myScaling);
model.Transform = tGroup;
```

ScaleTransform3D also supports scaling around a center point. Consider the example of a cube. If you rescale the cube, it will scale down toward, or up away from, one of its corners or, indeed, any location in space. However, you may want to scale it from a center point within the cube, evenly changing the size of the cube so it scales evenly out from or in to that center point. If the cube's center point is at PX,PY,PZ, you could define the transform thusly:

```
Transform3D myScaling = new ScaleTransform3D(1.01,1.01,1.01,PX,PY,PZ);
```

You can also define the scaling parameters using a vector instead of the scalar values as in the previous examples. Thus, you would build a Vector3D using {1.01,1.01,1.01} and use that Vector3D in the constructor of ScaleTransform3D to get the same effect:

```
Vector3D myVector = new Vector3D(1.01, 1.01, 1.01);
Transform3D myScaling = new ScaleTransform3D(myVector);
```

Using Rotation Transforms

You can perform two types of rotation on a model. These are rotating around an axis by a certain angle (using AxisAngleRotation3D) and rotating based on a quaternion (using QuaternionRotation3D). Each of these types is used to construct a RotateTransform3D, which you can then apply to your model.

When using AxisAngleRotation3D, you define your axis using a vector. You then have to define your actual rotation using the AxisAngleRotation3D class, passing it this vector and a double representing the number of degrees by which to rotate. You can then use this AxisAngleRotation3D to construct the RotateTransform3D to create the transformation. In this example, an axis is defined using the simple vector {1,1,1}, and this is used to define a five-degree rotation around this axis:

```
private void RotateModelByAxisandAngle()
{
  ModelVisual3D model =
    (ModelVisual3D)this.vpt.Children[0];
  Vector3D vAxis = new Vector3D(1, 1, 1);
  AxisAngleRotation3D myRotation =
    new AxisAngleRotation3D(vAxis, 5.0);
  Transform3D myRotationTransform =
    new RotateTransform3D(myRotation);
  tGroup.Children.Add(myRotationTransform);
  model.Transform = tGroup;
}
```

Quaternion mathematics is slightly more efficient for rotations because a quaternion represents an axis in 3D space along with a rotation around that axis. So, a single quaternion can represent the 1,1,1 axis and the five-degree rotation around that axis in a single object. They are particularly powerful in that they can be combined efficiently to get a single quaternion that contains the result of a compound rotation and then that result can be applied to the target model.

Here's how you could achieve the same rotation as previously shown using quaternions:

```
private void RotateModelByQuaternion()
{
  ModelVisual3D model = (ModelVisual3D)this.vpt.Children[0];
  Vector3D vAxis = new Vector3D(1, 1, 1);
  Quaternion myQuaternion = new Quaternion(vAxis, 5.0);
  QuaternionRotation3D myQRot =
    new  QuaternionRotation3D(myQuaternion);
  Transform3D myRotationTransform =
```

```
    new RotateTransform3D(myQRot);
  tGroup.Children.Add(myRotationTransform);
  model.Transform = tGroup;
}
```

To compound quaternions, you would simply define new ones and add them to the group as you did with this one. Here's an example:

```
QuaternionRotation3D myQRot2 =
    New QuaternionRotation3D(mySecondQuaternion);
QuaternionRotation3D myQRot3 =
  New QuarterionRotation3d(myThirdQuarterion);
tGroup.Children.Add(myQRot2);
tGroup.Children.Add(myQRot3);
```

Summary

This chapter gave you the foundations of developing 3D graphics with WPF. It barely scratched the surface of what is possible, but it took you through the basics of what you need to know. You looked at how you can use points and vertices to make the simplest possible 2D shape in 3D space (a triangle) and then at how you combine it with a normal to understand how that shape is to be lit.

Next, you used the ViewPort3D in XAML to define the viewing area of your 3D world—and it is the 2D surface onto which the scene is "projected" based on lighting, positioning, material, and camera position attributes. You looked at the different forms of lighting and material that you can apply to an object or scene, as well as how to make models of objects from meshes.

Finally, you built a model representing a simple landscape using triangles and used this model to understand how to use the different transforms: translation, rotation, and scaling.

From here you can use what you've learned to start building more sophisticated applications using this great and powerful API!

CHAPTER 10

■ ■ ■

Distributing Your WPF Applications

In Chapter 1, you looked briefly into the history of thick and thin client applications and how application development has swung between the two methodologies. Throughout this book you've seen the richness of the Windows Presentation Foundation (WPF) and how you can use it to drastically improve the user experience that your application clients will experience.

In this chapter, you'll build some applications from the ground up, so you may run into some territory you've seen before. Please feel free to skip over those sections, but you may also find them useful as a refresher. This chapter is a nice stand-alone reference that will give you a feel for building Windows applications and web applications with WPF in Visual Studio *and* that will take you through what you need to know to deploy, run, and maintain them using the ClickOnce deployment technology. You'll start with a Windows application designed in Visual Studio and look into deploying it for online and offline access as well as deploying it for online access only.

Deploying a WPF Windows Application

In this example, you will build a simple Windows application using WPF. This application will demonstrate how you can use each of the deployment methodologies—as an application that can be run online or offline and as an application that can be run online only.

To get started, launch Visual Studio 2005, and issue a File ➤ New Project request. You'll get the New Project dialog box, as shown in Figure 10-1.

If you have the Orcas development tools for WinFX installed, you'll see the WinFX project types, and within this you'll see the different templates for WinFX project development. Select Windows Application (WPF), as shown in Figure 10-1, and give your application a friendly name (for example, WinFXHelloWorld).

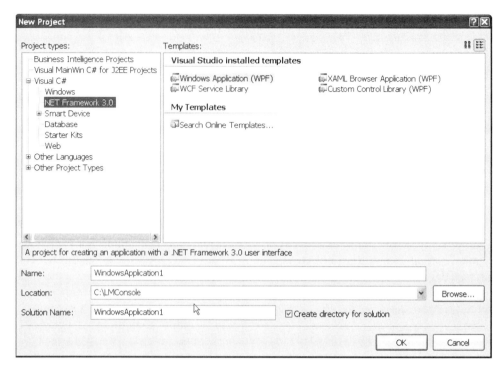

Figure 10-1. *The New Project dialog box*

When you click OK, Visual Studio will create the project file and launch the Cider designer for the WPF applications. You can see this in Figure 10-2.

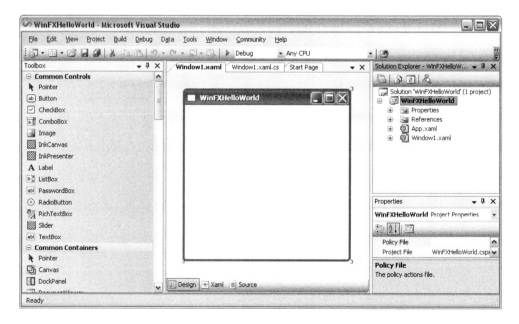

Figure 10-2. *A new application in Visual Studio 2005*

Now you are ready to start building your application. You'll build a simple one because I merely want to demonstrate the deployment and deployment management technologies. Add a button and a label to the form. Call these btnPush and lblWarning, respectively.

For the label, use the property settings shown in Table 10-1.

Table 10-1. *Properties for the Label*

Property	Content
Content	Do not push that button again!
FontSize	18
FontWeight	Bold
Foreground	#FFFF0000
Visibility	Hidden
Name	lblWarning

For the button, use the property settings shown in Table 10-2.

Table 10-2. *Properties for the Button*

Property	Content
Content	I am a button!
FontSize	18
Name	btnPush

When you are done, your screen should look like Figure 10-3.

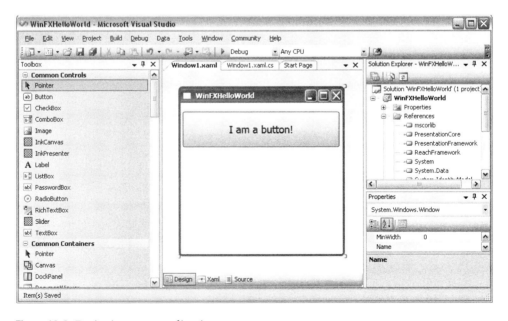

Figure 10-3. *Designing your application*

If you click the Xaml tab at the bottom of the designer, you can see the Extensible Application Markup Language (XAML) markup that corresponds to your application design. It should look something like Listing 10-1.

Listing 10-1. *XAML for WinFXHelloWorld*

```
<Window x:Class="WinFXHelloWorld.Window1"
    xmlns="http://schemas.microsoft.com/winfx/2006/xaml/presentation"
    xmlns:x="http://schemas.microsoft.com/winfx/2006/xaml"
    Title="WinFXHelloWorld"
    Height="300"
    Width="300">
    <Grid>
    <Button FontSize="18"
            Height="64"
            Margin="3,15,5,0"
            Name="btnPush"
            VerticalAlignment="Top">
            I am a button!</Button>
    <Label FontSize="18"
            FontWeight="Bold"
            Foreground="#FFFF0000"
            Margin="-3.63,102.723333333333,1,127"
            Name="lblWarning"
            Visibility="Hidden">Do not push that button again!!
    </Label>
  </Grid>
</Window>
```

You need to add an event handler to handle what happens when the user clicks the button. You specify this in XAML using the Click attribute. You'll change the <Button> declaration to look like this:

```
<Button Click="btnPush_Click"
        FontSize="18"
        Height="64"
        Margin="3,15,5,0"
        Name="btnPush"
        VerticalAlignment="Top">
        I am a button!</Button>
```

You can use any name for the event handler function. For consistency with previous programming models, I used the control name followed by an underscore followed by the event name, as in btnPush_Click.

Now you need to write the event handler code. Because the event handler was specified as being called btnPush_Click, you'll need to write a public void function with this name.

This function needs to accept two arguments: an object that represents the sender and a RoutedEventArgs that represents any arguments that are being passed to the function by the event handler. This function will make the label visible.

It should look something like this:

```
public void btnPush_Click(object sender, RoutedEventArgs e)
{
  lblWarning.Visibility - Visibility.Visible;
}
```

Now, when you run the application and click the button, the label becomes visible along with the friendly message asking you not to click the button again. This re-creates a scene from *The Hitchhiker's Guide to the Galaxy* when Arthur Dent first encounters the intergalactic user experience. And you thought your user interface (UI) was unfriendly!

Publishing for Online or Offline Mode

The next step is to publish the application to a web server. It's a good idea, if you don't have it already, to get Internet Information Services (IIS) running on your development box before continuing.

From the Build menu in Visual Studio 2005, select the Publish <ApplicationName> item, as shown in Figure 10-4.

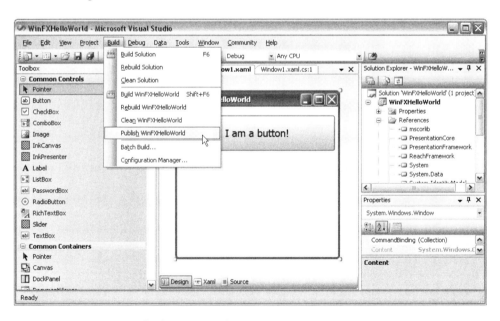

Figure 10-4. *Beginning to deploy your application*

When you select this option, you will be taken to the Application Publish Wizard. From here, you can select the four types of deployment supported by ClickOnce:

- Deploying to disk
- Deploying to a network share
- Deploying to a File Transfer Protocol (FTP) server
- Deploying to a web server

This example is using the web server deployment target, but feel free to experiment with the others. When publishing to a web server, you specify the location to which you want to publish the application. You, of course, will need to have rights to publish new web applications to this web server. To publish to your local web server, use `http://localhost/<ApplicationName>`, as in Figure 10-5.

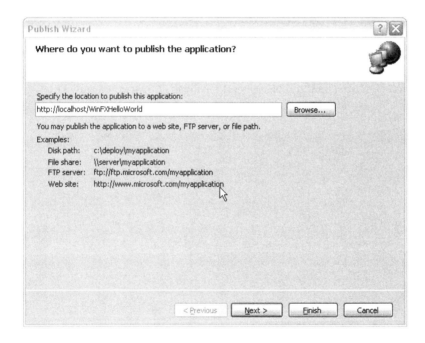

Figure 10-5. *Selecting the location to publish your application*

Clicking Next will take you to where you select how your application will be run by your users. You can select it to have online and offline mode or offline mode only. When you select the first option, your users get the richest experience, but it isn't for all applications. Applications that *benefit* from connectivity but still can be used in an offline experience fit this category.

Consider Microsoft Outlook—even though it is an online application, used for sending and receiving e-mail as well as updating calendars and task lists among others, you can use it offline. When you aren't connected, you can still read your local cache of e-mail messages and respond and manage your various mailboxes, calendars, and tasks. This is an application that has an online and an offline mode, and its behavior changes according to which one you are using.

Now, in comparison to this, consider an application such as Windows Live Local that provides mapping and local searching functionality—this cannot operate when you are offline and thus can run only in online mode. When using WPF, even though you are building forms-type applications, you can still build some that are smart enough to know they are online applications (by specifying it at this point in the wizard) and as such will not operate if your user is offline. You can see this dialog box in Figure 10-6.

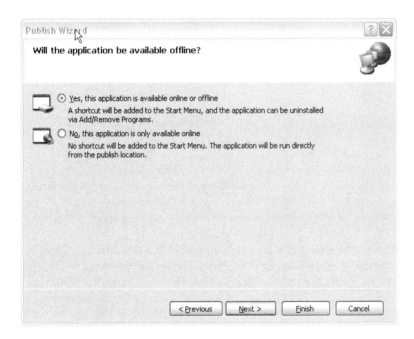

Figure 10-6. *Selecting application run mode*

You'll look into online-only applications later in the "Deploying a WPF Application in Online Mode Only" section. For now, select the option that allows your users to have the application online or offline, and move to the next step in the wizard by selecting Yes and clicking Next.

This loads the last step in the wizard—telling you that you are ready to publish your application. It was that easy! Clicking Finish will build and publish the application, and a few moments later your web browser should launch and show its published home page, as shown in Figure 10-7.

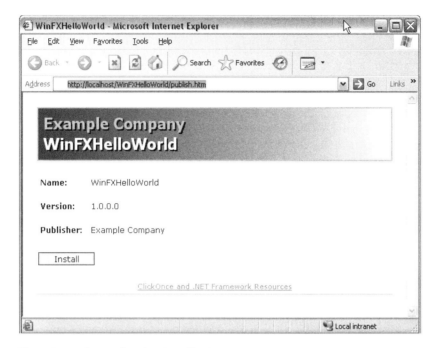

Figure 10-7. *The application installation page*

Your users would now be able to browse to a page like this to see your application install page. It contains your company name (as specified when you installed Visual Studio 2005), the application name, and the version. The version automatically revs up when you republish the application.

Clicking Install will begin the installation process. Remember, this was selected as an online and offline application, so you will get an entry on the Start menu when the installation is done. When the user clicks the Install button, ClickOnce will first verify that the system meets the installation requirements. Should it do so (that is, you are running on Windows Vista or an earlier version of Windows that has the WinFX runtime installed), the installation will proceed. See Figure 10-8.

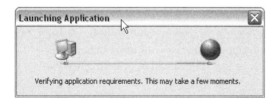

Figure 10-8. *Checking system requirements*

Once it has done this, the system will open a warning dialog box because the application was published without the certificate of a known certification authority (see Figure 10-9). Check the ClickOnce documentation for details on setting up a certification authority or obtaining a verified certificate from a third party if you want to avoid this dialog box. Refer to your project in Visual Studio 2005; you'll see that a temporary key was generated and put in your project. You would replace this with one that you get from the certification authority if you want your users to avoid the dialog box in Figure 10-9.

Figure 10-9. *The application isn't published with a trusted certificate.*

If they choose to install the application anyway, it will download and install itself and then run. You can see it running in Figure 10-10.

Figure 10-10. *The application installed and launched successfully.*

Because this application was designed for offline and online mode, you can see that it is present on the Add/Remove Programs Control Panel as well as on your Start menu.

To uninstall the application, you use the Add/Remove Programs Control Panel and select the application. The Change/Remove button will appear, as shown in Figure 10-11.

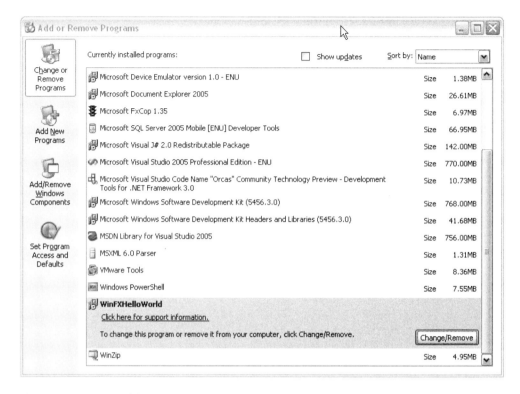

Figure 10-11. *Using Add/Remove Programs to uninstall the application*

When you click this button, you'll get taken into the ClickOnce maintenance dialog box that allows you to (in some cases) restore the application or (in all cases) remove the application, as shown in Figure 10-12.

Figure 10-12. *Uninstalling the application*

Clicking OK on this dialog box will then uninstall the application, removing it from the Control Panel and the Start menu.

Running and Updating the Application

If you ran through the uninstallation, return to the installation screen (as in Figure 10-7) and reinstall the application. It will run after the installation. Stop it from running, and take a look at your Start menu. You will see that the application is present in a folder that uses the same company name as you used when you installed Visual Studio 2005 (in this case, it is Example Company). Whenever you run the application from this location, it will check whether a newer version of itself is available, and if it is, it will give you the option to download and run it. Thus, when you are offline, you will continue to run your existing application, but as soon as you go online, you'll be given the facility to automatically update the application. This is a nice feature of ClickOnce that makes it much easier to keep your installation base synchronized on the same version of the application.

You can test this by making a change to the application and republishing it. To do this, return to Visual Studio .NET, and change something small. For example, change the font color on the button to something other than black. When you're ready, rebuild the solution, and go through the wizard to publish it again. (You start the wizard by selecting Publish <ApplicationName> from the Build menu).

When the Publication Wizard has finished, you'll see the browser launch with the same screen as you saw earlier; however, the version of the application has been revved up, as shown in Figure 10-13. Do *not* install the application at this time. Instead, go to the Start menu, and launch the application from there. You'll see a dialog box stating that the application has detected that it has an update ready and asks you whether you want to download and install it. If you click OK, it will take you through the installation process; if you click Skip, you'll run the version you currently have installed.

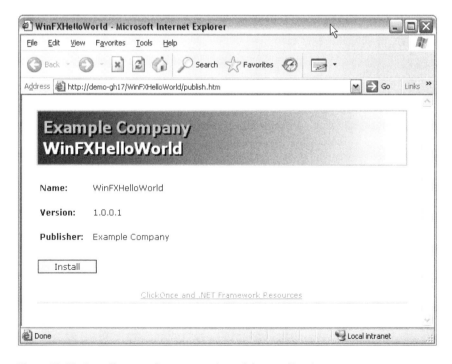

Figure 10-13. *Install screen for new version of the application*

Click OK, and you'll see the application download, install, and run the new version. Now that you have this version in hand, the next time you run it the new version will run, unless of course you update and publish another update in the interim, as shown in Figure 10-14.

Figure 10-14. *Application update screen*

Exploring the Installation

You can understand the installation a lot better if you explore what is going on in your system. To this point, you created a version 1.0.0.0 of your application, then created an update (version 1.0.0.1), and used the ClickOnce automatic update technology to rev it up. Now if you look at the Start menu item that you use to launch the application by dragging and dropping it onto Notepad, you'll see the following:

```
http://<servername>/WinFXHelloWorld/WinFXHelloWorld.application#
WinFXHelloWorld.application, Culture=neutral,
PublicKeyToken=00db07da2461ed5c,
processorArchitecture=msil
```

You can see that it is referring to the WinFXHelloWorld.application file—let's go to the directory for the application on the web server and see what is there. Figure 10-15 shows this directory in Windows Explorer Tiled view. I chose this because it shows how the application type is registered. You can see that WinFXHelloWorld.application is called the *application manifest*.

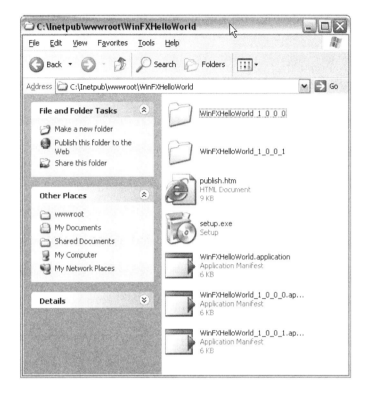

Figure 10-15. *Viewing the application web root*

Now, if you open this file in Notepad, you'll see the application manifest and how it works. Take a look for the following node in the XML:

```
<dependency>
  <dependentAssembly dependencyType="install"
      codebase="WinFXHelloWorld_1_0_0_1\WinFXHelloWorld.exe.manifest"
      size="7366">
    <assemblyIdentity name="WinFXHelloWorld.exe"
      version="1.0.0.1"
      publicKeyToken="00db07da2461ed5c"
      language="neutral"
      processorArchitecture="msil"
      type="win32" />
```

The first dependency you see is the install type—this is how the application checks to see whether a new rev is available. When the application was published, the codebase attribute was updated. The application knows its codebase attribute, sees that this one is different, and thus gives you the facility to launch the installer to update it.

The assemblyIdentity node contains the name of the application to launch. As you can see, it specifies the WinFXHelloWorld.exe file that is contained in the application directory, currently WinFXHelloWorld_1_0_0_1. The EXE originally resides on the server, not the client, and is copied to the client when you run it the first time. On subsequent runs, it checks the server to see whether a newer version exists. If one doesn't, it runs the local copy.

Finally, on this tour, let's look at a snippet from the deployment manifest. This is the WinFXHelloWorld.exe.manifest file in the latest deployment directory (in this case, WinFXHelloWorld_1_0_0_1). You can drag and drop it onto Notepad to view it. In it, you'll see lots of nodes like this one:

```
<dependency>
    <dependentAssembly dependencyType="preRequisite" allowDelayedBinding="true">
      <assemblyIdentity name="Microsoft.Windows.CommonLanguageRuntime"
                        version="2.0.50727.0" />
    </dependentAssembly>
  </dependency>
```

These specify what the installer should check your system for before installing the application. Should any of them be missing or be the wrong type, it will flag an error.

Deploying a WPF Windows Application in Online Mode Only

In the previous sections, you built and deployed a simple application to use the online and offline modes of publication that ClickOnce supports. In this section, you'll learn how to treat your application as a pure online application. To make sure everything is clean, you'll do this by building a completely new application and then testing that.

So, create a new Windows application project called WinFXWebHelloWorld. You'll use this project to design and build a multilingual "Hello, World!" application.

Listing 10-2 shows the XAML code that defines the UI for the application.

Listing 10-2. *XAML for Multilingual "Hello, World!"*

```
<Window x:Class="WinFXWebHelloWorld.Window1"
    xmlns="http://schemas.microsoft.com/winfx/2006/xaml/presentation"
    xmlns:x="http://schemas.microsoft.com/winfx/2006/xaml"
    Title="WinFXWebHelloWorld" Height="300" Width="300"
     xmlns:my="clr-namespace:System;assembly=mscorlib">
    <Grid>
    <Label Height="26.2766666666667" Margin="10.37,15.7233333333333,131,0"
             Name="label1" VerticalAlignment="Top">Select your language:
    </Label>
    <ComboBox SelectionChanged="cmbLanguage_Selected" Height="26"
             Margin="55,43,116,0" Name="cmbLanguage" VerticalAlignment="Top">
      <Label Content="English" />
      <Label Content="Irish" />
      <Label Content="French" />
```

```
      <Label Content="Chinese" />
      <Label Content="Japanese" />
      <Label Content="Hebrew" />
   </ComboBox>
   <Label FontSize="24" Foreground="#FFFF0000"
               Margin="13.37,96.7233333333333,9,45"
               Name="lblGreeting"></Label>
  </Grid>
</Window>
```

This defines two labels—one that simply says "Select your language" and the other that is used to render the "Hello, World!" greeting in the appropriate language. It also contains a ComboBox that is loaded with six labels, and each label represents a language to use.

The ComboBox defines an event handler to fire whenever the selection changes (using the SelectionChanged attribute no less!). The event handler is implemented by the cmbLanguage_Selected public void function. You can see the code for it in Listing 10-3.

Listing 10-3. *Handling the Drop-Down List*

```
    public void cmbLanguage_Selected(
               object sender,
               SelectionChangedEventArgs e)
    {
        string strGreeting;
        int nSelection = cmbLanguage.SelectedIndex;
        switch (nSelection)
        {
            case 0:
            {
                strGreeting = "Hello, World!";
                break;
            }
            case 1:
            {
                strGreeting = "Conas ata tu, domhain!";
                break;
            }
            case 2:
            {
                strGreeting = "Bonjour Monde!";
                break;
            }
            case 3:
            {
                strGreeting = "Leih ho ma?";
                break;
            }
            case 4:
```

```
                {
                    strGreeting = "Konichi wa, World!";
                    break;
                }
                case 5:
                {
                    strGreeting = "Boker Tov, World!";
                    break;
                }
                default:
                {
                    strGreeting = "Hello, World!";
                    break;
                }
            }
            lblGreeting.Content = strGreeting;
        }

}
```

Note that this function accepts a SelectedChangedEventArgs instead of a RoutedEventArgs because it is fired upon a list selection event.

If you run the application, you can see how it works—select a language from the drop-down list, and you'll get a greeting in that language, as shown in Figure 10-16.

Figure 10-16. *The multilingual "Hello, World!" application*

Now let's look at deploying the application as a web-only application. When you select the Publish <Application> entry from the Build menu, you are taken to the Application Publish Wizard. In the first dialog box, select http://localhost/WinFXWebHelloWorld as the destination. Then, in the next dialog box, when asked whether you want an online/offline application, select the second option, specifying that you want an online-only application. When you finish running the wizard, it will publish the application to the specified uniform resource locator (URL). Once it's done publishing, it will launch the browser and point it at the landing page for the application in that website. You can see this in Figure 10-17.

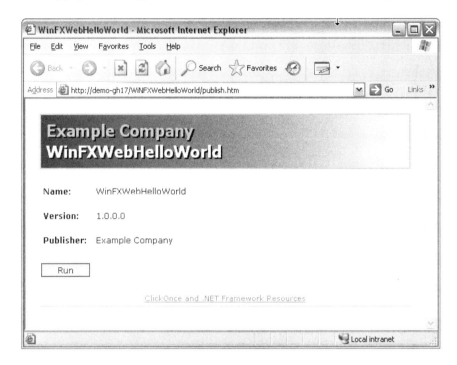

Figure 10-17. *Running your application on the Web*

You can see that this is similar to that for the online/offline application with one major difference—there is no concept of installation; you simply run the application straight from this page. Under the hood not much is different—the application is still downloaded to your machine and executed from there, but it isn't installed in the Add/Remove Programs Control Panel, and it doesn't have an icon on the Start menu.

The application is cached on your machine, but every time it launches, it checks itself against the latest version on the website. It's easy to try this. The first time you run the application, you'll get the Checking Dependencies dialog box, followed by the dialog box that shows the download progress before the application launches. On subsequent visits, you skip the middle part (that is, the download progress), because the application is already present. It checks dependencies, and then if nothing has changed, it launches.

You can test its behavior upon modification too. Make a simple change to the application, such as adding a new language. Then recompile and republish the application. After publication, the browser will launch, and you'll see that the application has increased a revision, as shown in Figure 10-18.

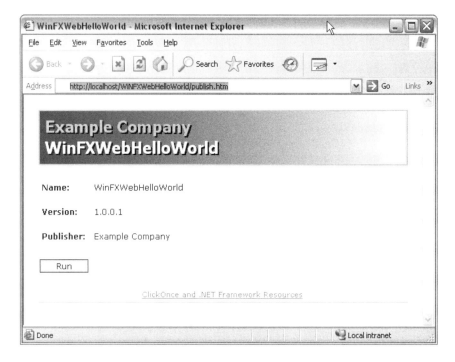

Figure 10-18. *The updated version of the application*

Now when you run your application, you'll see that it goes through the same download process as it did the first time. This shows how ClickOnce allows you to maintain versions of the application as it runs purely on the Web. See the "Deploying a WPF Windows Application" section of this chapter for a review of the different constraints of running the application in online only and online/offline modes for more details.

Building and Deploying a WinFX Web Application

It's easy to get confused amongst the myriad of options available to you. Thus far, you've looked at a *Windows* application that can be run in a mixed online/offline mode and a *Windows* application that can run only on the Web. This is not a *web* application. You can also build and deploy a web application using Visual Studio .NET. This is an application that runs within the browser, not its own stand-alone window like its web-based Windows application cousin that you saw in the previous section.

To make it even more confusing, you don't use File ➤ New Web Site like when creating a standard Web application; you still use the File ➤ New Project dialog box you saw way back in Figure 10-1. From this dialog box, select the WinFX Web Browser application template, and you'll be ready to go.

When you create a WinFX web application, you'll have a solution containing two XAML files. The first is called App.xaml, and this is roughly analogous to an App.config file from pre-WinFX development; it is used to configure your application, performing duties such as setting up the start page to load, as well as having the facility to store application-global variables. It also has a code-behind file that you can use for global code, amongst other things.

Here's an example of the basic App.xaml created by the integrated development environment (IDE):

```
<Application x:Class="WinFxBrowserApplication1.App"
    xmlns="http://schemas.microsoft.com/winfx/2006/xaml/presentation"
    xmlns:x="http://schemas.microsoft.com/winfx/2006/xaml"
    StartupUri="Page1.xaml">

    <Application.Resources>

    </Application.Resources>
</Application>
```

As you can see, the StartupUri attribute specifies the start-up page. When you created the application using the File ➤ New Project dialog box, Visual Studio also created a page called Page1.xaml, and this URI points to that page. When a WinFX web application runs, it reads App.xaml, finds the StartupUri, and then runs that page.

Listing 10-4 shows an example of a simple XAML page that can be loaded and run in this way.

Listing 10-4. *XAML Pig Latin Translator*

```
<Page x:Class="Chapter10BrowserApp.Page1"
    xmlns="http://schemas.microsoft.com/winfx/2006/xaml/presentation"
    xmlns:x="http://schemas.microsoft.com/winfx/2006/xaml"
    Title="Page1">
    <Grid>
        <Button Click="btnTranslate_Click"
                Height="28"
                HorizontalAlignment="Right"
                Margin="0,70,20,0"
                Name="btnTranslate"
                VerticalAlignment="Top"
                Width="109">And then push me
        </Button>
```

```
        <Label Height="25.2766666666667"
                     HorizontalAlignment="Left"
                     Margin="7.37,48.7233333333333,0,0"
                     Name="label1"
                     VerticalAlignment="Top"
                     Width="114.63">Enter your Name:
        </Label>
      <Label Height="28.2766666666667"
                     Margin="7.37,107.723333333333,118,0"
                     Name="label2"
                     VerticalAlignment="Top">Your name in Pig Latin is:
       </Label>
      <Label Margin="7.37,141.723333333333,8,99"
                     Name="lblPig"
                     FontSize="18"
                     FontWeight="Bold"
                     Foreground="#FFFF0000">
       </Label>
      <TextBox Height="25"
                       Margin="10,72,0,0"
                       Name="txtName"
                       VerticalAlignment="Top"
                       HorizontalAlignment="Left"
                       Width="154">
      </TextBox>
   </Grid>
</Page>
```

This provides a simple web application that allows the user to enter their name and have it translated into Pig Latin, which puts the first letter of the word at the end of the word and adds "ay" after it, so that John would become ohnJay and Paul would become aulPay. The code that does this is in the btnTranslate_Click event handler:

```
public void btnTranslate_Click(Object sender, RoutedEventArgs e)
        {
            string strTest = txtName.Text;
            string strTrans = strTest.Substring(1, strTest.Length - 1)
                                        + strTest.Substring(0, 1) + "ay";
            lblPig.Content = strTrans;


        }
```

When you run the application, you'll see something like that in Figure 10-19.

Figure 10-19. *Running the web application*

You'll notice that this web application is running directly from your file system and not from your localhost web server. This is because it hasn't yet been deployed or published to the web server. You publish it in the same manner as publishing a Windows application using the Publish <Application> entry on the Build menu.

In a similar manner to publishing a Windows WinFX application, you have the option to create an installer for an application that can be viewed online or offline or an application that is online only. As such, it would appear that the two application types are the same—and that there is no fundamental difference between a Windows WinFX application and a web WinFX application, after all—both of them can be run online only, and both of them have an offline mode. This is indicative of the blurring between traditional "desktop" applications and the emerging "connected" applications as outlined in the history of UI technology in Chapter 1.

The fundamental difference between the two lies beneath the surface—and it is in the permissibility of the application to access system resources. Despite that either application can be an online application, the one that is flagged as a WinFX desktop application will have superior access to system resources such as the registry and the file system for security reasons. The logic is that the desktop-style application is a powerful one, distributed to a controlled user base that will require these things, whereas the web-style application is a less powerful one, distributed to a wider, potentially anonymous user base that requires more security; that is, they will not want you accessing some system resources, and thus the technology to develop applications for these users will prevent you from doing so.

When you publish this type of application, you go through the familiar ClickOnce publication steps. These will generate the publish.htm file that gives some basic details of your application and allows your users to run it.

This is consistent with what you saw in the previous section, but now instead of running an executable (.application) file, as they did earlier, they will browse to a new type of application called an XBAP. See Figure 10-20 for the publish page. You can see that the Run button navigates to the .xbap file (see the status bar as the mouse is hovering over it).

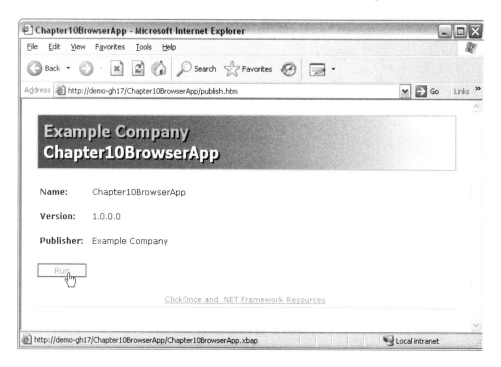

Figure 10-20. *The publish page for an XBAP web application*

XBAP is an acronym for *XAML browser application*, and it is, in fact, the deployment manifest file that describes where the executable code is located, what its dependencies are, and how it can be launched. When the user clicks Run, the browser will navigate to the XBAP URI and use this to download and launch the application. You can see the download process in Figure 10-21.

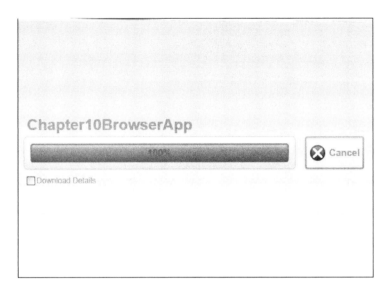

Figure 10-21. *Downloading and running the XBAP*

Once this is downloaded, the application will execute within the browser, as shown in Figure 10-19 earlier.

Configuring Web Applications for Trust

The major difference between the web application and the online Windows forms application is that the web application requires trust to be able to access system resources.

A WinFX Windows application will be set, by default, to *full trust*. In this mode, the code access security features of the .NET Framework will not be used—the application will be allowed do whatever the user executing it is allowed to do. In the case of a web application, the default is for *partial trust* where it is restricted in what it can do. If you look at the Security tab in the Project Properties dialog box, you can see how this is configured and change it if necessary. You access this dialog box by right-clicking the project (not the solution) in Solution Explorer and selecting Properties from the context menu. You then select the Security tab to see the code access security settings. See Figure 10-22.

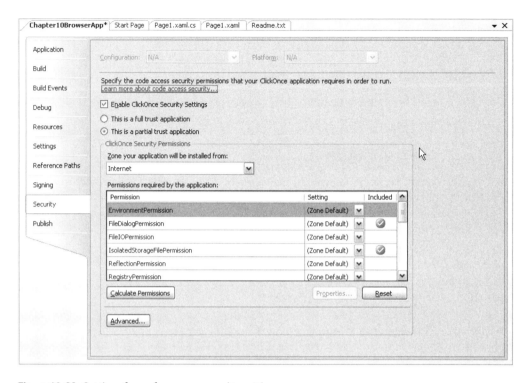

Figure 10-22. *Setting the code access security settings*

You can use this dialog box to then dictate the "zone" from which your application will be installed, and it will inherit the permissions that are allowed for that zone. As you can see in Figure 10-22, the application defaults to being hosted on the Internet zone and is thus restricted from doing many things. Should you want to deploy your application within the enterprise, you can change the default zone to Local Intranet, and the permission set that your application will be allowed grows accordingly. Finally, you can override these settings with a Custom zone that gives you fine-grained control over the permissibility of your application for various functions. You have a wealth of options and resulting implications that are way too much to go into for a *Foundations of WPF* book; however, for more information about code access security and how it can work with your applications, check the MSDN documentation or the excellent *Deploying .NET Applications: Learning MSBuild and ClickOnce* by Sayed Y. Hashimi and Sayed Ibrahim Hashimi (Apress, 2006).

Summary

In this chapter, you learned about the types of WinFX applications you can build using WPF and about how they can be deployed and managed at your end users' desktops. You looked at a WinFX Windows application, how it behaves when it is usable in both online and offline modes, and how you can use ClickOnce technology to allow it to smartly update itself. You also looked into how a WinFX Windows application can be a purely hosted, and thus centrally managed, application that has all the power and trustworthiness as well as the same user experience as an installed application. Then you looked at WinFX web applications—which themselves can be run in either mode (online/offline or online only). Because these applications are built on the same UI technology (WPF), they can have the similar rich experience as the WinFX Windows applications—limited only by the trustworthiness established at compile time.

Thus, you can see that WPF and ClickOnce offer you a plethora of options, but they also offer you the technology base to take your applications to the next level—gone are the days when you would use one technology, such as ActiveX or .NET controls, for rich desktop applications but would have to scale down the experience into Hypertext Markup Language (HTML) or JavaScript for the web experience. With WPF, you can now offer the same richness, from potentially the same code base to both types of users, and you can use a single deployment technology (ClickOnce) to handle installing and managing these deployed applications!

Index

Symbols

.NET *See* NET
3D. *See* three-dimensional (3D) graphics

A

accelerating and decelerating
    SplineDoubleKeyFrame class, 243
Activated event
    Application class, 26
ActiveX technology
    .NET as successor to, 7
    evolution of user interfaces, 6
Add New Item dialog box
    DataSet item, 81, 99
Add New Project dialog
    WinFX Windows Application template, 92
AdventureWorks browser application
    basic version, 35
AdventureWorks sample database
    data used in WPF project, 34
AmbientLight type, 274
animation, 205, 233
    animation types, 235–238
    assigning animations to events in
        Interactive Designer, 259–261
    getting started, 233–235
    keyframe-based animation, 238–247
    using Storyboards and TimeLine classes,
        248–249
    working with TimeLines and Interactive
        Designer, 250–259
Appearance palette, 56
    brushes available, 56
    filling rectangle with gradient color, 61
    Linear Gradient Brush, 57
    making List transparent, 64
Application class
    Activated event, 26
    Current property, 25
    Deactivated event, 26–27
    MainWindow property, 29
    programming WPF applications, 23–25
    SessionEnding event, 27
    ShutdownMode property, 29
    StartupUri property, 25
    Windows property, 29
Application definition file, 24
    <Application> tag, 25

application distribution, 17
    installed applications, 19
    XAML browser application, 17–19
application manifest files, 18
Application Publish Wizard
    deployment options, 294–295
<Application> tag, 25
arrange pass, 22
ASP.NET runtime, 9
AxisAngleRotation3D class, 287

B

background gradient
    setting for user interface, 55–58
Background property
    Button control, 154
BackGround property
    List control, 64
<BeginStoryBoard> tag
    starting a storyboard, 248
Bezier curves
    Path class, 217
binding for service, 73
BitmapImage class, 225–226
<BitmapImage> tag, 167
    DecodePixelHeight attribute, 164
    DecodePixelWidth attribute, 164
    Rotation attribute, 165
BitmapSource class, 225
BorderBrush property
    List control, 64
bounce effect
    LinearDoubleKeyFrame class, 241
Brush class, 206
Brush Transform tool, 57
brushes, 205–206
    using Fill property with a hex brush, 206
    using Fill property with a predefined
        brush, 206
    using ImageBrush class, 209
    using images as brushes, 230
    using LinearGradientBrush class, 208
    using RadialGradientBrush class, 208
    using SolidColorBrush class, 207
    using SystemColors class, 210
    using VisualBrush class, 211
Button control
    rich content, 152–154
    using, 151–152

Find it faster at http://superindex.apress.com/

You Need the Companion eBook

Your purchase of this book entitles you to buy the companion PDF-version eBook for only $10. Take the weightless companion with you anywhere.

We believe this Apress title will prove so indispensable that you'll want to carry it with you everywhere, which is why we are offering the companion eBook (in PDF format) for $10 to customers who purchase this book now. Convenient and fully searchable, the PDF version of any content-rich, page-heavy Apress book makes a valuable addition to your programming library. You can easily find and copy code — or perform examples by quickly toggling between instructions and the application. Even simultaneously tackling a donut, diet soda, and complex code becomes simplified with hands-free eBooks!

Once you purchase your book, getting the $10 companion eBook is simple:

❶ Visit **www.apress.com/promo/tendollars/**.

❷ Complete a basic registration form to receive a randomly generated question about this title.

❸ Answer the question correctly in 60 seconds, and you will receive a promotional code to redeem for the $10.00 eBook.

2560 Ninth Street • Suite 219 • Berkeley, CA 94710

eBookshop

THE EXPERT'S VOICE™

Offer valid through 5/20/07.